GW01375104

LEGENDARY FICTIONS OF THE IRISH CELTS

COLLECTED AND NARRATED BY
Patrick Kennedy

First published London & N.Y., 1891.
Facsimile reprint 1998 by
LLANERCH PUBLISHERS
FELINFACH

ISBN 1 86143 059 0

LEGENDARY FICTIONS

OF

THE IRISH CELTS

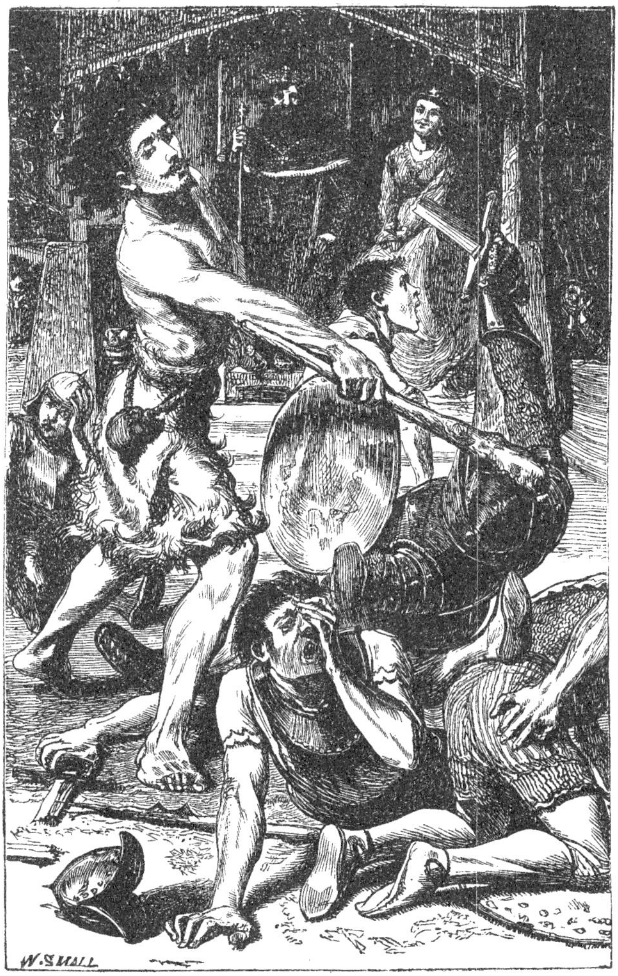
W.SMALL

GLOSSARY

ON looking through the work, the editor has found some words and passages not sufficiently explicit to the mere English reader. The deficiency is here made up.

Blue Cap, p. 217. Nickname of a woman among the old English settlers. Her people, ignorant of the custom just mentioned, buried her on the men's side of the churchyard : the coffin was raised and set upright against the church-door in the night. After two re-interments the Palatine family buried her on the other side of the stream, and there she was allowed to rest.

Bohyeen, p. 55. The reader anxious for the correct sound of the word must make one syllable out of *hyeen*, and give the *hy* the guttural sound of *ch*.

Bohyeen, p. 145, correctly *Borán* in the sense here given.

Booran, note, p. 149, should be Borrán.

Bowl Almanac, p. 16, an attempt at Bole Armeniæ. The editor has throughout the whole collection carefully abstained from inventing any mistakes for his characters. *Futhryom*, p. 78, is another case in point.

Bullawn a Rinka, p. 216, Plain of the Dance, the locality being used by the fairies for that purpose. Some few words, such as *Bullawn*, will not be found in Irish dictionaries.

Carlow, p. 219. The city guessed at was probably Dinrigh (*Dun Righ*, Fortress of the King), on the west bank of the Barrow, the ancient capital of South Leinster.

Cead Millia Mollaghart, p. 220, *Cead Mile Mollachd ort* (100,000 curses on you).

Colpa, p, 291. Drogheda was anciently called *Inver Colpa*, Colpa's Harbour, a Milesian chief of that name having been drowned there.

Culdees, p. 259, worshippers of God as distinguished from Pagans.

Ditch, p. 162, the high clay mound commonly overgrown with furze bushes : the ditch proper is called the *gripe* of the ditch.

File or *Fileadh*, p. 174, Bard or Poet ; *Scealuidhe*, Story-teller.

Fir and *Fear*, p. 180. *Fear* is the nominative case, *Fir* the genitive and vocative cases.

Gealach, p. 260, the Moon, bright, &c.

GLOSSARY

On looking through the work, the editor has found some words and passages not sufficiently explicit to the mere English reader. The deficiency is here made up.

Blue Cap, p. 217. Nickname of a woman among the old English settlers. Her people, ignorant of the custom just mentioned, buried her on the men's side of the churchyard: the coffin was raised and set upright against the church-door in the night. After two re-interments the Palatine family buried her on the other side of the stream, and there she was allowed to rest.

Bohyeen, p. 55. The reader anxious for the correct sound of the word must make one syllable out of *hyeen*, and give the *hy* the guttural sound of *ch*.

Bohyeen, p. 145, correctly *Borán* in the sense here given.

Booran, note, p. 149, should be Borrán.

Bowl Almanac, p. 16, an attempt at Bole Armeniæ. The editor has throughout the whole collection carefully abstained from inventing any mistakes for his characters. *Futhryom*, p. 78, is another case in point.

Bullawn a Rinka, p. 216, Plain of the Dance, the locality being used by the fairies for that purpose. Some few words, such as *Bullawn*, will not be found in Irish dictionaries.

Carlow, p. 219. The city guessed at was probably Dinrigh (*Dun Righ*, Fortress of the King), on the west bank of the Barrow, the ancient capital of South Leinster.

Cead Millia Mollaghart, p. 220, *Cead Mile Mollachd ort* (100,000 curses on you).

Colpa, p, 291. Drogheda was anciently called *Inver Colpa*, Colpa's Harbour, a Milesian chief of that name having been drowned there.

Culdees, p. 259, worshippers of God as distinguished from Pagans.

Ditch, p. 162, the high clay mound commonly overgrown with furze bushes: the ditch proper is called the *gripe* of the ditch.

File or *Fileadh*, p. 174, Bard or Poet; *Scealuidhe*, Story-teller.

Fir and *Fear*, p. 180. *Fear* is the nominative case, *Fir* the genitive and vocative cases.

Gealach, p. 260, the Moon, bright, &c.

TO

JOSEPH SHERIDAN LE FANU, Esq.

AUTHOR OF "UNCLE SILAS," ETC.

DEAR SIR,

I beg to offer this collection of Irish Legends to your acceptance, from respect for your high position among English writers, in consideration of your being a truly good man, and in gratitude for your kind encouragement of my own literary attempts. Without that encouragement I should probably never have an opportunity of penning a dedication to any one.

I am, dear Sir,

Your faithful Servant,

PATRICK KENNEDY.

LOUGH NA PIASTHA COTTAGE.

PREFACE

THOUGH the subject of this volume seems light and frivolous enough, it might be preceded, and accompanied, and concluded by grave and tiresome dissertations; and if our hopes were limited to its perusal by readers of an archæological turn, we would freely exhaust all the philosophy of fiction in our possession upon them. But from our early youth we have felt the deepest interest in the stories and legends which are peculiar to the Irish, or which they possess in common with all the Indo-European races, and our dearest wish is that their memory should not fade from the minds of the people. They have existed in one form or other from long before the Christian era, and have been mainly preserved by oral tradition among the unlettered.

Taking into consideration the diminishing of our population by want and emigration, and the general diffusion of book-learning, such as it is, and the growing taste for the rubbishy tales of the penny and halfpenny journals, we have in these latter times been haunted with the horrid thought that the memory of the tales heard in boyhood would be irrecoverably lost. To prevent an

PREFACE

evil of such magnitude (in our judgment to wit), we submitted some of the treasured lore to the editor of the *Dublin University Magazine* in the year 1862. Though his favourite walk in fiction, in which he is excelled by no living writer, admits only of the flesh and blood beings of our own times, he was not without sympathy for story tellers and story listeners who could be interested by the naïve and broadly-defined personages of the household story. So the "Leinster Folk Lore" was allowed an appearance in that national magazine, and now, through the liberality of our present publishers, we look to the preservation of a portion of our light literature which would otherwise be probably lost.

If the large-souled man cannot look upon anything human as foreign to his sympathies, he cannot but feel interest in inventions which, however artless in structure, improbable in circumstance, and apparently destitute of purpose, have engrossed the attention of fireside audiences probably since the days of Homer. This leads us to hope for the approbation of thoughtful and comprehensive minds as well as of that of the young, and as yet unvitiated by the exciting and demoralizing pictures of unmitigated wickedness abounding in modern fiction.

The greater part of the stories and legends in this volume are given as they were received from the storytellers with whom our youth was familiar. A few of them thus heard we read at a later period, and in an improved form, in the Bardic historians and in MSS., some kindly furnished us by the late estimable archæologist,

PREFACE

John Windele, of Cork. No story in the present collection is copied either in substance or form from any writer of the present or past generation. The subjects of some have of course been already used by other collectors, but they and the present compiler had a common source to draw from.

But to occupy the reader's attention with a long preface to a volume of light reading, would be worse than keeping a hungry company from a simple and scanty meal by a prolonged grace. If a fastidious reader fails to take pleasure or interest in the mere tales, and experiences contempt for the taste of those ancestors of ours who could have relished them so much as they evidently did, perhaps he may be induced to search into the history, and the polity, and the social usages of those easily-pleased folk, and discover the cause of their want of critical acumen. In this case the acquisition of archæological knowledge, more or less, will recompense the time lost in the perusal of a mere FOLK'S BOOK.

CONTENTS

	PAGE
DEDICATION	vii
PREFACE	ix

PART I.—HOUSEHOLD STORIES.

Jack and his Comrades	4
The Bad Stepmother	15
Adventures of " Gilla na Chreck an Gour "	21
Jack the Master and Jack the Servant	28
"I'll be Wiser the next Time"	35
The Three Crowns	39
The Corpse Watchers	48
The Brown Bear of Norway	52
The Goban Saor	61
The Three Advices which the King with the Red Soles gave to his Son	66

PART II.—LEGENDS OF THE "GOOD PEOPLE."

The Fairy Child	76
The Changeling and his Bagpipes	81
The Tobinstown Sheeoge	84
The Belated Priest	87
The Palace in the Rath	89
The Breton Version of the Palace in the Rath	94
The Fairy Nurse	96
The Recovered Bride	100
Faction-Fight among the Fairies	104
Jemmy Doyle in the Fairy Palace	104
The Fairy Cure	105

xiv CONTENTS

	PAGE
The Sea Fairies	109
The Black Cattle of Durzy Island	110
The Silkie Wife	110
The Pooka of Murroe	112
The Kildare Pooka	114
The Kildare Lurikeen	117
The Adventures of the " Son of Bad Counsel "	119

PART III.—WITCHCRAFT, SORCERY, GHOSTS, AND FETCHES.

The Long Spoon	131
The Prophet before his Time	132
The Bewitched Churn	135
The Ghosts and the Game of Football	137
The Cat of the Carman's Stage	140
Cauth Morrisy looking for Service	141
Black Stairs on Fire	146
The Witches' Excursion	148
The Crock found in the Rath	150
The Enchantment of Gearhoidh Iarla	153
Illan Eachtach and the Lianan	156
The Misfortunes of Barrett the Piper	158
The Woman in White	160
The Queen's County Ghost	162
The Ghost in Graigue	164
Droochan's Ghost	165
The Kilranelagh Spirit	167
The Doctor's Fetch	168
The Apparition in Old Ross	170

PART IV.—OSSIANIC AND OTHER EARLY LEGENDS.

Fann Mac Cuil and the Scotch Giant	179
How Fann Mac Cuil and his Men were bewitched	182
Qualifications and Duties of the Fianna Eirionn	184
The Battle of Ventry Harbour	187
The Fight of Castle Knoc	190
The Youth of Fion	193

CONTENTS

	PAGE
Fion's First Marriage	194
How Fion selected a Wife	196
Pursuit of Diarmuid and Grainne	197
The Flight of the Sluggard	199
Beanriogain na Sciana Breaca	200
Conan's Delusions in Ceash	205
The Youth of Oisin	207
The Old Age of Oisin	212
Legend of Loch na Piasta	215
The King with the Horse's Ears	219
The Story of the Sculloge's Son from Muskerry	225
An Braon Suan Or	240
The Children of Lir	245
Lough Neagh	248
Killarney	249
Legend of the Lake of Inchiquin	250
How the Shannon acquired its Name	251
The Origin of the Lake of Tiis	252
The Building of Ardfert Cathedral	253
How Donaghadee got its Name	255
The Borrowed Lake	256
Kilstoheen in the Shannon	257
The Isle of the Living	258
Fionntuin Mac Bochna	261
The Firbolgs and Danaans	266
Inis na Muic	268
The Bath of the White Cows	269
The Quest for the "Tain-Bo-Cuailgne"	273
The Progress of the Wicked Bard	275

PART V.—LEGENDS OF THE CELTIC SAINTS.

St. Patrick	282
How St. Patrick received the Staff of Jesus	283
The Fortune of Dichu	284
St. Patrick's Contest with the Druids	285
The Baptism of Aongus	288
The Decision of the Chariot	289
Conversion of the Robber Chief, Macaldus	290

CONTENTS

	PAGE
Baptism after Death	291
The Vision of St. Brigid	292
Death and Burial of St. Patrick	292
The Corpse-freighted Barque	294
St. Brigid's Cloak	296
St. Brigid and the Harps	297
"Arran of the Saints," and its Patrons	298
St. Fanchea's Visit to Arran	298
St. Brendain's Voyage	299
The Island of the Birds	300
The Sinner Saved	301
A Legend of St. Mogue of Ferns	302
O'Carroll's Warning	305
How St. Eloi was cured of Pride	306
St. Lateerin of Cullin	307
GLOSSARY	311

PART I

HOUSEHOLD STORIES

HOUSEHOLD STORIES

In this class is properly comprised those fictions which, with some variations, are told at the domestic gatherings of Celts, Teutons, and Slavonians, and are more distinguished by a succession of wild and wonderful adventures than a carefully-constructed framework. A dramatic piece exhibiting reflection, and judgment, and keen perception of character, but few incidents or surprises, may interest an individual who peruses it by his fireside, or as he saunters along a sunny river bank; but let him be one of an audience witnessing its performance, and he becomes sensible of an uncomfortable change. Presence in a crowd produces an uneasy state of expectation, which requires something startling or sensational to satisfy it. Thus it was with the hearth-audiences. It needed but few experiments to put the first story-tellers on the most effective way of amusing and interesting the groups gathered round the blaze, who for the moment felt their mission to consist in being agreeably excited, not in applying canons of criticism.

The preservation of these tales by unlettered people from a period anterior to the going forth of Celt or Teuton or Slave from the neighbourhood of the Caspian Sea is hard to be accounted for. The number of good

Scealuidhes dispersed through the country parts is but small compared to the mass of the people, and hundreds may be found who recollect the succession of events and the personages of a tale while utterly incapable of relating it.

In remote neighbourhoods, where the people have scarcely any communication with towns or cities, or access to books, stories will be heard identical with those told in the Brothers Grimm's German collection, or among the Norse tales gathered by MM. Asbjornsen and Moë. We cannot for a moment imagine an Irishman of former days speaking English or his native tongue communicating these household stories to Swede or German who could not understand him, or suppose the old dweller in Deutschland doing the good office for the Irishman. The ancestors both of Celt and Teuton brought the simple and wonderful narratives from the parent ancestral household in Central Asia. In consideration of the preference generally given by young students to stirring action rather than dry disquisition, we omit much we had to say on the earliest forms of fiction, and introduce a story known in substance to every Gothic and Celtic people in Europe. It is given in the jaunty style in which we first heard it from *Garrett* (Gerald) Forrestal of Bantry, in Wexford.

JACK AND HIS COMRADES.

Once there was a poor widow, and often there was, and she had one son. A very scarce summer came, and they didn't know how they'd live till the new potatoes would be fit for eating. So Jack said to his mother one evening, "Mother, bake my cake, and kill my cock, till I go seek my fortune; and if I meet it, never fear but I'll soon be back to share it with you." So she did as he asked her, and he set out at break of day on his journey. His mother came along with him to the *bawn* (yard) gate, and says she,—"Jack, which would you rather have, half the cake and half the cock with my blessing, or the whole of 'em with my curse?" "O musha, mother," says Jack, "why do you *ax* me that question? sure you know I wouldn't have your curse and Damer's[1] estate along with it." "Well, then, Jack," says she, "here's the whole *tote* (lot) of 'em, and my thousand blessings along with them." So she stood on the bawn *ditch* (fence) and blessed him as far as her eyes could see him.

Well, he went along and along till he was tired, and ne'er a farmer's house he went into wanted a boy.[2] At last his road led by the side of a bog, and there was a poor ass up to his shoulders near a big bunch of grass he was striving to come at. "Ah, then, Jack asthore," says he, "help me out or I'll be *dhrownded*." "Never say't twice," says Jack, and he pitched in big stones and *scraws* (sods) into the slob, till the ass got good ground under him. "Thank you, Jack," says he, when he was out on the hard road; "I'll do as much for you another time. Where are you going?" "Faith, I'm going to seek my fortune till harvest comes in, God bless it!" "And if you like," says the ass, "I'll go along with you; who knows what luck we may have!" "With all my heart; it's getting late, let us be jogging."

Well, they were going through a village, and a whole army of *gorsoons*[3] were hunting a poor dog with a *kittle* tied to his tail. He ran up to Jack for protection, and the ass let such a roar out of him, that the little thieves took to their heels as if the *ould boy* (the devil) was after them. "More power to you, Jack!" says the dog. "I'm much *obleeged* to you: where is the *baste*[4] and yourself

---

[1] A rich Dublin money-lender, contemporary with Dr. Jonathan Swift, and commemorated by him in an appropriate lament. Damer is to the Irish peasant what Crœsus was to the old Greeks.

[2] We must beg rigid grammarians to excuse some solecisms, without which the peasant idiom could not be truly given.

[3] *Garçons*, boys. In the counties of the Pale, the earliest colonized by the English, several Norman-French words and expressions, long obsolete in England, may still be heard.

[4] We are anxious in the expressions put into the mouths of

going?" "We're going to seek our fortune till harvest comes in." "And wouldn't I be proud to go with you!" says the dog, "and get *shut* (rid) of them ill-conducted boys; *purshuin'* to 'em!" "Well, well, throw your tail over your arm and come along."

They got outside the town, and sat down under an old wall, and Jack pulled out his bread and meat, and shared with the dog; and the ass made his dinner on a bunch of thistles. While they were eating and chatting, what should come by but a poor half-starved cat, and the *moll-row* he gave out of him would make your heart ache. "You look as if you saw the tops of nine houses since breakfast," says Jack; "here's a bone and something on it." "May your child never know a hungry belly!" says Tom; "it's myself that's in need of your kindness. May I be so bold as to ask where *yez* are all going?" "We're going to seek our fortune till the harvest comes in, and you may join us if you like." "And that I'll do with a heart and a half," says the cat, "and thank'ee for asking me."

Off they set again, and just as the shadows of the trees were three times as long as themselves, they heard a great cackling in a field inside the road, and out over the ditch jumped a fox with a fine black cock in his mouth. "Oh, you *anointed villian!*" says the ass, roaring like thunder. "At him, good dog!" says Jack, and the word wasn't out of his mouth when Coley was in full sweep after the *Moddhera Rua* (Red Dog). Reynard dropped his prize like a hot potato, and was off like shot, and the poor cock came back fluttering and trembling to Jack and his comrades. "O musha, *naybours!*" says he, "wasn't it the *hoith* o' luck that threw you in my way! Maybe I won't remember your

the characters to preserve the idiom, but not always to inflict the pronunciation on the reader. English youths and maidens are requested to recollect that the *g* in the final *ing* is seldom sounded; that *ea* and *ei* get the sound of *a* in *rare:* that *dr* and *tr* are pronounced *dhr* and *thr*, and *der* and *ter*, when not in the first syllable of a word, are sounded *dher* and *ther*. The Irish peasant never errs in the pronunciation of *ie*. So the reader may set down any sketch or story in which he finds *praste, belave, thafe,* as the composition of one thoroughly ignorant of Irish pronunciation or phraseology.

kindness if ever I find you in hardship; and where in the world are you all going?" "We're going to seek our fortune till the harvest comes in; you may join our party if you like, and sit on Neddy's crupper when your legs and wings are tired."

Well, the march began again, and just as the sun was gone down they looked around, and there was neither cabin nor farmhouse in sight. "Well, well," says Jack, "the worse luck now the better another time, and it's only a summer night after all. We'll go into the wood, and make our bed on the long grass." No sooner said than done. Jack stretched himself on a bunch of dry grass, the ass lay near him, the dog and cat lay in the ass's warm lap, and the cock went to roost in the next tree.

Well, the soundness of deep sleep was over them all, when the cock took a notion of crowing. "Bother you, *Cuileach Dhu* (Black Cock)!" says the ass: "you disturbed me from as nice a wisp of hay as ever I tasted. What's the matter?" "It's daybreak that's the matter: don't you see light yonder?" "I see a light indeed," says Jack, "but it's from a candle it's coming, and not from the sun. As you've roused us we may as well go over, and ask for lodging." So they all shook themselves, and went on through grass, and rocks, and briars, till they got down into a hollow, and there was the light coming through the shadow, and along with it came singing, and laughing, and cursing. "Easy, boys!" says Jack: "walk on your tippy toes till we see what sort of people we have to deal with." So they crept near the window, and there they saw six robbers inside, with pistols, and *blunderbushes*, and *cutlashes*, sitting at a table, eating roast beef and pork, and drinking mulled beer, and wine, and whisky punch.

"Wasn't that a fine haul we made at the Lord of Dunlavin's!" says one ugly-looking thief with his mouth full, "and it's little we'd get only for the honest porter: here's his purty health!" "The porter's purty health!" cried out every one of them, and Jack bent his finger at his comrades. "Close your ranks, my men," says he in a whisper, "and let every one mind the word of command." So the ass put his fore-hoofs on the sill of the window, the dog got on the ass's head, the cat got on the dog's head, and the cock on the cat's head. Then Jack made a sign, and they all sung out like mad. "Hee-haw, hee-haw!" roared the ass; "bow-wow!" barked the dog; "meaw-meaw!" cried the cat; "cock-a-doodle-doo!" crowed the cock. "Level your pistols!" cried Jack, "and make smithereens of 'em. Don't leave a mother's son of 'em alive; present, fire!" With that they gave another halloo, and smashed every pane in the window. The robbers were frightened out of their lives. They blew out the candles, threw down the table, and skelped out at the back door as if they were in earnest, and never drew rein till they were in the very heart of the wood.

Jack and his party got into the room, closed the shutters, lighted the candles, and ate and drank till hunger and thirst were gone. Then they lay down to rest;—Jack in the bed, the ass in the stable, the dog on the door mat, the cat by the fire, and the cock on the perch.

At first the robbers were very glad to find themselves safe in the thick wood, but they soon began to get vexed. "This damp grass is very different from our warm room," says one; "I was obliged to drop a fine pig's *crubeen* (foot)," says another; "I didn't get a *tay*-spoonful of my last tumbler," says another; "and all the Lord of Dunlavin's *goold* and silver that we left behind!" says the last. "I think I'll venture back," says the captain, "and see if we can recover anything." "That's a good boy!" said they all, and away he went.

The lights were all out, and so he groped his way to the fire, and there the cat flew in his face, and tore him with teeth and claws. He let a roar out of him, and made for the room door, to look for a candle inside. He trod on the dog's tail, and if he did, he got the marks of his teeth in his arms, and legs, and thighs. "*Millia murdher* (thousand murders)!" cried he; "I wish I was out of this unlucky house." When he got to the street door, the cock dropped down upon him with his claws and bill, and what the cat and dog *done* to him was only a *flay*-bite to what he got from the cock. " Oh, tattheration to you all, you unfeeling *vagabones !* " says he, when he recovered his breath ; and he staggered and spun round and round till he reeled into the stable, back foremost, but the ass received him with a kick on the broadest part of his small clothes, and laid him comfortably on the dunghill. When he came to himself, he scratched his head, and began to think what happened him ; and as soon as he found that his legs were able to carry him, he crawled away, dragging one foot after another, till he reached the wood.

"Well, well," cried *them* all, when he came within hearing, "any chance of our property ? " " You may say chance," says he, "and it's itself is the poor chance all out. Ah, will any of you pull a bed of dry grass for me ? All the sticking plaster in *Inniscorfy* (Enniscorthy) will be too little for the cuts and bruises I have on me. Ah, if you only knew what I have gone through for you ! When I got to the kitchen fire, looking for a sod of lighted turf, what should be there but a *colliach* (old woman) carding flax, and you may see the marks she left on my face with the cards. I made to the room door as fast as I could, and *who* should I stumble over but a cobbler and his seat, and if he did not work at me with his awls and his *pinchers* you may call me a rogue. Well, I got away from him somehow, but when I was passing through the door, it must be the *divel* himself that pounced down on me with his claws, and his teeth, that were equal to sixpenny nails, and his wings—ill luck be in his road ! Well, at last I reached the stable, and there, by way of salute, I got a pelt from a sledge-hammer that sent me half a mile off. If you don't believe me, I'll give you leave to go and judge for yourselves." "Oh, my poor captain," says they, "we believe you *to the nines*. Catch us, indeed, going within a hen's race of that unlucky cabin ! "

Well, before the sun shook his doublet next morning, Jack and his comrades were up and about. They made a hearty breakfast on what was left the night before, and then they all agreed to set off to the castle of the Lord of Dunlavin, and give him back all his gold and silver.

Jack put it all in the two ends of a sack, and laid it across Neddy's back, and all took the road in their hands. Away they went, through bogs, up hills, down dales, and sometimes along the *yalla* high road, till they came to the hall door of the Lord of Dunlavin, and who should be there, airing his powdered head, his white stockings, and his red breeches, but the thief of a porter.

He gave a cross look to the visitors, and says he to Jack, "What do you want here, my fine fellow? there isn't room for you all." "We want," says Jack, "what I'm sure you haven't to give us—and that is, common civility." "Come, be off, you lazy *geochachs* (greedy strollers)!" says he, "while a cat 'ud be licking her ear, or I'll let the dogs at you." "Would you tell a body," says the cock that was perched on the ass's head, "who was it that opened the door for the robbers the other night?" Ah! maybe the porter's red face didn't turn the colour of his frill, and the Lord of Dunlavin and his pretty daughter, that were standing at the parlour window *unknownst* to the porter, put out their heads. "I'd be glad, Barney," says the master, "to hear your answer to the gentleman with the red comb on him." "Ah, my lord, don't believe the rascal; sure I didn't open the door to the six robbers." "And how did you know there were six, you poor innocent?" said the lord. "Never mind, sir," says Jack, "all your gold and silver is there in that sack, and I don't think you will *begrudge* us our supper and bed after our long march from the wood of *Athsalach* (muddy ford)." "Begrudge, indeed! Not one of you will ever see a poor day if I can help it."

So all were welcomed to their hearts' content, and the ass, and the dog, and the cock got the best posts in the farmyard, and the cat took possession of the kitchen. The lord took Jack in hand, dressed him from top to toe in broadcloth, and frills as white as snow, and turn-pumps, and put a watch in his fob. When they sat down to dinner, the lady of the house said Jack had the air of a born gentleman about him, and the lord said he'd make him his steward. Jack brought his mother, and settled her comfortably near the castle, and all were as happy as you please. The old woman that told me the story said Jack and the young lady were married; but if they were, I hope he spent two or three years getting the *edication* of a gentleman. I don't think that a country boy would feel comfortable, striving to find *discoorse* for a well-bred young lady, the length of a summer's day, even if he had the *Academy of Compliments* and the *Complete Letter Writer* by heart.[1]

Our archæologists, who are of opinion that beast worship prevailed in Erin as well as in Egypt, cannot but be well pleased with our selection of this story, seeing the domestic animals endowed with such intelligence, and acting their parts so creditably in the stirring little drama. This animal *cultus* must have been of a fetish character, for among the legendary remains we find no acts of beneficence ascribed to serpent, or boar, or cat, but the contrary. The number of places in the country named from animals is very great. A horse cleared the Shannon at its mouth (a leap of nine miles); one of the Fenian hounds sprung across the river Roe in the North, and the town built on the locality gets its name from the circumstance (*Limavaddy*—Dog's leap). We have more than one large pool deriving its name from having been infested by a worm or a serpent in the days of the heroes. Fion M'Cumhaill killed several of these. A Munster champion slew a terrible specimen in the Duffrey (Co. Wexford), and the pool in which it sweltered is yet called Loch-na-Piastha. Near that remarkable piece of water is a ridge, called Kilach dermid (*Cullach Diarmuid*, Diarmuid's Boar). Even the domestic hen gives a name to a mountain in Lon-

[1] Two chap or pedler's books, great favourites among our populace during the last century, and still finding some readers. The concluding observations, as well as the body of the story, are in the words of the original narrator.

donderry, *Sliabh Cearc*,[1] and to a castle in Connaught, *Caislean na Cearca*. The dog has a valley in Roscommon (*Glann na Moddha*) to himself, and the pig (*muc*), among his possessions, owns more than one line of vale. Fion's exploits in killing terrible birds with his arrows, the boar that ravaged the great valley in Munster, and the various "piasts" in the lakes, bring him on a line with the Grecian Hercules. And as the old Pagans of that country and of Italy, along with a wholesome dread and hatred of the Stymphalides, hydras, and lions, warred on by Hercules, together with the Harpies and Cerberus, entertained for them a certain fetish reverence, so it is not to be wondered at if the secluded Celts of Ireland regarded their boars, and serpents, and cats, with similar feelings. Mr. Hackett relates a legend of a monster (genus and species not specified) who levied black mail in the form of flesh meat on a certain district in Cork to such an amount that they apprehended general starvation. In this exigency they applied to a holy man, and acting under his directions, they called the terrible tax-collector to a parley. They represented to him that they were nearly destitute of means to furnish his honour with another meal, but that if he consented to enter a certain big pot, and sleep till Monday, they would scatter themselves abroad, and collect such a supply of fish and flesh as would satisfy his appetite for a twelvemonth. Thinking the offer reasonable, he got into his crib, which was securely covered by his wily constituents, and dropped into an exceedingly deep hole in the neighbouring river. He looked on this as a strange proceeding, but kept his opinion to himself until next Monday. Then he roared

---

[1] In Celtic words *c* and *g* have uniformly a hard sound: they are never pronounced as *c* in *cent* or *g* in *gem*.

out to be set at liberty, but the unprincipled party with whom he had to do, stated that the time appointed had not arrived, seeing that Doomsday was the period named in the covenant. He insisted that Monday was the word, but learned, to his great disgust, that the Celtic name, besides doing duty for that first of working days, also implied the Day of Judgment. He gave a roar, and stupidly vented his rage in a stanza of five lines, to the effect that if he was once more at liberty he would not only eat up the whole country, but half the world into the bargain; and bitterly bewailed his ignorance of the perfidies of the Gaelic tongue, that had made him a wretched prisoner.

These observations on animal worship cannot be better brought to a close than by the mention of the cat who reigned over the Celtic branch of the feline race at Knobba, in Meath. The talented and very ill-tempered chief bard, Seanchan, satirized the mice in a body, and the cats also, including their king, for allowing the contemptible vermin to thrust their whiskers into the egg intended for his dinner. He was at Cruachan in Connaught at the time, but the venom of his verse disagreeably affected King *Irusan*, in his royal cave at Knowth, on the Boyne. He (the cat) took the road, and never stopped for refreshment, till, in the presence of the full court at Cruachan, he seized on the pestilent poet, and throwing him on his back, swept eastwards across the Shannon in full career. His intent was to take him home and make a sumptuous meal of him, assisted by Madame Sharptooth, his spouse, their daughter of the same name, and Roughtooth and the Purrer, their sons. However, as he was cantering through Clonmacnois, St. Kiaran, who, like his Saxon brother, St. Dunstan, was a skilful worker in metals, espied him while hammering on a long red-hot bar of iron. The saint set very small value on Seanchan as a bard, but, regarding him as a baptized man, he determined to disappoint the revengeful Irusan. Rushing out of his workshop, and assuming the correct attitude of a spear-thrower, he launched the flaming bar, which, piercing the cat near the flank, an inch behind the helpless body of the bard, passed through and through, stretched the feline king expiring in agony, and gave the ill-conditioned poet a space for repentance.

Not only can a general resemblance be traced in all the fictions of the great Japhetian divisions of the human race, but an enthusiastic and diligent explorer would be able to find a relationship between these and the stories current among the Semitic races, and even the tribes scattered over the great continent of Africa, subject to the variations arising from climate, local features, and the social condition of the people. One instance must suffice. In the cold north the fox persuaded the bear to let down his tail into a pond to catch fish, just as the frost was setting in. When a time sufficient for Reynard's purpose had elapsed he cried out, "Pull up the line, you have got a bite." The first effort was to no purpose. "Give a stouter pull—there is a great fish taken;" and now the bear put such a will in his strain that he left his tail under the ice. Since that time the family of Bruin are distinguished by stumpy tails. In Bournou, in Africa, where ice is rather scarce, the weasel said to the hyena, "I've just seen a large piece of flesh in such a pit. It is too heavy for me, but you can dip down your tail and I will fasten the meat to it, and then you have nothing to do but give a pull." "All right," said the hyena. When the tail was lowered, the weasel fastened it to a stout cross-stick, and gave the word for heaving. No success at first; then he cried out, "The meat is heavy—pull as if you were in earnest." At the second tug the tail was left behind, and ever since, hyenas have no tails worth mentioning.

The chief incidents of the following household tale would determine its invention to a period subsequent to the introduction of Christianity; but it would not have been difficult for a Christian story-teller to graft the delay of the baptism on some Pagan tale. It is slightly connected with the "Lassie and her Godmother" in the Norse collection. An instance of the rubbing-down process to which these old-world romances are subject in their descent through the generations of story-tellers, is the introduction of the post-office and its unworthy officer, long before the round ruler and the strip of parchment formed the writing apparatus of the kings of Sparta or their masters, the Ephori.

THE BAD STEPMOTHER.

Once there was a king, and he had two fine children, a girl and a boy; but he married again after their mother died, and a very wicked woman she was that he put over them. One day when he was out hunting, the stepmother came in where the daughter was sitting all alone, with a cup of poison in one hand and a dagger in the other, and made her swear that she would never tell any one that ever was christened what she would see her doing. The poor young girl—she was only fifteen—took the oath, and just after the queen took the king's favourite dog and killed him before her eyes.

When the king came back, and saw his pet lying dead in the hall, he flew into a passion, and axed who *done*[1]

---

[1] The reader must calculate on finding the perfect participle doing duty for the imperfect tense, and a total neglect of the pluperfect tense, when the story is given in the words of the original teller.

it; and says the queen, says she—"Who done it but your favourite daughter? There she is—let her deny it if she can!" The poor child burst out a crying, but wasn't able to say anything in her own defence *bekase* of her oath. Well, the king did not know what to do or to say. He cursed and swore a little, and hardly ate any supper. The next day he was out a hunting the queen killed the little son, and left him standing on his head on the window-seat of the lobby.

Well, whatever way the king was in before, he went mad now in earnest. "Who done this?" says he to the queen. "Who but your pet daughter?" "Take the vile creature," says he to two of his footmen, "into the forest, and cut off her two hands at the wrists, and maybe that'll teach her not to commit any more murders. Oh, Vuya, Vuya!" says he, stamping his foot on the boarded floor, "what a misfortunate king I am to lose my childher this way, and had only the two. Bring me back the two hands, or your own heads will be off before sunset."

When he stamped on the floor a splinter ran up into his foot through the sole of his boot; but he didn't mind it at first, he was in such grief and anger. But when he was taking off his boots, he found the splinter fastening one of them on his foot. He was very hardset to get it off, and was obliged to send for a surgeon to get the splinter out of the flesh; but the more he cut and probed, the further it went in. So he was obliged to lie on a *sofia* all day, and keep it poulticed with *bowl-almanac* or some other plaster.

Well, the poor princess, when her arms were cut off, thought the life would leave her: but she knew there was a holy well off in the wood, and to it she made her way. She put her poor arms into the moss that was growing over it, and the blood stopped flowing, and she was eased of the pain, and then she washed herself as well as she could. She fell asleep by the well, and the spirit of her mother appeared to her in a dream, and told her to be good, and never forget to say her prayers night and morning, and that she would escape every snare that would be laid for her.

When she awoke next morning she washed herself

again, and said her prayers, and then she began to feel hungry. She heard a noise, and she was so afraid that she got into a low broad tree that hung over the well. She wasn't there long till she saw a girl with a piece of bread and butter in one hand, and a pitcher in the other, coming and stooping over the well. She looked down through the branches, and if she did, so sure the girl saw her face in the water, and thought it was her own. She looked at it again and again, and then, without waiting to eat her bread or fill her pitcher, she ran back to the kitchen of a young king's palace that was just at the edge of the wood. "Where's the water?" says the housekeeper. "Wather!" says she; "it 'ud be a purty business for such handsome girl as I grew since yesterday, to be fetchin' wather for the likes of the people that's here. It's married to the young prince I ought to be." "Oh! to Halifax with you," says the housekeeper, "I'll soon cure your impedence." So she locked her up in the store-room, an' kep' her on bread and water.

To make a long story short, two other girls were sent to the well, and all were in the same story when they cum back. An' there was such a *thravally*[1] ruz in the kitchen about it at last, that the young king came to hear the rights of it. The last girl told him what happened to herself, and nothing would do the prince but go to the well to see about it. When he came he stooped and saw the *shadow* of the beautiful face; but he had sense enough to look up, and he found the princess in the tree.

Well, it would take me too long to tell yez all the fine things he said to her, and how modestly she answered him, and how he handed her down, and was almost ready to cry when he seen her poor arms. She would not tell him who she was, nor the way she was persecuted on account of her oath; but the short and the long of it was, that he took her home, and couldn't live if she didn't marry him. Well, married they were; and in course of time they had a fine little boy; but the

[1] Corruption of *reveillé*. This and many other Anglo-Saxon and Anglo-Norman words, such as *bon-grace*, "bonnet," *brief*, a corruption of "rife;" *grisset*, for "cresset," &c., are still in use in the counties of the Pale. *Ruz*, "arose."

strangest thing of all was that the young queen begged her husband not to have the child baptized till he'd be after coming home from the wars that the King of Ireland had just then with the Danes.

He agreed, and set off to the camp, giving a beautiful jewel to her just as his foot was in the stirrup. Well, he wrote to her every second day, and she wrote to him every second day, and dickens a letter ever came to the hands of him or her. For the wicked stepmother had her watched all along, from the very day she came to the well till the king went to the wars; and she gave such a bribe to the postman (!) that she got all the letters herself. Well, the poor king didn't know whether he was standing on his head or his feet, and the poor queen was crying all the day long.

At last there was a letter delivered to the king; and this was wrote by the wicked stepmother herself, as if it was from the young queen to one of the officers, asking him to get a furlough, and come and meet her at such a well, naming the one in the forest. He got this officer, that was as innocent as the child unborn, put in irons, and sent two of his soldiers to put the queen to death, and bring him his young child safe. But the night before, the spirit of the queen's mother appeared to her in a dream, and told her the danger that was coming. "Go," said she, "with your child to-morrow morning to the well, and dress yoursel in your maid's clothes before you leave the house; wash your arms in the well once more, and take a bottle of the water with you, and return to your father's palace. Nobody will know you. The water will cure him of a disorder he has, and I need not say any more."

Just as the young queen was told, just so she done; and when she was after washing her face and arms, lo and behold! her nice soft hands were restored; but her face that was as white as cream was now as brown as a berry. So she fell on her knees and said her prayers, and then she filled her bottle, and set out for her father's court with her child in her arms. The sentries at the palace gates let her pass when she said she was coming to cure the king; and she got to where he was lying in pain before the stepmother knew anything about it, for herself was sick at the time.

Before she opened her mouth the king loved her, she looked so like his former queen and his lost daughter, though her face was so swarthy. She hardly washed his wound with the water of the holy well when out came the splinter, and he was as strong on his limbs as a new ditch.

Well, hadn't he great *cooramuch* about the brown-faced woman and her child, and nothing that the wicked queen could do would alter his opinion of her. The old rogue didn't know who she was, especially as she wasn't without the hands; but it was her nature to be jealous of every one that the king cared for.

In two or three weeks the wars was over, and the young king was returning home, and the road he took brought him by his father-in-law's. The old king would not let him pass by without giving him an entertainment for all his bravery again' the Danes, and there was great huzzaing and cheering as he was riding up the avenue and through the courtyard. Just as he was alighting, his wife held up his little son to him, with the jewel in his little hand.

He got a wonderful fright. He knew his wife's features, but they were so tawny, and her pretty brown hands were to the good, and the child was his own picture, but still she couldn't be his false princess. He kissed the child, and passed on, but hardly said a word till dinner was over. Then says he to the old king, "Would you allow a brown woman and her child that I saw in the palace yard, to be sent for, till I speak to her?" "Indeed an' I will," said the other; "I owe my life to her." So she came in, and the young king made her sit down very close to him. "Young woman," says he, "I have a particular reason for asking who you are, and who is the father of that child." "I can't tell you that, sir," said she, "because of an oath I was obliged to take never to tell my story to any one that was christened. But my little boy was never christened, and to him I'll tell everything. My little son, you must know that my wicked stepmother killed my father's favourite dog, and killed my own little brother, and made me swear never to tell any one that ever received baptism, about it. She got my own father to have my hands chopped off, and I'd die only I washed them in the holy well in the forest. A king's son made me his wife, and she got him by forged letters to send orders to have me killed. The spirit of my mother watched over me; my hands were restored; my father's wound was healed; and now I place you in your own father's arms. Now, you may be baptized, thank God! and that's the story I had to tell you."

She took a wet towel, and wiped her face, and she became as white and red as she was the day of her marriage. She had like to be hurt with her husband and her father pulling her from each other; and such laughing and crying never was heard before or since. If the wicked stepmother didn't make her escape, she was torn between wild horses; and if they all didn't live happy after—that you and I may!

We heard the following household narrative only once. The narrator, Jemmy Reddy, was a young lad whose father's garden was on the line between the rented land of Ballygibbon, and the Common of the White Mountain (the boundary between Wexford and Carlow counties), consequently on the very verge of civilization. He was gardener, ploughman, and horseboy to the Rev. Mr. M. of Coolbawn, at the time of the learning of this tale. We had once the misfortune to be at a wake, when the adventures of another fellow with a goat-skin, not at all decent, were told by a boy with a bald head, rapidly approaching his eightieth year. Jemmy Reddy's story has nothing in common with it but the name. We recognized the other in Mr. Campbell's *Tales of the Highlands*, very much disguised; but, even in that tolerably decent garb, not worth preserving. The following avowal is made with some reluctance. Forty or fifty years since, several very vile tales—as vile as could be found in the *Fabliaux*, or the *Decameron*, or any other dirty collection, had a limited circulation among farm-servants and labourers, even in the respectable county of Wexford. It was one of these that poor old T. L. told. Let us hope that it has vanished from the collections still extant in our counties of the Pale.

ADVENTURES OF GILLA NA CHRECK AN GOUR.[1]

Long ago, a poor widow woman lived down near the iron forge, by Enniscorthy, and she was so poor, she had no clothes to put on her son; so she used to fix him in the ash-hole, near the fire, and pile the warm ashes about him; and according as he grew up, she sunk the pit deeper. At last, by hook or by crook, she got a goat-skin, and fastened it round his waist, and he felt quite grand, and took a walk down the street. So says she to him next morning, "Tom, you thief, you never done any good yet, and you six foot high, and past nineteen;—take that rope, and bring me a *bresna* from the wood." "Never say 't twice, mother," says Tom—"here goes."

When he had it gathered and tied, what should come up but a big *joiant*, nine foot high, and made a lick of a club at him. Well become Tom, he jumped a-one side, and picked up a ram-pike; and the first crack he gave the big fellow, he made him kiss the clod. "If you have e'er a prayer," says Tom, "now's the time to say it, before I make *brishe*[2] of you." "I have no prayers," says the giant; "but if you spare my life I'll give you that club; and as long as you keep from sin, you'll win every battle you ever fight with it."

Tom made no bones about letting him off; and as soon as he got the club in his hands, he sat down on the bresna, and gave it a tap with the kippeen, and says, "Bresna, I had a great trouble gathering you, and run the risk of my life for you; the least you can do is to carry

---

[1] Correctly, "Giolla na Chroicean Gobhar." (The Fellow with the Goat-skin.)

[2] A corruption of an old word still in use—root, *briser*, "to break."

me home." And sure enough, the wind o' the word was all it wanted. It went off through the wood, groaning and cracking, till it came to the widow's door.

Well, when the sticks were all burned, Tom was sent off again to pick more; and this time he had to fight with a giant that had two heads on him. Tom had a little more trouble with him—that's all; and the prayers *he* said, was to give Tom a fife, that nobody could help dancing when he was playing it. *Begonies*, he made the big fagot dance home, with himself sitting on it. Well, if you were to count all the steps from this to Dublin, dickens a bit you'd ever arrive there. The next giant was a beautiful boy with three heads on him. He had neither prayers nor catechism no more *nor* the others; and so he gave Tom a bottle of green ointment, that wouldn't let you be burned, nor scalded, nor wounded. "And now," says he, "there's no more of us. You may come and gather sticks here till little *Lunacy Day* in Harvest, without giant or fairy-man to disturb you."

Well, now, Tom was prouder nor ten paycocks, and used to take a walk down street in the heel of the evening; but some o' the little boys had no more manners than if they were Dublin jackeens, and put out their tongues at Tom's club and Tom's goat-skin. He didn't like that at all, and it would be mean to give one of them a clout. At last, what should come through the town but a kind of a bellman, only it's a big bugle he had, and a huntsman's cap on his head, and a kind of a painted shirt. So this—he wasn't a bellman, and I don't know what to call him—bugle-man, maybe, proclaimed that the King of Dublin's daughter was so melancholy that she didn't give a laugh for seven years, and that her father would grant her in marriage to whoever could make her laugh three times. "That's the very thing for me to try," says Tom; and so, without burning any more daylight, he kissed his mother, curled his club at the little boys, and off he set along the yalla highroad to the town of Dublin.

At last Tom came to one of the city gates, and the guards laughed and cursed at him instead of letting him in. Tom stood it all for a little time, but at last one of them—out of fun, as he said—drove his *bagnet* half an inch or so into his side. Tom done nothing but take the fellow by the scruff o' the neck and the waistband of his corduroys, and fling him into the canal. Some run to pull the fellow out, and others to let manners into the vulgarian with their swords and daggers; but a tap from his club sent them headlong into the moat or down on the stones, and they were soon begging him to stay his hands.

So at last one of them was glad enough to show Tom the way to the palace-yard; and there was the king, and the queen, and the princess, in a gallery, looking at all sorts of wrestling, and sword-playing, and *rinka-fadhas* (long dances), and mumming,[1] all to please the princess; but not a smile came over her handsome face.

Well, they all stopped when they seen the young giant, with his boy's face, and long black hair, and his short, curly beard—for his poor mother couldn't afford to buy *razhurs*—and his great strong arms, and bare legs, and no covering but the goatskin that reached from his waist to his knees. But an envious wizened *basthard*[2] of a fellow, with a red head, that wished to be married to the princess, and didn't like how she opened her eyes at Tom, came forward, and asked his business very snappishly. "My business," says Tom, says he, "is to make the beautiful princess, God bless her, laugh three times." "Do you see all them merry fellows and skilful swordsmen," says the other, "that could eat you up with a grain of salt, and not a mother's soul of 'em ever got a laugh from her these seven years?" So the fellows gathered round Tom, and the bad man aggravated him till he told them he didn't care a pinch o' snuff for the whole bilin' of 'em; let 'em come on, six at a time, and try what they could do. The king, that was too far off to hear what they were saying, asked what did the

[1] Jemmy and the editor of these stories had witnessed the *rinka-fadha*, with the vizarded, goat-bearded clown, and his wife (Tom Blanche the tailor), and May-boys and May-girls at Castle Boro, and had in their time enjoyed the speeches of mummers and the clashing of cudgels in *Droghedy's March*. So let no one accuse us of putting words unwarranted into the mouth of our story-teller.

[2] Contemptible, not necessarily illegitimate.

stranger want. "He wants," says the red-headed fellow, "to make hares of your best men." "Oh!" says the king, "if that's the way, let one of 'em turn out and try his mettle." So one stood forward, with *soord* and pot-lid, and made a cut at Tom. He struck the fellow's elbow with the club, and up over their heads flew the sword, and down went the owner of it on the gravel from a thump he got on the helmet. Another took his place, and another, and another, and then half-dozen at once, and Tom sent swords, helmets, shields, and bodies, rolling over and over, and themselves bawling out that they were kilt, and disabled, and damaged, and rubbing their poor elbows and hips, and limping away. Tom contrived not to kill any one; and the princess was so amused, that she let a great sweet laugh out of her that was heard over all the yard. "King of Dublin," says Tom, "I've quarter your daughter." And the king didn't know whether he was glad or sorry, and all the blood in the princess's heart run into her cheeks.

So there was no more fighting that day, and Tom was invited to dine with the royal family. Next day, Redhead told Tom of a wolf, the size of a yearling heifer, that used to be *serenading* (sauntering) about the walls, and eating people and cattle; and said what a pleasure it would give the king to have it killed. "With all my heart," says Tom; "send a jackeen to show me where he lives, and we'll see how he behaves to a stranger." The princess was not well pleased, for Tom looked a different person with fine clothes and a nice green *birredh* over his long curly hair; and besides he'd got one laugh out of her. However, the king gave his consent; and in an hour and a half the horrible wolf was walking into the palace-yard, and Tom a step or two behind, with his club on his shoulder, just as a shepherd would-be walking after a pet lamb.

The king and queen and princess were safe up in their gallery, but the officers and people of the court that wor *padrowling* about the great bawn, when they saw the big baste coming in, gave themselves up, and began to make for doors and gates; and the wolf licked his chops, as if he was saying, "Wouldn't I enjoy a breakfast off a couple of yez!" The king shouted out, "O Gilla na Chreck an Gour, take away that terrible wolf, and you must have all my daughter." But Tom didn't mind him a bit. He pulled out his flute and began to play like vengeance; and dickens a man or boy in the yard but began shovelling away heel and toe, and the wolf himself was obliged to get on his hind legs and dance *Tatther Jack Walsh*, along with the rest. A good deal of the people got inside, and shut the doors, the way the hairy fellow wouldn't pin them; but Tom kept playing, and the outsiders kept dancing and shouting, and the wolf kept dancing and roaring with the pain his legs were giving him: and all the time he had his eyes on Redhead, who was shut out along with the rest. Wherever Redhead went, the wolf followed, and kept one eye on him and the other on Tom, to see if he would give him leave to eat him. But Tom shook his head, and never stopped the tune, and Redhead never stopped dancing and bawling, and the wolf dancing and roaring, one leg up and the other down, and he ready to drop out of his standing from fair tiresomeness.

When the princess seen that there was no fear of any one being kilt, she was so divarted by the stew that Redhead was in, that she gave another great laugh; and, well become Tom, out he cried, "King of Dublin, I have two halves of your daughter." "Oh, halves or alls," says the king, "put away that divel of a wolf, and we'll see about it." So Gilla put his flute in his pocket, and says he to the baste that was sittin' on his currabingo ready to faint, "Walk off to your mountain, my fine fellow, and live like a respectable baste; and if I ever find you come within seven miles of any town, I'll——." He said no more, but spit in his fist, and gave a flourish of his club. It was all the poor divel wanted: he put his tail between his legs, and took to his pumps without looking at man or mortial, and neither sun, moon, or stars ever saw him in sight of Dublin again.

At dinner every one laughed but the foxy fellow; and sure enough he was laying out how he'd settle poor Tom next day. "Well, to be sure!" says he, "King of Dublin, you are in luck. There's the Danes moidhering us to no end. D—— run to Lusk wid 'em! and if any one can save us from 'em, it is this gentleman with the goatskin. There is a flail hangin' on the collar-beam in hell, and neither Dane nor devil can stand before it." "So," says Tom to the king, "will you let me have the other half of the princess if I bring you the flail?" "No, no," says the princess; "I'd rather never be your wife than see you in that danger."

But Redhead whispered and nudged Tom about how shabby it would look to reneague the adventure. So he asked which way he was to go, and Redhead directed him through a street where a great many bad women lived, and a great many sheebeen houses were open, and away he set.

Well, he travelled and travelled, till he came in sight of the walls of hell; and, bedad, before he knocked at the gates, he rubbed himself over with the greenish ointment. When he knocked, a hundred little imps popped their heads out through the bars, and axed him what he wanted. "I want to speak to the big divel of all," says Tom: "open the gate."

It wasn't long till the gate was *thrune* open, and the Ould Boy received Tom with bows and scrapes, and axed his business. "My business isn't much," says Tom. "I only came for the loan of that flail that I see hanging on the collar-beam, for the King of Dublin to give a thrashing to the Danes." "Well," says the other, "the Danes is much better customers to me; but since you walked so far I won't refuse. Hand that flail," says he to a young imp; and he winked the far-off eye at the same time. So, while some were barring the gates, the young devil climbed up, and took down the flail that had the handstaff and booltheen both made out of red-hot iron. The little vagabond was grinning to think how it would burn the hands off o' Tom, but the dickens a burn it made on him, no more nor if it was a good oak sapling. "Thankee," says Tom. "Now would you open the gate for a body, and I'll give you no more trouble." "Oh, tramp!" says Ould Nick; "is that the way? It is easier getting inside them gates than getting out again. Take that tool from him, and give him a dose of the oil of stirrup." So one fellow put out his claws to seize on the flail, but Tom gave him such a welt of it on the side of the head that he broke off one of his horns, and made him roar like a devil as he was. Well, they rushed at Tom but he gave them, little and big, such a thrashing as they didn't forget for a while. At last says the ould thief of all, rubbing his elbow, "Let the fool out; and woe to whoever lets him in again, great or small."

So out marched Tom, and away with him, without minding the shouting and cursing they kept up at him from the tops of the walls; and when he got home to the big bawn of the palace, there never was such running and racing as to see himself and the flail. When he had his story told, he laid down the flail on the stone steps, and bid no one for their lives to touch it. If the king, and queen, and princess, made much of him before, they made ten times more of him now; but Redhead, the mean scruffhound, stole over, and thought to catch hold of the flail to make an end of him. His fingers hardly touched it, when he let a roar out of him as if heaven and earth were coming together, and kept flinging his arms about and dancing, that it was pitiful to look at him. Tom run at him as soon as he could rise, caught his hands in his own two, and rubbed them this way and that, and the burning pain left them before you could reckon one. Well, the poor fellow, between the pain that was only just gone, and the comfort he was in, had the comicalest face that ever you see, it was such a mixtherum-gatherum of laughing and crying. Everybody burst out a laughing—the princess could not stop no more than the rest; and then says Gilla, or Tom, "Now, ma'am, if there were fifty halves of you, I hope you'll give me them all." Well, the princess had no mock modesty about her. She looked at her father, and by my word, she came over to Gilla, and put her two delicate hands into his two rough ones, and I wish it was myself was in his shoes that day!

Tom would not bring the flail into the palace. You may be sure no other body went near it; and when the early risers were passing next morning, they found two long clefts in the stone, where it was after burning itself an opening downwards, nobody could tell how far. But a messenger came in at noon and said that the Danes were so frightened when they heard of the flail coming into Dublin, that they got into their ships, and sailed away.

Well, I suppose, before they were married, Gilla got some man, like Pat Mara of Tomenine, to larn him the "principles of politeness," fluxions, gunnery and fortification, decimal fractions, practice, and the rule of three direct, the way he'd be able to keep up a conversation with the royal family. Whether he ever lost his time larning them sciences, I'm not sure, but it's as sure as fate that his mother never more saw any want till the end of her days.

Let not the present compiler be censured for putting this catalogue of learned branches into the mouth of an uneducated boy. We have seen Reddy, and half the congregation of Rathnure Chapel, swallowing with eyes, mouths, and ears, the enunciation of the *master's* assumed stock of knowledge, ornamented with flourishes, gamboge, verdigris, and vermilion, and set forth in the very order observed in the text.

In the *Volksmärchen* (People's Stories), *Hans* (the diminutive of Johannes) performs the greater part of the exploits. His namesake *Jack* is the hero of the household stories of the more English counties of Ireland. The following is a fair specimen of the class :—

JACK THE MASTER AND JACK THE SERVANT.

There was once a poor couple, and they had three sons, and the *youngest's* name was Jack. One harvest day, the eldest fellow threw down his hook, and says he, "What's the use to be slaving this way? I'll go seek my fortune." And the second son said the very same; and says Jack, "I'll go seek my fortune along with you, but let us first leave the harvest stacked for the old couple."

Well, he over-persuaded them, and bedad, as soon as it was safe, they kissed their father and mother, and off they set, every one with three pounds in his pocket, promising to be home again in a year and a day. The first night they had no better lodging than a fine dry dyke of a ditch, outside of a churchyard. Before they went to sleep, the youngest got inside to read the tombstones. What should he stumble over but a coffin and the sod was just taken off where the grave was to be. "Some poor body," says he, "that was without friends to put him in consecrated ground : he mustn't be left this way." So he threw off his coat, and had a couple of feet cleared out, when a terrible giant walked up. "What are you at ? " says he ; "The corpse owed me a guinea, and he sha'n't be buried till it is paid." "Well, here is your guinea," says Jack, "and leave the churchyard, it's nothing the better for your company." Well, he got down a couple of feet more, when another uglier giant again, with two heads on him, came and stopped Jack with the same story, and got his guinea ; and when the grave was six feet down, the third giant looks on him, and he had three heads. So Jack was obliged to part with his three guineas before he could put the sod over the poor man. Then he went and lay down by his brothers, and slept till the sun began to shine on their faces next morning.

They soon came to a cross-road, and there every one took his own way. Jack told them how all his money was gone, but not a farthing did they offer him. Well, after some time, Jack found himself hungry, and so he sat down by the road side, and pulled out a piece of cake and a lump of bacon. Just as he had the first bit in his mouth, up comes a poor man, and asks something of him for God's sake. "I have neither brass, gold, nor silver about me," says Jack ; "and here's all the provisions I'm master of. Sit down and have a share." Well the poor man didn't require much pressing, and when the meal was over, says he, "Sir, where are you bound for?" "Faith, I don't know," says Jack ; "I'm going to seek my fortune." "I'll go with you for your servant," says the other. "Servant *inagh* (forsooth) ! bad I want a servant—I, that's looking out for a place myself." "No matter. You gave Christian burial to my poor brother yesterday evening. He appeared to me in a dream, and told me where I'd find you, and that I was to be your servant for a year. So you'll be Jack the master, and I Jack the servant." "Well, let it be so."

After sunset, they came to a castle in a wood, and "Here," says the servant, "lives the giant with one head, that wouldn't let my poor brother be buried." He took hold of a club that hung by the door, and gave two or three *thravallys* on it. "What do yous want?" says the giant, looking out through a grating. "Oh, sir, honey!" says Jack, "we want to save you. The king is sending 100,000 men to take your life for all the wickedness you ever done to poor travellers, and that. So because you let my brother be buried, I came to help you." "Oh, murdher, murdher, what'll I do at all at all?" says he. "Have you e'er a hiding-place?" says Jack. "I have a cave seven miles long, and it opens into the bawn." "That'll do. Leave a good supper for the men, and then don't stir out of your pew till I call you." So they went in, and the giant left a good supper for the army, and went down, and they shut the trap-door down on him.

Well, they ate and they drank, and then Jack *gother* all the horses and cows, and drove them *over an hether* the trap-door, and such fighting and shouting, whinnying and lowing, as they had, and such noise as they made! Then Jack opened the door, and called out, "Are you there, sir?" "I am," says he, from a mile or two inside. "Wor you frightened, sir?" "You may say frightened. Are they gone away?" "Dickens a go they'll go till you give them your sword of sharpness." "Cock them up with the sword of sharpness. I won't give them a smite of it." "Well, I think you're right. Look out. They'll be down with you in the twinkling of a harrow pin. Go to the end of the cave, and they won't have your head for an hour to come." "Well, that's no great odds; you'll find it in the closet inside the parlour. D—— do 'em good with it." "Very well," says Jack; "when they're all cleared off, I'll drop a big stone on the trap-door." So the two Jacks slept very *combustible* in the giant's bed—it was big enough for them; and next morning, after breakfast, they dropped the big stone on the trap-door, and away they went.

That night they slept at the castle of the two-headed giant, and got his cloak of darkness in the same way; and the next night they slept at the castle of the three-headed giant, and got his shoes of swiftness; and the next night they were near the king's palace. "Now," says Jack the servant, "this king has a daughter, and she was so proud that twelve princes killed themselves for her, because she would not marry any of them. At last the King of *Moróco* thought to persuade her, and the dickens a bit of him she'd have no more nor the others. So he fell on his sword, and died; and the *old boy* got leave to give him a kind of life again, to punish the proud lady. Maybe it's an imp from hell is in his appearance. He lives in a palace one side of the river, and the king's palace is on the other, and he has got power over the princess and her father; and when they have the heads of twelve *courtiers* over the gate, the King of Moróco will have the princess to himself, and maybe the evil spirit will have them both. Every young man that offers himself has to do three things, and if he fails in all, up goes his head. There you see them—eleven, all black and white, with the sun and rain. You must try your hand. God is stronger than the devil."

So they came to the gate. "What do you want?" says the guard. "I want to get the princess for my wife." "Do you see them heads?" "Yes; what of that?" "Yours will be along with them before you're a week older." "That's my own look out." "Well, go on. God help all foolish people!" The king was on his throne in the big hall, and the princess sitting on a golden chair by his side. "Death or my daughter, I suppose," says the king to Jack the master. "Just so, my liege," says Jack. "Very well," says the king. "I don't know whether I'm glad or sorry," says he. "If you don't succeed in the three things, my daughter must marry the King of Moróco. If you do succeed, I suppose we'll be eased from the dog's life we are leading. I'll leave my daughter's scissors in your bedroom to-night, and you'll find no one going in till morning. If you have the scissors still at sunrise, your head will be safe for that day. Next day you must run a race against the King of Moróco, and if you win, your head will be safe that day too. Next day you must bring me the King of Moróco's head, or your own head, and then all this bother will be over one way or the other."

Well, they gave the two a good supper, and one time the princess would look sweet at Jack, and another time sour; for you know she was under enchantment. Sometimes she'd wish him killed, sometimes she'd like him to be saved.

When they went into their bedroom, the king came in along with them, and laid the scissors on the table. "Mind that," says he, "and I'm sure I don't know whether I wish to find it there to-morrow or not." Well, poor Jack was a little frightened, but his man encouraged him. "Go to bed," says he; "I'll put on the cloak of darkness, and watch, and I hope you'll find the scissors there at sunrise." Well, bedad he couldn't go to sleep. He kept his eye on the scissors till the dead hour, and the moment it struck twelve no scissors could he see: it vanished as clean as a whistle. He looked here, there, and everywhere—no scissors. "Well," says he, "there's hope still. Are you there, Jack?" but no answer came. "I can do no more," says he. "I'll go to bed." And to bed he went, and slept.

Just as the clock was striking, Jack in the cloak saw the wall opening, and the princess walking in, going over to the table, taking up the scissors, and walking out again. He followed her into the garden, and there he saw herself and her twelve maids going down to the boat that was lying by the bank. "I'm in," says the princess; "I'm in," says one maid; and "I'm in," says another; and so on till all were in; and "I'm in," says Jack. "Who's that?" says the last maid. "Go look," says Jack. Well, they were all a bit frightened. When they got over, they walked up to the King of Moróco's palace, and there the King of Moróco was to receive them, and give them the best of eating and drinking, and make his musicianers play the finest music for them.

When they were coming away, says the princess, "Here's the scissors; mind it or not as you like." "Oh, won't I mind it!" says he. "Here you go," says he again, opening a chest, and dropping it into it, and locking it up with three locks. But before he shut down the lid, my brave Jack picked up the scissors, and put it safe into his pocket. Well, when they came to the boat, the same things were said, and the maids were frightened again.

When Jack the master awoke in the morning, the first thing he saw was the scissors on the table, and the next thing he saw was his man lying asleep in the other bed, the next was the cloak of darkness hanging on the bed's foot. Well, he got up, and he danced, and he sung, and he hugged Jack; and when the king came in with a troubled face, there was the scissors safe and sound. "Well, Jack," says he, "you're safe for one day more." The king and princess were more *meentrach* (loving) to Jack to-day than they were yesterday, and the next day the race was to be run.

At last the hour of noon came, and there was the King of Moróco with tight clothes on him—themselves, and his hair, and his eyes as black as a crow, and his face as yellow as a kite's claw. Jack was there too, and on his feet were the shoes of swiftness. When the bugle blew, they were off, and Jack went seven times round the course while the king went one: it was like the fish in the water, the arrow from a bow, the stone from a sling, or a star shooting in the night. When the race was won, and the people were shouting, the black king looked at Jack like the very devil himself, and says he, "Don't holloa till you're out of the wood—to-morrow your head or mine." "Heaven is stronger than hell," says Jack.

And now the princess began to wish in earnest that Jack would win, for two parts of the charm were broke. So some one from her told Jack the servant that she and her maids should pay their visit to the Black Fellow at midnight like every other night past. Jack the servant was in the garden in his cloak when the hour came, and they all said the same words, and rowed over, and went up to the palace like as they done before.

The king was in a great state of fear and anger, and scolded the princess, and she didn't seem to care much about it; but when they were leaving she said, "You know to-morrow is to have your head or Jack's head off. I suppose you will stay up all night!" He was standing on the grass when they were getting into the boat, and just as the last maid had her foot on the edge of it, Jack swept off his head with the sword of sharpness just as if it was the head of a thistle, and put it under his cloak. The body fell on the grass and made no noise. Well, the same moment the princess felt any liking she had for him all gone like last year's snow, and she began to sob and cry for fear of anything happening to Jack. The maids were not very good at all, and so, from the moment they got out of the boat, Jack kept knocking the head against their faces and their legs, and made them roar and bawl till they were inside of the palace.

The first thing Jack the master saw when he woke in the morning, was the black head on the table, and didn't he jump up in a hurry. When the sun was rising, every one in the palace, great and small, were in the bawn before Jack's window, and the king was at the door. "Jack," said he, "if you haven't the King of Moróco's head on a gad, your own will be on a spear, my poor fellow." But just at the moment he heard a great shout from the bawn. Jack the servant was after opening the window, and holding out the King of Moróco's head by the long black hair.

So the princess, and the king, and all were in joy, and maybe they didn't keep the wedding long a-waiting. A year and a day after Jack left home, himself and his wife were in their coach at the cross-roads, and there were the two poor brothers, sleeping in the ditch with their reaping-hooks by their sides. They wouldn't believe Jack at first that he was their brother, and then they were ready to eat their nails for not sharing with him that day twelvemonth. They found their father and mother alive, and you may be sure they left them comfortable. So you see what a good thing in the end it is to be charitable to the poor, dead or alive.

In some versions of "Jack the Master," &c., Jack the servant is the spirit of the buried man. He aids and abets his master in leaving the giants interred alive in their caves, and carrying off their gold and silver, and he helps him to cheat his future father-in-law at cards, and bears a hand in other proceedings, most disgraceful to any ghost encumbered with a conscience. As originally told, the anxiety of the hero to bestow sepulchral rites on the corpse, arose from his wish to rescue the soul from its dismal wanderings by the gloomy Styx. In borrowing these fictions from their heathen predecessors, the Christian storytellers did not take much trouble to correct their laxity on the subject of moral obligations. Theft, manslaughter, and disregard of marriage vows, often pass uncensured by the free and easy narrator.

Silly as the poor hero of the next tale may appear, he is kept in countenance by the German "Hans in Luck," by the world-renowned Wise Men of Gotham, and even the sage Gooroo, of Hindoostan. In a version of the legend given by a servant girl, who came from the *Roer* in Kilkenny, and had only slight knowledge of English, Thigue distinguished himself by an exploit more worthy of his character than any in the text. He stood in the market, with a web of cloth under his arm for sale. "Bow wow," says a dog, looking up at him. "Five pounds," says Thigue; "Bow wow," says the dog again. "Well, here it is for you," says Thigue. His reception by his mother at eventide may be guessed.

I'LL BE WISER THE NEXT TIME.

Jack was twenty years old before he done any good for his family. So at last his mother said it was high time for him to begin to be of some use. So the next market day she sent him to Bunclody (Newtownbarry), to buy a billhook to cut the furze. When he was coming back he kep' cutting gaaches with it round his head, till at last it flew out of his hand, and killed a lamb that a neighbour was bringing home. Well, if he did, so sure was his mother obliged to pay for it, and Jack was in disgrace. "Musha, you fool," says she, "couldn't you lay the billhook in a car, or stick it into a bundle of hay or straw that any of the neighbours would be bringing home?" "Well, mother," said he, "it can't be helped now; I'll be wiser next time."

"Now, Jack," says she, the next Saturday, "you behaved like a fool the last time; have some wit about you now, and don't get us into a hobble. Here is a fi'penny bit, and buy me a good pair (set) of knitting needles, and fetch 'em home safe." "Never fear, mother." When Jack was outside the town, coming back, he overtook a neighbour sitting on the side-lace of his car, and there was a big bundle of hay in the bottom of it. "Just the safe thing," says Jack, sticking the needles into it. When he came home he looked quite proud of his good management. "Well, Jack," says his mother, "where's the needles?" "Oh, faith! they're safe enough. Send any one down to Jem Doyle's, and he'll find them in the bundle of hay that's in the car." "Musha, purshuin to you, Jack! why couldn't you stick them in the band o' your hat? What searching there will be for them in the hay!" "Sure you said I ought to put any things I was bringing home in a car, or stick 'em in hay or straw. Anyhow I'll be wiser next time."

Next week Jack was sent to a neighbour's house about a mile away, for some of her nice fresh butter. The day was hot, and Jack remembering his mother's words, stuck the cabbage leaf that held the butter between his hat and the band. He was luckier this turn than the other turns, for he brought his errand safe in his hair and down along his clothes. There's no pleasing some people, however, and his mother was so vexed that she was ready to beat him.

There was so little respect for Jack's gumption in the whole village after this, that he wasn't let go to market for a fortnight. Then his mother trusted him with a pair of young fowl. "Now don't be too eager to snap at the first offer you'll get; wait for the second any way, and above all things keep your wits about you." Jack got to the market safe. "How do you sell them fowl, honest boy?" "My mother bid me ax three shillings for 'em, but sure herself said I wouldn't get it." "She never said a truer word. Will you have eighteen pence?" "In throth an' I won't; she ordhered me to wait for a second offer." "And very wisely she acted; here is a shilling." "Well now, I think it would be wiser to take the eighteen pence, but it is better for me at any rate to go by her bidding, and then she can't blame me."

Jack was in disgrace for three weeks after making that bargain; and some of the neighbours went so far as to say that Jack's mother didn't show much more wit than Jack himself.

She had to send him, however, next market day to sell a young sheep, and says she to him, "Jack, I'll have your life if you don't get the highest penny in the market for that baste." "Oh, won't I!" says Jack. Well, when he was standing in the market, up comes a jobber, and asks him what he'd take for the sheep. "My mother won't be satisfied," says Jack, "if I don't bring her home the highest penny in the market." "Will a guinea note do you?" says the other. "Is it the highest penny in the market?" says Jack. "No, but here's the highest penny in the market," says a sleeveen that was listenin', getting up on a high ladder that was restin' again' the market house: "here's the highest penny, and the sheep is mine."

Well, if the poor mother wasn't heart-scalded this time it's no matter. She said she'd never lose more than a shilling a turn by him again while she lived; but she had to send him for some groceries next Saturday for all that, for it was Christmas eve. "Now, Jack," says she, "I want some cinnamon, mace, and cloves, and half a pound of raisins; will you be able to think of 'em?" "Able, indeed! I'll be repatin' 'em every inch o' the way, and that won't let me forget them." So he never stopped as he ran along, saying "cinnamon, mace, and cloves, and half a pound of raisins;" and this time he'd have come home in glory, only he struck his foot again' a stone, and fell down, and hurt himself.

At last he got up, and as he went limping on he strove to remember his errand, but it was changed in his mind to "pitch, and tar, and turpentine, and half a yard of sacking"—"pitch, and tar, and turpentine, and half a yard of sacking." These did not help the Christmas dinner much, and his mother was so tired of minding him that she sent him along with a clever *black man* (match-maker), up to the county Carlow, to get a wife to take care of him.

Well, the black man never let him open his mouth all the time the coortin' was goin' on; and at last the whole party—his friends, and her friends, were gathered into the priest's parlour. The black man stayed close to him for 'fraid he'd do a bull; and when Jack was married half a-year, if he thought his life was bad enough before, he thought it ten times worse now; and told his mother if she'd send his wife back to her father, he'd never make a mistake again going to fair or market. But the wife cock-crowed over the mother as well as over Jack; and if they didn't live happy, THAT WE MAY!

The ensuing household story has rather more of a Norse than Celtic air about it, though there are apparently no traces of it in Grimm's or Dasent's collections, except in the circumstances of the flight. Parts of the story may be recognised in the West Highland Tales, but we have met with the tale in full nowhere in print. Jemmy Reddy, Father Murphy's servant, the relater of the "Adventures of Gilla na Chreck an Gour," told it to the occupants of the big kitchen hearth in Coolbawn, one long winter evening, nearly in the style in which it is here given, and no liberty at all has been taken with the incidents. The underground adventures seem to point to the Celtic belief in the existence of the "Land of Youth," under our lakes. If it were ever told in

Scandinavia, the spacious caverns of the Northern land would be substituted for our Tir-na-n-Oge, with the bottom of the sea for its sky, and its own sun, moon, and stars. The editor of this series never heard a second recitation of this household story.

THE THREE CROWNS.

There was once a king, some place or other, and he had three daughters. The two eldest were very proud and uncharitable, but the youngest was as good as they were bad. Well, three princes came to court them, and two of them were the *moral* of the eldest ladies, and one was just as lovable as the youngest. They were all walking down to a lake, one day, that lay at the bottom of the lawn, just like the one at Castleboro', and they met a poor beggar. The king wouldn't give him anything, and the eldest princes wouldn't give him anything, nor their sweethearts; but the youngest daughter and her true love did give him something, and kind words along with it, and that was better *nor* all.

When they got to the edge of the lake, what did they find but the beautifulest boat you ever saw in your life; and says the eldest, "I'll take a sail in this fine boat;" and says the second eldest, "I'll take a sail in this fine boat;" and says the youngest, "I won't take a sail in that fine boat, for I am afraid it's an enchanted one.' But the others overpersuaded her to go in, and her father was just going in after her, when up sprung on the deck a little man only seven inches high, and he ordered him to stand back. Well, all the men put their hands to their soords; and if the same soords were only thraneens they weren't able to draw them, for all *sthrenth* was left their arms. *Seven Inches* loosened the silver chain that fastened the boat, and pushed away; and after grinning at the four men, says he to them, "Bid your daughters and your brides farewell for awhile. That wouldn't have happened you three, only for your want of charity. You," says he to the youngest, "needn't fear, you'll recover your princess all in good time, and you and she will be as happy as the day is long. Bad people, if they were rolling stark naked in gold, would not be rich. *Banacht lath.*" Away they sailed, and the ladies stretched out their hands but weren't able to say a word.

Well, they weren't crossing the lake while a cat 'ud be lickin' her ear, and the poor men couldn't stir hand or foot to follow them. They saw *Seven Inches* handing the three princesses out o' the boat, and letting them down by a nice basket and *winglas* into a draw-well that was convenient, but king nor princes ever saw an opening before in the same place. When the last lady was out of sight, the men found the strength in their arms and legs again. Round the lake they ran, and never drew rein till they came to the well and windlass; and there was the silk rope rolled on the axle, and the nice white basket hanging to it. "Let me down," says the youngest prince; "I'll die or recover them again." "No," says the second daughter's sweetheart, "I'm entitled to my turn before you." And says the other, "I must get first turn, in right of my bride." So they gave way to him, and in he got into the basket, and down they let him. First they lost sight of him, and then, after winding off a hundred perches of the silk rope, it slackened, and they stopped turning. They waited two hours, and then they went to dinner, because there was no chuck made at the rope.

Guards were set till next morning, and then down went the second prince, and sure enough, the youngest of all got himself let down on the third day. He went down perches and perches, while it was as dark about him as if he was in a big pot with the cover on. At last he saw a glimmer far down, and in a short time he felt the ground. Out he came from the big lime-kiln, and lo and behold you, there was a wood, and green fields, and a castle in a lawn, and a bright sky over all. "It's in Tir-na-n-Oge I am," says he. "Let's see what sort of people are in the castle." On he walked, across fields and lawn, and no one was there to keep him out or let him into the castle; but the big hall door was wide open. He went from one fine room to another that was finer, and at last he reached the handsomest of all, with a table in the middle; and such a dinner as was laid upon it! The prince was hungry enough, but he was too mannerly to go eat without being invited. So he sat by the fire, and he did not wait long till he heard steps, and in came *Seven Inches* and the youngest sister by the hand. Well, prince and princess flew into one another's arms, and says the little man, says he, "Why aren't you eating?" "I think, sir," says he, "it was only good manners to wait to be asked." "The other princes didn't think so," says he. "Each o' them fell to without leave or licence, and only gave me the rough side o' their tongue when I told them they were making more free than welcome. Well, I don't think they feel much hunger now. There they are, good *marvel* instead of flesh and blood," says he, pointing to two statues, one in one corner, and the other in the other corner of the room. The prince was frightened, but he was afraid to say anything, and *Seven Inches* made him sit down to dinner between himself and his bride; and he'd be as happy as the day is long, only for the sight of the stone men in the corner. Well, that day went by, and when the next came, says *Seven Inches* to him: "Now, you'll have to set out that way," pointing to the sun; "and you'll find the second princess in a giant's castle this evening, when you'll be tired and hungry, and the eldest princess to-morrow evening; and you may as well bring them here with you. You need not ask leave of their masters; they're only housekeepers with the big fellows. I suppose, if they ever get home, they'll look on poor people as if they were flesh and blood like themselves."

Away went the prince, and bedad, it's tired and hungry he was when he reached the first castle, at sunset. Oh, wasn't the second princess glad to see him! and if she didn't give him a good supper, it's a wonder. But she heard the giant at the gate, and she hid the prince in a closet. Well, when he came in, he snuffed, an' he snuffed, an' says he, "*Be* (by) the life, I smell fresh mate." "Oh," says the princess, "it's only the calf I got killed to-day." "Ay, ay," says he, "is supper ready?" "It is," says she; and before he ruz from the table he hid three-quarters of the calf, and a cag of wine. "I think," says he, when all was done, "I smell fresh mate still." "It's sleepy you are," says she, "go to bed." "When will you marry me?" says the giant. "You're puttin' me off too long." "St. Tibb's Eve," says she. "I wish I knew how far off that is," says he; and he fell asleep, with his head in the dish.

Next day, he went out after breakfast, and she sent the prince to the castle where the eldest sister was. The same thing happened there; but when the giant was snoring, the princess wakened up the prince, and they saddled two steeds in the stables, and *magh go bragh* (the field for ever) with them. But the horses' heels struck the stones outside the gate, and up got the giant, and after them he made. He roared and he shouted, and the more he shouted, the faster ran the horses; and just as the day was breaking, he was only twenty perches behind. But the prince didn't leave the castle of *Seven Inches* without being provided with something good. He reined in his steed, and flung a short, sharp knife over his shoulder, and up sprung a thick wood between the giant and themselves. They caught the wind that blew before them, and the wind that blew behind them did not catch them. At last they were near the castle where the other sister lived; and there she was, waiting for them under a high hedge, and a fine steed under her.

But the giant was now in sight, roaring like a hundred lions, and the other giant was out in a moment, and the chase kept on. For every two springs the horses gave, the giants gave three, and at last they were only seventy perches off. Then the prince stopped again, and flung the second skian behind him. Down went all the flat field, till there was a quarry between them a quarter of a mile deep, and the bottom filled with black water; and before the giants could get round it, the prince and princesses were inside the domain of the great magician, where the high thorny hedge opened of itself to every one that he chose to let in.

Well, to be sure, there was joy enough between the three sisters, till the two eldest saw their lovers turned into stone. But while they were shedding tears for them, *Seven Inches* came in, and touched them with his rod.

So they were flesh, and blood, and life once more, and there was great hugging and kissing, and all sat down to a nice breakfast, and *Seven Inches* sat at the head of the table.

When breakfast was over, he took them into another room, where there was nothing but heaps of gold, and silver, and diamonds, and silks, and satins; and on a table there was lying three sets of crowns: a gold crown was in a silver crown, and that was lying in a copper crown. He took up one set of crowns, and gave it to the eldest princess; and another set, and gave it to the second youngest princess; and another, and gave it to the youngest of all; and says he, "Now you may all go to the bottom of the pit, and you have nothing to do but stir the basket, and the people that are watching above will draw you up. But remember, ladies, you are to keep your crowns safe, and be married in them, all the same day. If you be married separately, or if you be married without your crowns, a curse will follow—mind what I say."

So they took leave of him with great respect, and walked arm-in-arm to the bottom of the draw-well. There was a sky and a sun over them, and a great high wall, covered with ivy, rose before them, and was so high they could not see to the top of it; and there was an arch in this wall, and the bottom of the draw-well was inside the arch. The youngest pair went last; and says the princess to the prince, "I'm sure the two princes don't mean any good to you. Keep these crowns under your cloak, and if you are obliged to stay last, don't get into the basket, but put a big stone, or any heavy thing inside, and see what will happen."

So, when they were inside the dark cave, they put in the eldest princess first, and stirred the basket, and up she went, but first she gave a little scream. Then the basket was let down again, and up went the second princess, and then up went the youngest; but first she put her arms round her prince's neck, and kissed him, and cried a little. At last it came to the turn of the youngest prince, and well became him;—instead of going into the basket, he put in a big stone. He drew on one side and listened, and after the basket was drawn up about twenty perch, down came itself and the stone like thunder, and the stone was made brishe of on the flags.

Well, my poor prince had nothing for it but to walk back to the castle; and through it and round it he walked, and the finest of eating and drinking he got, and a bed of bog-down to sleep on, and fine walks he took through gardens and lawns, but not a sight could he get, high or low, of *Seven Inches*. Well, I don't think any of *us* would be tired of this fine way of living for ever. Maybe we would. Anyhow the prince got tired of it before a week, he was so lonesome for his true love; and at the end of a month he didn't know what to do with himself.

One morning he went into the treasure room, and took notice of a beautiful snuff-box on the table that he didn't remember seeing there before. He took it in his hands, and opened it, and out *Seven Inches* walked on the table. "I think, prince," says he, "you're getting a little tired of my castle?" "Ah!" says the other, "if I had my princess here, and could see you now and then, I'd never see a dismal day." "Well, you're long enough here now, and you're wanting there above. Keep your bride's crowns safe, and whenever you want my help, open this snuff-box. Now take a walk down the garden, and come back when you're tired."

Well, the prince was going down a gravel walk with a quickset hedge on each side, and his eyes on the ground, and he thinking on one thing and another. At last he lifted his eyes, and there he was outside of a smith's bawn-gate that he often passed before, about a mile away from the palace of his betrothed princess. The clothes he had on him were as ragged as you please, but he had his crowns safe under his old cloak.

So the smith came out, and says he, "It's a shame for a strong, big fellow like you to be on the *sthra*, and so much work to be done. Are you any good with hammer and tongs? Come in and bear a hand, and I'll give you diet and lodging, and a few thirteens when you earn them." "Never say't twice," says the prince; "I want nothing but to be employed." So he took the sledge, and pounded away at the red-hot bar that the smith was turning on the anvil to make into a set of horse-shoes.

Well, they weren't long powdhering away, when a *sthronshuch* (idler) of a tailor came in; and when the smith asked him what news he had, he got the handle of the bellows and began to blow, to let out all he had heard for the last two days. There was so many questions and answers at first, that if I told them all, it would be bedtime afore I'd be done. So here is the substance of the discourse; and before he got far into it, the forge was half-filled with women knitting stockings, and men smoking.

"Yous all heard how the two princesses were unwilling to be married till the youngest would be ready with her crowns and her sweetheart. But after the windlass loosened *accidentally* when they were pulling up her bridegroom that was to be, there was no more sign of a well, or a rope, or a windlass, than there is on the palm of your hand. So the buckeens that wor coortin' the eldest ladies, wouldn't give peace or ease to their lovers nor the king, till they got consent to the marriage, and it was to take place this morning. Myself went down out o' curosity; and to be sure I was delighted with the grand dresses of the two brides, and the three crowns on their heads—gold, silver, and copper, one inside the other. The youngest was standing by mournful enough in white, and all was ready. The two bridegrooms came in as proud and grand as you please, and up they were walking to the altar rails, when, my dear, the boards opened two yards wide under their feet, and down they went among the dead men and the coffins in the vaults. Oh, such screeching as the ladies gave! and such running and racing and peeping down as there was; but the clerk soon opened the door of the vault, and up came the two heroes, and their fine clothes covered an inch thick with cobwebs and mould."

So the king said they should put off the marriage, "For," says he, "I see there is no use in thinking of it till my youngest gets her three crowns, and is married along with the others. I'll give my youngest daughter for a wife to whoever brings three crowns to me like the others; and if he doesn't care to be married, some other one will, and I'll make his fortune." "I wish," says the smith, "I could do it: but I was looking at the crowns after the princesses got home, and I don't think there's a black or a white smith on the face o' the earth could imitate them." "Faint heart never won fair lady," says the prince. "Go to the palace and ask for a quarter of a pound of gold, a quarter of a pound of silver, and a quarter of a pound of copper. Get one crown for a pattern; and my head for a pledge, I'll give you out the very things that are wanted in the morning." "Ubbabow!" says the smith, "are you in earnest?" "Faith, I am so," says he. "Go! worse than lose you can't."

To make a long story short, the smith got the quarter of a pound of gold, and the quarter of a pound of silver, and the quarter of a pound of copper, and gave them and the pattern crown to the prince. He shut the forge door at nightfall, and the neighbours all gathered in the bawn, and they heard him hammering, hammering, hammering, from that to daybreak; and every now and then he'd pitch out through the window, bits of gold, silver, and copper; and the idlers scrambled for them, and cursed one another, and prayed for the good luck of the workman.

Well, just as the sun was thinking to rise, he opened the door, and brought out the three crowns he got from his true love, and such shouting and huzzaing as there was! The smith asked him to go along with him to the palace, but he refused; so off set the smith, and the whole townland with him; and wasn't the king rejoiced when he saw the crowns! "Well," says he to the smith, "you're a married man; what's to be done?" "Faith, your majesty, I didn't make them crowns at all; it was a big *shuler* (vagrant) of a fellow that took employment with me yesterday." "Well, daughter, will you marry the fellow that made these crowns?" "Let me see them first, father." So when she examined them, she knew them right well, and guessed it was her true-love that sent them. "I will marry the man that these crowns came from," says she.

"Well," says the king to the eldest of the two princes, "go up to the smith's forge, take my best coach, and bring home the bridegroom." He was very unwilling to do this, he was so proud, but he did not wish to refuse. When he came to the forge, he saw the prince standing at the door, and beckoned him over to the coach. "Are you the fellow," says he, "that made them crowns?" "Yes," says the other. "Then," says he, "maybe you'd give yourself a brushing, and get into that coach; the king wants to see you. I pity the princess." The young prince got into the carriage, and while they were on the way, he opened the snuff-box, and out walked *Seven Inches*, and stood on his thigh. "Well," says he, "what trouble is on you now?" "Master," says the other, "please to let me be back in my forge, and let this carriage be filled with paving stones." No sooner said than done. The prince was sitting in his forge, and the horses wondered what was after happening to the carriage.

When they came into the palace yard, the king himself opened the carriage door, to pay respect to his new son-in-law. As soon as he turned the handle, a shower of small stones fell on his powdered wig and his silk coat, and down he fell under them. There was great fright and some tittering, and the king, after he wiped the blood from his forehead, looked very cross at the eldest prince. "My liege," says he, "I'm very sorry for this *accidence*, but I'm not to blame. I saw the young smith get into the carriage, and we never stopped a minute since." "It's uncivil you were to him. Go," says he, to the other prince, "and bring the young smith here, and be polite." "Never fear," says he.

But there's some people that couldn't be good-natured if they were to be made heirs of Damer's estate. Not a bit civiller was the new messenger than the old, and when the king opened the carriage door a second time, it's a shower of mud that came down on him; and if he didn't fume, and splutter, and shake himself, it's no matter. "There's no use," says he, "going on this way. The fox never got a better messenger than himself."

So he changed his clothes, and washed himself, and

out he set to the smith's forge. Maybe he wasn't polite to the young prince, and asked him to sit along with himself. The prince begged to be allowed to sit in the other carriage, and when they were half-way, he opened his snuff-box. "Master," says he, "I'd wish to be dressed now according to my rank." "You shall be that," says *Seven Inches*. "And now I'll bid you farewell. Continue as good and kind as you always were; love your wife, and that's all the advice I'll give you." So *Seven Inches* vanished; and when the carriage door was opened in the yard—not by the king though, for a burnt child dreads the fire—out walks the prince as fine as hands and pins could make him, and the first thing he did was to run over to his bride, and embrace her very heartily.

Every one had great joy but the two other princes. There was not much delay about the marriages that were all celebrated on the one day. Soon after, the two elder couples went to their own courts, but the youngest pair stayed with the old king, and they were as happy as the happiest married couple you ever heard of in a story.

The next tale is one which was repeated oftenest in our hearing during our country experience. It probably owed its popularity to the bit of a rhyme, and the repetition of the adventures of the three sisters, nearly in the same words. It may seem strange that this circumstance, which would have brought *ennui* and discomfort on our readers, should have recommended it to the fireside audiences. Let it be considered that they expected to sit up to a certain hour, and that listening to a story was the pleasantest occupation they could fancy for the time. Length, then, in a tale was a recommendation, and these repetitions contributed to that desirable end.

THE CORPSE WATCHERS.

There was once a poor woman that had three daughters, and one day the eldest said, "Mother, bake my cake and kill my cock, till I go seek my fortune." So she did, and when all was ready, says her mother to her, "Which will you have—half of these with my blessing, or the whole with my curse?" "Curse or no curse," says she, "the whole is little enough." So away she set, and if the mother didn't give her her curse, she didn't give her her blessing.

She walked and she walked till she was tired and hungry, and then she sat down to take her dinner. While she was eating it, a poor woman came up, and asked for a bit. "The dickens a bit you'll get from me," says she; "it's all too little for myself;" and the poor woman walked away very sorrowful. At nightfall she got lodging at a farmer's, and the woman of the house told her that she'd give her a spade-full of gold and a shovel-full of silver if she'd only sit up and watch her son's corpse that was waking in the next room. She said she'd do that; and so, when the family were in their bed, she sat by the fire, and cast an eye from time to time on the corpse that was lying *under* the table.

All at once the dead man got up in his shroud, and stood before her, and said, "All alone, fair maid!" She gave him no answer, and when he said it the third time, he struck her with a switch, and she became a grey flag.

About a week after, the second daughter went to seek her fortune, and she didn't care for her mother's blessing no more *nor* her sister, and the very same thing happened to her. She was left a grey flag by the side of the other.

At last the youngest went off in search of the other two, and she took care to carry her mother's blessing with her. She shared her dinner with the poor woman on the road, and *she* told her that she would watch over her.

Well, she got lodging in the same place as the others, and agreed to mind the corpse. She sat up by the fire with the dog and cat, and amused herself with some apples and nuts the mistress gave her. She thought it a pity that the man under the table was a corpse, he was so handsome.

But at last he got up, and says he, "All alone, fair maid!" and she wasn't long about an answer :—

> "All alone I am not,
> I've little dog Douse and Pussy, my cat;
> I've apples to roast, and nuts to crack,
> And all alone I am not."

"Ho, ho!" says he, "you're a girl of courage, though you wouldn't have enough to follow me. I am now going to cross the quaking bog, and go through the burning forest. I must then enter the cave of terror, and climb the hill of glass, and drop from the top of it into the Dead Sea." "I'll follow you," says she, "for I engaged to mind you." He thought to prevent her, but she was as stiff as he was stout.

Out he sprang through the window, and she followed him till they came to the "Green Hills," and then says he :—

"Open, open, Green Hills, and let the Light of the Green Hills through;"
"Aye," says the girl, "and let the fair maid, too."

They opened, and the man and woman passed through, and there they were, on the edge of a bog.

He trod lightly over the shaky bits of moss and sod; and while she was thinking of how she'd get across, the old beggar appeared to her, but much nicer dressed, touched her shoes with his stick, and the soles spread a foot on each side. So she easily got over the shaky marsh. The burning wood was at the edge of the bog, and there the good fairy flung a damp, thick cloak over her, and through the flames she went, and a hair of her head was not singed. Then they passed through the dark cavern of horrors, where she'd have heard the most horrible yells, only that the fairy stopped her ears with wax. She saw frightful things, with blue vapours round them, and felt the sharp rocks, and the slimy backs of frogs and snakes.

When they got out of the cavern, they were at the mountain of glass; and then the fairy made her slippers so sticky with a tap of her rod, that she followed the young corpse easily to the top. There was the deep sea a quarter of a mile under them, and so the corpse said to her, "Go home to my mother, and tell her how far you came to do her bidding: farewell." He sprung head foremost down into the sea, and after him she plunged, without stopping a moment to think about it.

She was stupefied at first, but when they reached the waters she recovered her thoughts. After piercing down a great depth, they saw a green light towards the bottom. At last they were below the sea, that seemed a green sky above them; and sitting in a beautiful meadow, she half asleep, and her head resting against his side. She couldn't keep her eyes open, and she couldn't tell how long she slept: but when she woke, she was in bed at his house, and he and his mother sitting by her bedside, and watching her.

It was a witch that had a spite to the young man, because he wouldn't marry her, and so she got power to keep him in a state between life and death till a young woman would rescue him by doing what she had just done. So at her request, her sisters got their own shape again, and were sent back to their mother, with their spades of gold and shovels of silver. Maybe they were better after that, but I doubt it much. The youngest got the young gentleman for her husband. I'm sure she deserved him, and, if they didn't live happy, THAT WE MAY!

The succeeding story is met with, in some shape or other, in almost every popular collection. It happened, however, that we never met with it in a complete form except from the recital of Mrs. K., of the Duffrey, a lady in heart and deed, though a farmer's wife. The reader will find the word *serenade* doing duty for "surround;" but the circumstance having remained fixed in our memory, we have not ventured on a supposed improvement. The scarcity of proper names is a remarkable feature in these old monuments. We have always, even at the risk of tautology and circumlocution, respected this characteristic.

THE BROWN BEAR OF NORWAY.

There was once a king in Ireland, and he had three daughters, and very nice princesses they were. And one day that their father and themselves were walking in the lawn, the king began to joke on them, and to ask them who they would like to be married to. "I'll have the King of Ulster for a husband," says one; "and I'll have the King of Munster," says another; "and," says the youngest, "I'll have no husband but the Brown Bear of Norway." For a nurse of hers used to be telling her of an enchanted prince that she called by that name, and she fell in love with him, and his name was the first name on her lips, for the very night before she was dreaming of him. Well, one laughed, and another laughed, and they joked on the princess all the rest of the evening. But that very night she woke up out of her sleep in a great hall that was lighted up with a thousand lamps; the richest carpets were on the floor, and the walls were covered with cloth of gold and silver, and the place was full of grand company, and the very beautiful prince she saw in her dreams was there, and it wasn't a moment till he was on one knee before her, and telling her how much he loved her, and asking her wouldn't she be his queen. Well, she hadn't the heart to refuse him, and married they were the same evening.

"Now, my darling," says he, when they were left by themselves, "you must know that I am under enchantment. A sorceress, that had a beautiful daughter, wished me for her son-in-law; and because I didn't keep the young girl at the distance I ought, the mother got power over me, and when I refused to marry her daughter, she made me take the form of a bear by day, and I was to continue so till a lady would marry me of her own free will, and endure five years of great trials after."

Well, when the princess woke in the morning, she missed her husband from her side, and spent the day very sorrowful. But as soon as the lamps were lighted in the grand hall, where she was sitting on a sofa covered with silk, the folding doors flew open, and he was sitting by her side the next minute. So they spent another evening so happy, and he took an opportunity of warning her that whenever she began to tire of him, or not to have any confidence in him, they would be parted for ever, and he'd be obliged to marry the witch's daughter.

So she got used to find him absent by day, and they spent a happy twelvemonth together, and at last a beautiful little boy was born; and as happy as she was before, she was twice as happy now, for she had her child to keep her company in the day when she couldn't see her husband.

At last, one evening, when herself, and himself and her child, were sitting with a window open because it was a sultry night, in flew an eagle, took the infant's sash in his beak, and flew up in the air with him. She screamed, and was going to throw herself out through the window after him, but the prince caught her, and looked at her very seriously. She bethought of what he said soon after their marriage, and she stopped the cries and complaints that were on her lips. She spent her days very lonely for another twelvemonth, when a beautiful little girl was sent to her. Then she thought to herself she'd have a sharp eye about her this time; so she never would allow a window to be more than a few inches open.

But all her care was in vain. Another evening, when they were all so happy, and the prince dandling the baby, a beautiful greyhound bitch stood before them, took the child out of the father's hand, and was out of the door before you could wink. This time she shouted, and ran out of the room, but there was some of the servants in the next room, and all declared that neither child nor dog passed out. She felt, she could not tell how, to her husband, but still she kept command over herself, and didn't once reproach him.

When the third child was born, she would hardly allow a window or a door to be left open for a moment; but she wasn't the nearer to keep the child to herself. They were sitting one evening by the fire, when a lady appeared standing by them. She opened her eyes in a great fright, and stared at her, and while she was doing so, the appearance wrapped a shawl round the baby that was sitting in its father's lap, and either sunk through the ground with it, or went up through the wide chimney. This time the mother kept her bed for a month.

"My dear," said she to her husband, when she was beginning to recover, "I think I'd feel better if I was after seeing my father, and mother, and sisters once more. If you give me leave to go home for a few days, I'd be glad." "Very well," said he, "I will do that; and whenever you feel inclined to return, only mention your wish when you lie down at night." The next morning when she awoke, she found herself in her own old chamber in her father's palace. She rung the bell, and in a short time she had her mother, and father, and married sisters about her, and they laughed till they cried for joy at finding her safe back again.

So in time she told them all that happened to her, and they didn't know what to advise her to do. She was as fond of her husband as ever, and said she was sure that he couldn't help letting the children go; but still she was afraid beyond the world to have another child to be torn from her. Well, the mother and sisters consulted a wise woman that used to bring eggs to the castle, for they had great confidence in her wisdom. She said the only plan was to secure the bear's skin that the prince was obliged to put on every morning, and get it burned, and then he couldn't help being a man night and day, and then the enchantment would be at an end.

So they all persuaded her to do that, and she promised she would; and after eight days she felt so great a longing to see her husband again, that she made the wish the same night, and when she woke three hours after, she was in her husband's palace, and himself was watching over her. There was great joy on both sides, and they were happy for many days.

Now she began to reflect how she never felt her husband leaving her of a morning, and how she never found him neglecting to give her a sweet drink out of a gold cup just as she was going to bed.

So one night she contrived not to drink any of it, though she pretended to do so; and she was wakeful enough in the morning, and saw her husband passing out through a panel in the wainscot, though she kept her eyelids nearly closed. The next night she got a few drops of the sleepy posset that she saved the evening before, put into her husband's night drink, and that made him sleep sound enough. She got up after midnight, passed through the panel, and found a beautiful brown bear's hide hanging in an alcove. She stole back, and went down to the parlour fire, and put the hide into the middle of it, and never took eyes off it till it was all fine ashes. She then lay down by her husband, gave him a kiss on the cheek, and fell asleep.

If she was to live a hundred years, she'd never forget how she wakened next morning, and found her husband looking down on her with misery and anger in his face. "Unhappy woman," said he, "you have separated us for ever! Why hadn't you patience for five years? I am now obliged, whether I like or no, to go a three days' journey to the witch's castle, and live with her daughter. The skin that was my guard you have burned it, and the egg-wife that gave you the counsel was the witch herself. I won't reproach you: your punishment will be severe enough without it. Farewell for ever!"

He kissed her for the last time, and was off the next minute walking as fast as he could. She shouted after him, and then seeing there was no use, she dressed herself and pursued him. He never stopped, nor stayed, nor looked back, and still she kept him in sight; and when he was on the hill she was in the hollow, and when he was in the hollow she was on the hill. Her life was almost leaving her, when just as the sun was setting, he turned up a *bohyeen* (lane), and went into a little house. She crawled up after him, and when she got inside there was a beautiful little boy on his knees, and he kissing and hugging him. "Here, my poor darling," says he, "is your eldest child, and there," says he, pointing to a nice middle-aged woman that was looking on with a smile on her face, "is the eagle that carried him away." She forgot all her sorrows in a moment, hugging her child, and laughing and crying over him. The Vanithee washed their feet, and rubbed them with an ointment that took all the soreness out of their bones, and made them as fresh as a daisy. Next morning, just before sunrise, he was up, and prepared to be off. "Here," said he to her, "is a thing which may be of use to you. It's a scissors, and whatever stuff you cut with it will be turned into rich silk. The moment the sun rises, I'll lose all memory of yourself and the children, but I'll get it at sunset again; farewell." But he wasn't far gone till she was in sight of him again, leaving her boy behind. It was the same to-day as yesterday: their shadows went before them in the morning, and followed them in the evening. He never stopped, and she never stopped, and as the sun was setting, he turned up another lane, and there they found their little daughter. It was all joy and comfort again till morning, and then the third day's journey commenced.

But before he started, he gave her a comb, and told her that whenever she used it, pearls and diamonds would fall from her hair. Still he had his full memory from sunset to sunrise; but from sunrise to sunset he travelled on under the charm, and never threw his eye behind. This night they came to where the youngest baby was, and the next morning, just before sunrise, the prince spoke to her for the last time. "Here, my poor wife," said he, "is a little hand-reel, with gold thread that has no end, and the half of our marriage ring. If you can ever get to my bed, and put your half ring to mine, I will recollect you. There is a wood yonder, and the moment I enter it, I will forget everything that ever happened between us, just as if I was born yesterday. Farewell, dear wife and child, for ever." Just then the sun rose, and away he walked towards the wood. She saw it open before him, and close after him, and when she came up, she could no more get in than she could break through a stone wall. She wrung her hands, and shed tears, but then she recollected herself, and cried out, "Wood, I charge you by my three magic gifts—the scissors, the comb, and the reel—to let me through;" and it opened, and she went along a walk till she came in sight of a palace, and a lawn, and a woodman's cottage in the edge of the wood where it came nearest the palace.

She went into this lodge, and asked the woodman and his wife to take her into their service. They were not willing at first; but she told them she would ask no wages, and would give them diamonds, and pearls, and silk stuffs, and gold thread whenever they wished for them. So they agreed to let her stay.

It wasn't long till she heard how a young prince, that was just arrived, was living in the palace as the husband of the young mistress. Herself and her mother said that they were married fifteen years before, and that he was charmed away from them ever since. He seldom stirred abroad, and every one that saw him remarked how silent and sorrowful he went about, like a person that was searching for some lost thing.

The servants and conceited folk at the big house began to take notice of the beautiful young woman at the lodge, and to annoy her with their impudent addresses. The head-footman was the most troublesome, and at last she invited him to *come luke tea* with her. Oh, how rejoiced he was, and how he bragged of it in the servants' hall! Well, the evening came, and the footman walked into the lodge, and was shown to her sitting-room; for the lodge-keeper and his wife stood in great awe of her, and gave her two nice rooms to herself. Well, he sat down as stiff as a ramrod, and was talking in a grand style about the great doings at the castle, while she was getting the tea and toast ready. "Oh," says she to him, "would you put your hand out at the window, and cut me off a sprig or two of honey-suckle?" He got up in great glee, and put out his hand and head; and said she, "By the virtue of my magic gifts, let a pair of horns spring out of your head, and *serenade* the lodge." Just as she wished, so it was. They sprung from the front of each ear, and tore round the walls till they met at the back. Oh, the poor wretch! and how he bawled, and roared! and the servants that he used to be boasting to, were soon flocking from the castle, and grinning, and huzzaing, and beating tunes on tongs, and shovels, and pans; and he cursing and swearing, and the eyes ready to start out of his head, and he so black in the face, and kicking out his legs behind like mad.

At last she pitied his case, and removed the charm, and the horns dropped down on the ground, and he would have killed her on the spot, only he was as weak as water, and his fellow-servants came in, and carried him up to the big house.

Well, some way or other, the story came to the ears of the prince, and he strolled down that way. She had only the dress of a country-woman on her as she sat sewing at the window, but that did not hide her beauty, and he was greatly puzzled and disturbed, after he had a good look at her features, just as a body is perplexed to know whether something happened to him when he was young, or if he only dreamed it. Well, the witch's daughter heard about it too, and she came to see the strange girl; and what did she find her doing, but cutting out the pattern of a gown from brown paper; and as she cut away, the paper became the richest silk she ever saw. The lady looked on with very covetous eyes, and, says she, "What would you be satisfied to take for that scissors?" "I'll take nothing," says she, "but leave to spend one night in the prince's chamber, and I'll swear that we'll be as innocent of any crime next morning as we were in the evening." Well, the proud lady fired up, and was going to say something dreadful; but the scissors kept on cutting, and the silk growing richer and richer every inch. So she agreed, and made her take a great oath to keep her promise.

When night came on she was let into her husband's chamber, and the door was locked. But, when she came in a tremble, and sat by the bed-side, the prince was in such a dead sleep, that all she did couldn't awake him. She sung this verse to him, sighing and sobbing, and kept singing it the night long, and it was all in vain :—

"Four long years I was married to thee;
Three sweet babes I bore to thee;
Brown Bear of Norway, won't you turn to me?"

At the first dawn, the proud lady was in the chamber, and led her away, and the footman of the horns put out his tongue at her as she was quitting the palace.

So there was no luck so far; but the next day the prince passed by again, and looked at her, and saluted her kindly, as a prince might a farmer's daughter, and passed on; and soon the witch's daughter came by, and found her combing her hair, and pearls and diamonds dropping from it.

Well, another bargain was made, and the princess spent another night of sorrow, and she left the castle at daybreak, and the footman was at his post, and enjoyed his revenge.

The third day the prince went by, and stopped to talk with the strange woman. He asked her could he do anything to serve her, and she said he might. She asked him did he ever wake at night. He said that he was rather wakeful than otherwise; but that during the last two nights, he was listening to a sweet song in his dreams, and could not wake, and that the voice was one that he must have known and loved in some other world long ago. Says she, "Did you drink any sleepy posset either of these evenings before you went to bed?" "I did," said he. "The two evenings my wife gave me something to drink, but I don't know whether it was a sleepy posset or not." "Well, prince," said she, "as you say you would wish to oblige me, you can do it by not tasting any drink this afternoon." "I will not," says he, and then he went on his walk.

Well, the great lady was soon after the prince, and found the stranger using her hand-reel and winding threads of gold off it, and the third bargain was made.

That evening the prince was lying on his bed at twilight, and his mind much disturbed; and the door opened, and in his princess walked, and down she sat by his bed-side, and sung:—

> "Four long years I was married to thee;
> Three sweet babes I bore to thee;
> Brown Bear of Norway, won't you turn to me?"

"Brown Bear of Norway!" said he: "I don't understand you." "Don't you remember, prince, that I was your wedded wife for four years?" "I do not," said he, "but I'm sure I wish it was so." "Don't you remember our three babes, that are still alive?" "Show me them. My mind is all a heap of confusion." "Look for the half of our marriage ring, that hangs at your neck, and fit it to this." He did so, and the same moment the charm was broken. His full memory came back on him, and he flung his arms round his wife's neck, and both burst into tears.

Well, there was a great cry outside, and the castle walls were heard splitting and cracking. Every one in the castle was alarmed, and made their way out. The prince and princess went with the rest, and by the time all were safe on the lawn, down came the building, and made the ground tremble for miles round. No one ever saw the witch and her daughter afterwards. It was not long till the prince and princess had their children with them, and then they set out for their own palace. The kings of Ireland, and of Munster and Ulster, and their wives, soon came to visit them, and may every one that deserves it be as happy as the Brown Bear of Norway and his family.

The *Goban Saor*, pronounced Gubawn Seer (free smith, free mason, or free carpenter, in fact), is a relative of Wayland Smith, or Vœlund, in the Vœlundar Quida; but with equal skill he is endowed with more mother wit than the Northern craftsman. Unconnected adventures of this character are met with in every country of Europe. It is probable that a more complete legend concerning this celebrated *gow* (Smith) would be met with in Mayo or Kerry. Vulcan or Prometheus was the original craftsman; perhaps Dædalus might dispute the honour with them. These old-world legends have reached our time and our province in an unsatisfactory and degraded state. All that remains to us is to make the most we can of our materials.

Our smith is a more moral, as well as a more fortunate man, than the Vœlund of the Northern saga. Vœlund returns evil for evil, and the master smith of MM. Asbjornsen and Moë is altogether unprincipled. He cuts off horses' legs to shoe them with the greater ease to himself, and sets an old woman in his furnace, in the vague hope that he may hammer her into a fresh young lass.when she is hot enough.

THE GOBAN SAOR.

It is a long time since the Goban Saor was alive. Maybe it was *him* that built the Castle of Ferns; part of the walls are thick enough to be built by any goban, or gow, that ever splintered wood, or hammered red-hot iron, or cut a stone. If he didn't build Ferns, he built other castles for some of the five kings or the great chiefs. He could fashion a spear-shaft while you'd count five, and the spear-head at three strokes of a hammer. When he wanted to drive big nails into beams that were ever so high from the ground, he would pitch them into their place, and, taking a fling of the hammer at their heads, they would be drove in as firm as the knocker of Newgate, and he would catch the hammer when it was falling down.

At last it came to the King of Munster's turn to get his castle built, and to Goban he sent. Goban knew that, in other times far back, the King of Ireland killed the celebrated architects, Rog, Robog, Rodin, and Rooney, the way they would never build another palace equal to his, and so he mentioned something to his wife privately before he set out. He took his son along with him, and the first night they got lodging at a farmer's house. The farmer told them they might leave their beasts to graze all night in any of his fields they pleased. So they entered one field, and says Goban, "Tie the bastes up for the night." "Why?" says the son; "I can't find anything strong enough." "Well, then, let us try the next field. Now," says he, "tie up the horses if you can." "Oh! by my word, here's a thistle strong enough this time." "That will do."

The next night they slept at another farmer's house, where there were two young daughters—one with black hair, very industrious; the other with fair complexion, and rather liking to sit with her hands across, and listen to the talk round the fire, than to be doing any work. While they were chatting about one thing and another, says the Goban, "Young girls, if I'd wish to be young again, it would be for the sake of getting one of you for a wife; but I think very few old people that do be thinking at all of the other world, ever wish to live their lives over again. Still I wish that you may have good luck in your choice of a husband, and so I give you three bits of advice. Always have the head of an old woman by the hob; warm yourselves with your work in the morning; and, some time before I come back, take the skin of a newly-killed sheep to the market, and bring itself and the price of it home again." When they were leaving next morning, the Goban said to his son, "Maybe one of these girls may be your wife some day."

As they were going along, they met a poor man striving to put a flat roof over a mud-walled round cabin, but he had only three joists, and each of them was only three-quarters of the breadth across. Well, the Goban put two nicks near one end of every joist on opposite sides; and when these were fitted into one another, there was a three-cornered figure formed in the middle, and the other ends rested on the mud wall, and the floor they made was as strong as anything. The poor man blessed the two men, and they went on. That night they stopped at a house where the master sat by the fire, and hardly opened his mouth all the evening. If he didn't talk, a meddlesome neighbour did, and interfered about everything. There was another chance lodger besides the Goban and his son, and when the evening was half over, the Goban said he thought he would go farther on his journey as it was a fine night. "You may come along with us, if you like," says he to the other man ; but he said he was too tired. The two men slept in a farmer's house half a mile farther on ; and the next morning the first news they heard, when they were setting out, was, that the man of the house they left the evening before was found murdered in his bed, and the lodger taken up on suspicion. Says he to his son, "Never sleep a night where the woman is everything, and the man nothing." He stopped a day or two, however, and by cross-examining and calling witnesses, he got the murder tracked to the woman and the busy neighbour.

The next day they came to a ford, where a dozen of carpenters were puzzling their heads about setting up a wooden bridge that would neither have a peg nor a nail in any part of it. The king would give a great reward to them if they succeeded, and if they didn't, he'd never give one of them a job again. "Give us a hatchet and a few sticks," says the Goban, "and we'll see if we have any little genius that way." So he squared a few posts and cross-bars, and made a little bridge on the sod ; and it was so made, that the greater weight was on it, and the stronger the stream of water, the solider it would be.[1]

Maybe the carpenters warn't thankful, except one envious, little, ould basthard of a fellow, that said any child might have thought of the plan (it happened he didn't think of it though), and would make the Goban and his son drink a cag of whisky, only they couldn't delay their journey.

[1] If a curious reader wishes to know the secret of the roofing of the round cabin, let him get three twigs, cut a notch within half an inch of one end of each, and another about an inch and a half from that, but on the opposite side. Let him get a hat, or a large mug, or anything else he pleases, and by adapting the notched ends to each other, he will find the plan of making a roof-support to his model cabin after some essays, more or less, and some healthy trials of his patience. The editor of these sketches will not attempt to decide whether the Goban or Julius Cæsar was the inventor of the peg-less and nail-less bridge, but the mode of construction may be learned from the Commentaries on the Gallic War.

At last they came to where the King of Munster kep' his coort, either at Cashel or Limerick, or some place in Clare, and the Goban burned very little daylight till he had a palace springing up like a flagger. People came from all parts, and were in admiration of the fine work; but as they were getting near the eaves, one of the carpenters that were engaged at the wooden bridge came late one night into the Goban's room, and told him what himself was suspecting, that just as he would be setting the coping stone, the scaffolding would, somehow or other, get loose, himself fall down a few stories and be kilt, the king wring his hands, and shed a few crocodile tears, and the like palace never be seen within the four seas of Ireland.

"*Sha gu dheine*,"[1] says the Goban to himself; but next day he spoke out plain enough to the king. "Please your Majesty," says he, "I am now pretty near the end of my work, but there is still something to be done before we come to the wall-plate that is to make all sure and strong. There is a bit of a charm about it, but I haven't the tool here—it is at home, and my son got so sick last night, and is lying so bad, he is not able to go for it. If you can't spare the young prince, I must go myself, for my wife wouldn't intrust it to any one but of royal blood." The king, rather than let the Goban out of his sight, sent the young prince for the tool. The Goban told him some outlandish name in Irish, which his wife would find at his bed's head, and bid him make all the haste he could back.

In a week's time, back came two of the poor attendants that were with the prince, and told the king that his son was well off, with the best of eating and drinking, and chess-playing and sword exercise, that any prince could wish for, but that out of her sight the Goban's wife nor her people would let him, till she had her husband safe and sound inside of his own threshold.

Well, to be sure, how the king fumed and raged! but what's the use of striving to tear down a stone wall with your teeth? He could do without his palace being finished, but he couldn't do without his son and heir.

[1] "That's it," or "Is that it?"

The Goban didn't keep spite; he put the finishing touch to the palace in three days, and, in two days more, himself and his son were sitting at the farmer's fireside where the two purty young girls wor.

"Well, my colleen bawn," says he to the one with the fair hair, "did you mind the advice I gev you when I was here last?" "Indeed I did, and little good it did me. I got an old woman's skull from the churchyard, and fixed it in the wall near the hob, and it so frightened every one, that I was obliged to have it taken back in an hour." "And how did you warm yourself with your work in the cold mornings?" "The first morning's work I had was to card flax, and I thrune some of it on the fire, and my mother gave me such a raking for it, that I didn't offer to warm myself that way again." "Now for the sheep-skin." "That was the worst of all. When I told the buyers in the market that I was to bring back the skin and the price of it, they only jeered at me. One young buckeen said, if I'd go into the tavern and take share of a quart of mulled beer with him, he'd make that bargain with me, and that so vexed me that I turned home at once." "Well, that was the right thing to do, anyhow. Now my little *Ceann Dhu* (black head), let us see how you fared. The skull?" "Och!" says an old woman, sitting close to the fire in the far corner, "I'm a distant relation that was left desolate, and this," says she tapping the side of her poor head, "is the old woman's skull she provided." "Well, now for the warming of yourself in the cold mornings." "Oh, I kept my hands and feet going so lively at my work that it was warming enough." "Well, and the sheep-skin?" "That was easy enough. When I got to the market, I went to the crane, plucked the wool off, sold it, and brought home the skin."

"Man and woman of the house," says the Goban, "I ask you before this company, to give me this girl for my daughter-in-law; and if ever her husband looks crooked at her, I'll beat him within an inch of his life." There was very few words, and no need of a black man to make up the match; and when the prince was returning home, he stopped a day to be at the wedding. If I hear of any more of the Goban's great doings, I'll tell 'em some other time.

Intermixed with tales of the wild and wonderful, we sometimes meet in the old Gaelic collections with a few of a more commonplace character, illustrative of the advantage of observing certain moral maxims or time-honoured proverbs. The MS. from which we have obtained the following story does not explain what the colour of the soles of the dying king had to do in the narrative.

THE THREE ADVICES WHICH THE KING WITH THE RED SOLES GAVE TO HIS SON.[1]

When the chief of the *Bonna Dearriga* was on his death-bed he gave his son three counsels, and said misfortune would attend him if he did not follow them. The first was never to bring home a beast from a fair after having been offered a fair price for it; the second, never to call in ragged clothes on a friend when he wanted a favour from him; the third not to marry a wife with whose family he was not well acquainted.

The name of the young chief was Illan, called Don, from his brown hair, and the first thing he set about doing after the funeral, was to test the wisdom of his father's counsels. So he went to the fair of Tailtean[2] with a fine mare of his, and rode up and down. He asked twenty gold rings for his beast, but the highest bid he got was only nineteen. To work out his design he would not abate a *screpal*, but rode home on her back in the evening. He could have readily crossed a ford that lay in his way near home; for sheer devilment he leaped the river higher up, where the banks on both sides were steep. The poor beast stumbled as she came near the edge, and was flung head foremost into the rocky bed,

---

[1] This in the corrupt wording of our MS. is "Sceal Re Bonna Dearriga na tri chourla do hug she dha mac."

[2] Now Telltown in Meath. Centuries before the Christian era meetings were held there for the purpose of negotiating marriages, and hiring servants, and transacting other matters of business.

and killed. He was pitched forward, but his fall was broken by some shrubs that were growing in the face of the opposite bank. He was as sorry for the poor mare as any young fellow, fond of horses and dogs, could be. When he got home he sent a giolla to take off the animal's two four-legs at the knee, and these he hung up in the great hall of his dun, having first had them properly dried and prepared.

Next day he repaired again to the fair, and got into conversation with a rich chief of Oriel, whose handsome daughter had come to the meeting to purchase some cows. Illan offered his services, as he knew most of the bodachs and the bodachs' wives who were there for the object of selling. A word to them from the handsome and popular young chief,—and good bargains were given to the lady. So pleased was her father, ay and she too, with this civility that he forthwith received an invitation to hunt and fish at the northern rath, and very willingly he accepted it. So he returned home in a very pleasant state of mind, and was anxious that this second experiment should succeed better than the first.

The visit was paid, and in the mornings there were pleasant walks in the woods with the young lady, while her little brother and sister were chasing one another through the trees, and the hunting and fishing went on afterwards, and there were feasts of venison, and wild boar, and drinking of wine and mead in the evenings, and stories in verse recited by bards, and sometimes moonlight walks on the ramparts of the fort, and at last marriage was proposed and accepted.

One morning as Illan was musing on the happiness that was before him, an attendant on his promised bride walked into his room. "Great must be your surprise, O Illan Don," said she, " at this my visit, but my respect for you will not allow me to see you fall into the pit that is gaping for you. Your affianced bride is an unchaste woman. You have remarked the deformed Fergus Rua, who plays on the small clarsech, and is the possessor of thrice fifty stories. He often attends in her room late in the evening to play soft music to her, and to put her to sleep with this soft music and his stories of the Danaan druids. Who would suspect the weak deformed creature, or the young lady of noble birth? By your hand, O Illan of the brown hair, if you marry her, you will bring disgrace on yourself and your clan. You do not trust my words! Then trust to your own senses. She would most willingly break off all connexion with the lame wretch since she first laid eyes on you, but he has sworn to expose her before you and her father. When the household is at rest this night, wait at the entrance of the passage that leads to the women's apartments. I will meet you there. To-morrow morning you will require no one's advice for your direction."

Before the sun tinged the purple clouds, next morning, Illan was crossing the outer moat of the lios, and lying behind him on the back of his trusty steed was some long object carefully folded in skins. "Tell your honoured chief," said he to the attendant who was conducting him, "that I am obliged on a sudden to depart, and that I request him by his regard for me to return my visit a fortnight hence, and to bring his fair daughter with him." On he rode, and muttered from time to time, "Oh, had I slain the guilty pair, it would be a well-merited death! the deformed wretch! the weak lost woman! Now for the third trial!"

Illan had a married sister, whose rath was about twelve of our miles distant from his. To her home he repaired next day, changing clothes with a beggar whom he met on the road. When he arrived, he found that they were at dinner, and several neighbouring families with them in the great hall. "Tell my sister," said he to a giolla who was lounging at the door, "that I wish to speak with her." "Who is your sister?" said the other in an insolent tone, for he did not recognise the young chief in his beggar's dress. "Who should she be but the *Bhan a Teagh*, you rascal!" The fellow began to laugh, but the open palm of the irritated young man coming like a sledge stroke on his cheek, dashed him on the ground, and set him a-roaring. "Oh, what has caused this confusion?" said the lady of the house, coming out from the hall. "I," said her brother, "punishing your giolla's disrespect." "Oh, brother, what has reduced you to such a condition?" "An attack on my house, and a creagh made on my lands in my absence. I have neither gold nor silver vessels in my dun, nor rich cloaks, nor ornaments, nor arms for my followers. My cattle have been driven from my lands, and all as I was on a visit at the house of my intended bride. You must come to my relief; you will have to send cattle to my ravaged fields, gold and silver vessels, and ornaments and furs, and rich clothes to my house, to enable me to receive my bride and her father in a few days." "Poor dear Illan!" she answered, "my heart bleeds for you. I fear I cannot aid you, nor can I ask you to join our company within in these rags. But you must be hungry; stay here till I send you some refreshment."

She quitted him, and did not return again, but an attendant came out with a griddle-cake in one hand, and a porringer with some Danish beer in it in the other. Illan carried them away to the spot where he had quitted the beggar, and gave him the bread, and made him drink the beer. Then changing clothes with him he rewarded him, and returned home, bearing the porringer as a trophy.

On the day appointed with the father of his affianced, there were assembled in Illan's hall, his sister, his sister's husband, his affianced, her father, and some others. When an opportunity offered after meat and bread, and wine had gone the way of all food, Illan addressed his guests: "Friends and relations, I am about confessing some of my faults before you, and hope you will be bettered by the hearing. My dying father charged me never to refuse a fair offer for horse, cow, or sheep, at a fair. For refusing a trifle less than I asked for my noble mare, there was nothing left to me but those bits of her fore-legs you see hanging by the wall. He advised me never to put on an air of want when soliciting a favour. I begged help of my sister for a pretended need, and because I had nothing better than a beggar's cloak on me, I got nothing for my suit but the porringer that you see dangling by the poor remains of my mare. I wooed a strange lady to be my wife, contrary to my dying father's injunction, and after seeming to listen favourably to my suit, she at last said I should be satisfied with the crutches of her lame and deformed harper: there they are!" The sister blushed, and was ready to sink through the floor for shame. The bride was in a much more wretched state, and would have fainted, but it was not the fashion of the day. Her father stormed, and said this was but a subterfuge on the part of Illan. He deferred to her pleasure, but though torn with anguish for the loss of the young chief's love and respect, she took the blame on herself.

The next morning saw the rath without a visitor; but within a quarter of a year the kind-faced, though not beautiful daughter of a neighbouring *Duine Uasal* (gentleman) made the fort cheerful by her presence. Illan had known her since they were children. He was long aware of her excellent qualities, but had never thought of her as a wife till the morning after his speech. He was fonder of her a month after his marriage than he was on the marriage morning, and much fonder when a year had gone by, and presented his house with an heir.

PART II

LEGENDS OF THE "GOOD PEOPLE"

LEGENDS OF THE "GOOD PEOPLE"

ALL our superstitions, and a great part of our legendary lore, have descended to us from our pagan ancestors. Aphrodite and Artemis selected lovers from among mortals;—Melusina, Viviana, Morgana, and other beautiful and celebrated fairies, followed their example in enthralling Christian knights. The *Lianhan Sighe* (Fairy love) still attaches herself to some favoured mortal, who is thenceforward lost to human affection, and becomes what in pagan times would have been called a Nympholept. Juno and the three Fates assisted at the births of mortals—so do the fairies. The inflexible destinies were called the Parcæ (merciful);—the timorous cottager propitiates the fairies by addressing them as the *Duine Matha*, "The Good People." Hephæstion, and his swart Cyclops, forged impregnable armour for favoured heroes;—the dwarf workers in the Northern mines did the same for the terrible sea-kings. In the penetralia, at each side of the fire, were the Lares and Penates to keep blessings about the abode of the master. The Kobolds frequented favoured houses to bless the servants' efforts, or even do their work. Apollo and Hercules got much trouble destroying great hydras;—Fion MacCumhail murdered piasts in nearly every lake in Ireland. Achilles was rendered invulnerable in every part of his body except his heel;—Siegfried, the dragon slayer, could not be wounded except at a portion of his back, the size of a small leaf. The Golden Fleece brought misery to its possessors;—so did the Nibelungen hoard. The three goddesses so reverenced among the Gauls and Germans, and the Druidic priestesses afterwards substituted for them, became at last the fairies or Breton Korigans; and the herbs of Druidic rites still retain their power at All-Hallow Tide, in furnishing truthful visions of their future husbands to superstitious damsels.

The name Fairy has given rise to long disquisitions. The nearest root, in sound at least, is the Persian Peri. Then we have for the correct name, Fay, the Fata, or Destinies, which became Fada in the Provençal, and Hada in the Spanish tongues. The Greek language furnishes Μοῖραι (the Fates), and the propitiating title Parcæ (merciful), applied to the Destinies, has its representative in the "Good People," applied to the Fays in Ireland. The Gaelic name is Sighe, which is not found out of Ireland and the Highlands, except at *La font de Scée*, in Poitou. The Breton Korigan may derive from κούρη, young maid, or, perhaps, the Celtic *corrig*, a hill. The word Fairy, or Faërie, is properly the state or condition of the Fays.

Even as the Parcæ or other female divinities assisted at the births of Achilles, Meleager, &c., so, in the romances of the Middle Ages, fairies were present at the births of Holger the Dane, Oberon, Tristrem, &c., and endowed them with valuable gifts, or predicted their future fortunes. Till our own days the Bretons would have a feast laid out in an adjoining room on these occasions for their visitors. Aurora carried away the favoured Tithonus into her glowing palace of the morning. Calypso retained Ulysses in the happy isle of

Ogygia. King Arthur was borne to the isle of Avalon by Morgana. Lanval was conducted into the same isle by his fairy love; Ossian was kept in the "Land of Youth" under the Atlantic for a hundred and fifty years, by Nea of the Golden Hair; and the fairies contemporary with our fathers and mothers stole away to their Sighe-mounts as many mortals as they could get into their power. The druidical bowl of inspiration, and the symbolic lance, sought by Peredur in pagan Brittany, became, in the hands of the Christian romancers, the *sangraal* or bowl used at the last supper, and the spear which pierced our Saviour's side; and Sir Percival went forth in quest of them. Error varies its form, but its essence is indestructible. There is scarcely a legend or article of belief of the Greek or Roman mythology which, in some modification, may not be traced in the fairy systems of all the countries of Europe.

In connecting fairy superstition with paganism once prevailing over Europe, one circumstance remains to be noticed. The progeny of a god or goddess when residing among mortals, was distinguished by super-excellent qualities; any of the fairy race that have abode among men are noticeable for peculiarities the very reverse. They are gluttonous, peevish, ungrateful, and spiteful, and are never found to develop into anything better than rickety children. At the introduction of Christianity, Crom, Odin, Frea, Zeus, Aphrodite, and Bacchus the Intemperate, were obliged to forego adoration and even respect. They lost a good deal of their beauty, and the best part of their amiability, and even frolicsome Pan degenerated into the hoofed and horned devil. Their proceedings towards man became of a capricious, if not baleful character, and their interference in human affairs was deprecated by all right-minded and timorous people. The next legend will illustrate these remarks, Mrs. K., of the Duffrey, being our informant:—

THE FAIRY CHILD.

There was a sailor that lived up in Grange when he was at home; and one time, when he was away seven or eight months, his wife was brought to bed of a fine boy. She expected her husband home soon, and she wished to put off the christening of the child till he'd be on the spot. She and her husband were not natives of the country, and they were not as much afraid of leaving the child unchristened as our people would be.

Well, the child grew and throve, and the neighbours all bothered the woman to take him to Father M.'s to be baptized, and all they said was no use. "Her husband would be soon home, and then they'd have a joyful christening."

There happened to be no one sick up in that neighbourhood for some time, so the priest did not come to the place, nor hear of the birth, and none of the people about her could make up their minds to tell upon her, it is such an ugly thing to be informing; and then the child was so healthy, and the father might be on the spot any moment.

So the time crept on, and the lad was a year and a half old, and his mother up to that time never lost five nights' rest by him; when one evening that she came in from binding after the reapers, she heard wonderful *whingeing* and lamenting from the little bed where he used to sleep. She ran over to him and asked him what ailed him. "Oh, mammy, I'm sick, and I'm hungry, and I'm cold; don't pull down the blanket." Well, the poor woman ran and got some boiled bread and milk as soon as she could, and she asked her other son, that was about seven years old, when he took sick. "Oh, mother," says he, "he was as happy as a king, playing near the fire about two hours ago, and I was below in the room, when I heard a great rush like as if a whole number of fowls were flying down the chimley. I heard my brother giving a great cry, and then another sound like as if the fowls were flying out again; and when I got into the kitchen there he was, so miserable-looking that I hardly knew him, and he pulling his hair, and his clothes, and his poor face so dirty. Take a look at him, and try do you know him at all."

So when she went to feed him she got such a fright, for his poor face was like an old man's, and his body, and legs, and arms, all thin and hairy. But still he resembled the child she left in the morning, and " mammy, mammy," was never out of his mouth. She heard of people being fairy-struck, so she supposed it was that that happened to him, but she never suspected her own child to be gone, and a fairy child left in its place.

Well, it's he that kept the poor woman awake many a night after, and never let her have a quiet day, crying for bread and milk, and mashed pitaytees, and stirabout; and it was still " mammy, mammy, mammy," and the *glows* and the moans were never out of his mouth. Well, he had like to eat the poor woman out of house and home, and the very flesh off her bones with watching and sorrow. Still nothing could persuade her that it wasn't her own child that was in it.

One neighbour and another neighbour told her their minds plain enough. " Now, ma'am, you see what it is to leave a child without being christened. If you done your duty, fairy, nor spirit, nor divel, would have no power over your child. That *ounkran* (cross creature) in the bed is no more your child nor I am, but a little imp that the *Duiné Sighe* (fairy people)—God between us and harm!—left you. By this and by that, if you don't whip him up and come along with us to Father M.'s, we'll go, hot foot, ourselves, and tell him all about it. Christened he must be before the world is a day older."

So she went over and soothered him, and said, " Come, alanna, let me dress you, and we'll go and be christened." And such roaring and screeching as came out of his throat would frighten the Danes. " I haven't the heart," says she at last; " and sure if we attempted to take him in that state we'd have the people of the three townlands follying us to the priest's, and I'm afeard he'd take it very badly."

The next day when she came in, in the evening, she found him quite clean and fresh-looking, and his hair nicely combed. "Ah, Pat," says she to her other son, "was it you that done this?" Well, he said nothing till he and his mother were up at the fire, and the *angashore* (wretch) of a child in his bed in the room. "Mother," says he then, in a whisper, "the neighbours are right, and you are wrong. I was out a little bit, and when I was coming round by the wall at the back of the room, I heard some sweet voices as if they were singing inside; and so I went to the crack in the corner, and what was round the bed but a whole parcel of nicely-dressed little women, with green gowns; and they singing, and dressing the little fellow, and combing his hair, and he laughing and crowing with them. I watched for a long time, and then I stole round to the door, but the moment I pulled the string of the latch I hears the music changed to his whimpering and crying, and when I got into the room there was no sign of anything only himself. He was a little better looking, but as cantankerous as ever." "Ah," says the mother, "you are only joining the ill-natured neighbours; you're not telling a word of truth."

Next day Pat had a new story. "Mother," says he, "I was sitting here while you were out, and I began to wonder why he was so quiet, so I went into the room to see if he was asleep. There he was, sitting up with his old face on him, and he frightened the life out of me, he spoke so plain. 'Paudh,' says he, 'go and light your mother's pipe, and let me have a shough; I'm tired o' my life lying here.' 'Ah, you thief,' says I, 'wait till you hear what she'll say to you when I tell her this.' 'Tell away, you pick-thanks,' says he; 'she won't believe a word you say.'" "And neither do I believe one word from you," said the mother.

At last a letter came from the father, that was serving on board the *Futhryom* (Le Foudroyant?), saying he'd be home after the letter as soon as coaches and ships could carry him. "Now," says the poor woman, "we'll have the christening any way." So the next day she went to

New Ross to buy sugar and tay, and beef and pork, to give a grand let-out to welcome her husband; but bedad the long-headed neighbours took that opportunity to gain their ends of the fairy imp. They gathered round the house, and one stout woman came up to the bed, promiskis-like, and wrapped him up in the quilt before he had time to defend himself, and away down the lane to the Boro she went, and the whole townland at her heels. He thought to get away, but she held him pinned as if he was in a vice: and he kept roaring, and the crowd kept laughing, and they never crack-cried till they were at the stepping-stones going to Ballybawn from Grange.

Well, when he felt himself near the water he roared like a score of bulls, and kicked like the divel, but my brave woman wasn't to be daunted. She got on the first stepping-stone, and the water, as black as night from the turf-*mull* (mould), running under her. He felt as heavy as lead, but she held on to the second. Well, she thought she'd go down there with the roaring, and the weight, and the dismal colour of the river, but she got to the middlestone, and there down through the quilt he fell as a heavy stone would through a muslin handkerchief. Off he went, whirling round and round, and letting the frightfulest laughs out of him, and showing his teeth and cracking his fingers at the people on the banks. "Oh, yous think yous are very clever, now," says he. "You may tell that fool of a woman from me that all I'm sorry for is that I didn't choke her, or do worse for her, before her husband comes home; bad luck to yous all!"

Well, they all came back joyful enough, though they were a little frightened. But weren't they rejoiced to meet the poor woman running to them with her fine healthy child in her arms, that she found in a delightful sleep when she got back from the town. You may be sure the next day didn't pass over him till he was baptized, and the next day his father got safe home. Well, I needn't say how happy they were; but bedad the woman was a little ashamed of herself next Sunday at Rathnure Chapel while Father James was preaching about the wickedness of neglecting to get young babies baptized as soon as possible after they're born.

Life among the Icelandic elves only partially resembles that among the Celtic fairies. The process of getting rid of one of them when introduced into a human family is, however, much the same among Celts and Scandinavians. The Breton or Irish housewife being incommoded by a squalling, rickety brat, collects a number of eggs ; and after throwing away the contents, places the shells carefully in a pot set over the fire. He looks with wonder on the operation; and when, in reply to his question, she explains that she is going to extract beer from them, he cries out, " I remember when they were building Babel, and never heard before of a brewery of egg-shells." Being now sure of his quality she summons her relations, and they get rid of him by taking him on a shovel, and *landing* him comfortably in the middle of the dung-lough at the bottom of the bawn, and letting him cry his fill. His fairy relations come to his rescue with little loss of time, and he vents his rage at not having done more mischief while he had been in such comfortable quarters.

Ión Arnason tells us, in his " Icelandic Legends " lately published by Mr. Bentley, that a Northern woman, under the same circumstances, sets a pot, furnished with some eatable, on the fire ; and having fastened many twigs in continuation of a spoon handle till the end of the shank appears above the chimney, she inserts the bowl in the mess. This excites the curiosity of the imp, and he is dislodged in the same way as his far-off brother in Galway. It would be, perhaps, trying the patience of the reader unduly to enlarge on all the ingenious devices practised for the ejectment of different intruders, so we will, using a story-teller's privilege, surround one case with the circumstances which waited on three or four.

THE CHANGELING AND HIS BAGPIPES.

A certain youth whom we shall here distinguish by the name of Rickard the Rake, amply earned his title by the time he lost in fair-tents, in dance-houses, in following hunts, and other unprofitable occupations, leaving his brothers and his aged father to attend to the concerns of the farm, or neglect them as they pleased. It is indispensable to the solemnities of a night dance in the country, to take the barn door off its hinges, and lay it on the floor to test the skill of the best dancers in the room in a single performance. In this was Rickard eminent, and many an evening did he hold the eyes of the assembly intent on his flourishes, lofty springs and kicks, and the other fashionable variations taught by the departed race of dancing-masters.

One evening while earning the applause of the admiring crowd, he uttered a cry of pain, and fell on his side on the hard door. A wonderful scene of confusion ensued,—the groans of the dancer, the pitying exclamations of the crowd, and their endeavours to stifle the sufferer in their eagerness to comfort him. We must suppose him carried home and confined to his bed for weeks, the complaint being a stiffness in one of his hip joints, occasioned by a fairy-dart. Fairy-doctors, male and female, tried their herbs and charms on him in vain; and more than one on leaving the house said to one of his family, "God send it's not one of the sheeoges yous are nursing, instead of poor wild Rickard!"

And indeed there seemed to be some reason in the observation. The jovial, reckless, good-humoured buck was now a meagre, disagreeable, exacting creature, with pinched features, and harsh voice, and craving appetite; and for several weeks he continued to plague and distress his unfortunate family. By the advice of a fairy-man a pair of bagpipes was accidentally left near his bed, and ears were soon on the stretch to catch the dulcet notes of the instrument from the room. It was well known that he was not at all skilled in the musical art; so if a well-played tune were heard from under his fingers, the course to be adopted by this family was clear.

But the invalid was as crafty as they were cunning; groans of pain and complaints of neglect formed the only body of sound that issued from the sick chamber. At last, during a hot harvest afternoon when every one should be in the field, and a dead silence reigned through the house, and yard, and out-offices, some one that was watching from an unsuspected press saw an anxious, foxy face peep out from the gently opened door of the room, and draw itself back after a careful survey of the great parlour into which it opened, and which had the large kitchen on the other side. Soon after, the introductory squeal of the instrument was heard, but of a sweeter quality than the same pipes ever uttered before or after that day. Then followed a strain of such wild and sweet melody as held in silent rapture about a dozen of the people of the house and some neighbours who had been apprised of the experiment, and who, till the first enchanting sound breathed through the house, had kept themselves quiet in the room above the kitchen, consequently the farthest from the changeling's station.

While they stood or sat entranced as air succeeded to air, and the last still the sweetest, they began to distinguish whispers, and the nearly inaudible rustle of soft and gauzy dresses seemingly brushing against each other, and such subdued sounds as a cat's feet might cause, swiftly pacing along a floor. They were unable to stir, or even move their lips, so powerful was the charm of the fairy's music on their wills and their senses, till at last the fairy-man spoke—the only person who had the will or the capacity to hold conference with him being the fairy-woman from the next townland.

He.—Come, come! this must be put a stop to.

The words were not all uttered when a low whistling noise was heard from the next room, and the moment after there was profound stillness.

She.—Yes, indeed; and what would you advise us to do first with the *anointed* sheeoge?

He.—We'll begin easy. We'll take him neck and crop

and hold his head under the water in the turnhole till we'll dhrive the divel out of him.

She.—That 'ud be a great deal too easy a punishment for the thief. We'll *hate* the shovel red-hot, put it under his currabingo, and land him out in the dung-lough.

He.—Ah, now; can't you thry easier punishments on him? I'll put the tongs in the fire till the claws are as hot as the divel, and won't I hould his nasty crass nose between them till he'll know the difference between a *fiery faces* and a *latchycock*.[1]

She.—No, no! Say nothing, and I'll go and bring my liquor, drawn from the leaves of the lussmore;[2] and if he was a sheeoge forty times, it will put the inside of him, into such a state that he'd give the world he could die. Some parts of him will be as if he had red-hot saws rasping him asunder, and others as if needles of ice were crossing and crossing each other in his bowels; and when he's dead, we'll give him no better grave nor the bog-hole, or the outside of the churchyard.

He.—Very well; let's begin. I'll bring my red-hot tongs from the kitchen fire, and you your little bottle of lussmore water. Don't any of yez go in, neighbours, till we have them ingradients ready.

There was a pause in the outer room while the fairy-man passed into the kitchen and back. Then there was a rush at the door, and a bursting into the room; but there was no sign of the changeling on the bed, nor under the bed, nor in any part of the room. At last one of the women shouted out in terror, for the face of the fiend was seen at the window, looking in, with such scorn and hate on the fearful features as struck terror into the boldest. However, the fairy-man dashed at him with his burning tongs in hand; but just as it was on the point of gripping his nose, a something between a laugh and a scream, that made the blood in their veins run cold, came from him. Face and all vanished, and

---

[1] Attempts at two law terms. The author has been acquainted with peasants to whom law terms and processes were as familiar as ever they were to poor Peter Peebles.

[2] *Great Herb.* The *Purpureus Digitalis*, Fairy-finger, or Fox-glove.

that was the last that was seen of him. Next morning, Rickard, now a reformed rake, was found in his own bed. Great was the joy at his recovery, and great it continued, for he laid aside his tobacco-pipe, and pint and quart measures. He forsook the tent and the sheebeen house, and took kindly to his reaping-hook, his spade, his plough, and his prayer-book, and blessed the night he was fairy-struck on the dance floor.

The mutual proceedings of the intruding fairies and the intruded-on mortals, are not always of the hostile character hitherto described. It is with some pleasure that we record an instance where the desirable re-exchange was effected without those disagreeable agencies resorted to in the case of "Rickard the Rake."

THE TOBINSTOWN SHEEOGE.

In the pleasant valley of the Duffrey, sheltered from the north-west winds by the huge pile of Mount Leinster, lie two villages separated by a turf bog. The western cluster is called Kennystown, and the eastern, Tobinstown.[1] The extensive Rath of Cromogue commands the bog on the north, and the over-abounding moisture in the holes and drains finds its way to the noisy Glasha on the south. The elder inhabitants of these villages spoke the Irish tongue at the close of the last century and the beginning of this. About the year 1809, the inhabitants of the whole valley spent a Sunday afternoon on the dry tussocks of the bog, sounding the dark pools with long poles and fishing spears, to stir up a descendant of the serpent that had laid the country waste in the days of Brian Boroimhe. Some intelligent person had seen it lying on the surface of Lough na Piastha about half a

---

[1] Let no incautious reader suppose that these villages were respectively inhabited by Tobins and Kennys. There was one family of Tobins extant, we forget in which village, but no Kenny in either. Thus Forrestalstown was filled by O'Learys, the Forrestals occupying a village in Gurawn entirely to themselves.

mile off, a day or two before, and a still more intelligent person had seen it tearing across the intermediate fields on Saturday night, with sparks of fire flashing from its tail. If the young piast was at the bottom of a bog-hole he remained there quietly enough. The enthusiastic crowd was obliged to separate at nightfall, no incident having rewarded their expectations beyond the fall of a little boy into a turf-pool, his rescue and consequent punishment by a loving but irritable parent. This, however, is no better than a digression.

Katty Clarke of Tobinstown was once happy in the possession of a fine boy, the delight of her eyes and heart, till one unlucky day, when she happened to sleep too long in the morning, and, consequently, had not time to say her prayers. Mr. Clarke, coming in from the fields, was annoyed at not finding the stirabout ready, and opened his mind on the subject. Katty was vexed with him and herself, and cursed a little, as was customary sixty years since among men and women in remote districts of our country. All these annoyances prevented her from remembering the holy water, and from sprinkling some drops on her little son, and making the sign of the cross on his innocent forehead. When the men and boys left the house for their out-door work after breakfast, Katty took a pailful of soiled linen to the spot where the stream formed a little pool, and where the villagers had fixed a broad and flat "beetling" stone. While she was employed in cleaning the clothes, she let her child sit or roll about on the grassy slope behind her.

All at once she heard a scream from the boy, and when she turned, and ran to him, she found him in convulsions. She ran home with him, administered salt and water, and the other specifics popular in the country. The fit passed away, but she was grieved to perceive that the weazened, pained expression still remained on his face, and that his whimpering and whining did not abate—in fact, to use a well-worn Irish expression, "the cry was never out of his mouth." He ate as much as would suffice a full-grown man, and was always ready for food both at regular meal-times and between them.

After a week of this state of things, the neighbours came to the conclusion that it was a sheeoge that Katty was slaving her life out for. Katty's family came next into the same persuasion, and lastly, but with some doubts, Katty herself.

At a family and neighbourly council, held round the fire, after the children had been sent to bed, they proceeded to get rid of the little wretch, and this was the order of the ceremonial:—

A neighbour took the shovel, rubbed it clean, laid it on the floor, and his wife, seizing on the supposed fairy, placed it sitting on the broad iron blade. She held it there stoutly, notwithstanding its howls, while her husband, raising it gently, proceeded to the bawn, accompanied by the assembly, and, despite all opposition on its part, placed it on a wisp of straw which crowned the manure heap. The luxury of the seat did not succeed in arresting his outcries, but his audience not taking much notice, joined hands, and in their own parlance *serenaded* the crowned heap three times, while the fairy-man, who had been summoned from Bawnard (high court), recited an incantation in Irish, of which we give a literal version:—

> "Come at our call, O Sighe mother!
> Come and remove your offspring.
> Food and drink he has received,
> And kindness from the Ben-a-teagh.[1]
> Here he no longer shall stay,
> But depart to the Duiné Matha.
> Restore the lost child, O Bean-Sighe![2]
> And food shall be left for thy people
> When the cloth is spread on the harvest-field,
> On the short grass newly mown.
> Food shall be left on the dresser-shelf,
> And the hearthstone shall be clean,
> When the Clann Sighe come in crowds,
> And sweep in rings round the floor,
> And hold their feast at the fire.
> Restore the mortal child, O Bean-Sighe!
> And receive thine own at our hands."

The charm and the third round ending at the same time, all re-entered the house, and closed the door.

[1] Woman of the house. [2] Lady fairy.

They soon felt the air around them sweep this way and that, as if it was stirred by the motion of wings, but they remained quiet and silent for about ten minutes. Opening the door, they then looked out, and saw the bundle of straw on the heap, but neither child nor fairy. "Go into your bedroom, Katty," said the fairy-man, "and see if there's anything left on the bed." She did so, and they soon heard a cry of joy, and Katty was among them in a moment, kissing and hugging her own healthy-looking child, who was waking and rubbing his eyes, and wondering at the lights and all the eager faces.

Whatever hurry Katty might be in of a morning after that, she never left her bedside till she had finished, as devoutly as she could, her five Paters and five Aves, and her Apostles' Creed and her Confiteor. And she never cursed or swore except when she was surprised by a sudden fit of passion.

In one point of elvish mythology, Teuton and Celt are agreed,—viz., that whether the supernatural beings of the old superstition be called fairies, elves, nixes, trolls, korigans, or duergars, they all live in fear of utter condemnation at the Day of Judgment. Their dislike of the human race arises from envy of their destiny, which they regard as the filling of the heavenly seats lost by themselves. Sometimes they experience a slight hope that their place may not be with Satan and his angels, and then they become urgent with holy and wise mortals, to give judgment on their case. This phase of fairy life will be illustrated by the local legend of—

THE BELATED PRIEST.

A very lonesome road connects the village of Ballindaggin, in the Duffrey, with the townland of Mangan, on the Bantry side of the brawling Urrin, and outside these intermediate stations it leads to Kaim and Castleboro, on one side, and the high road from Bunclody to

Ross on the other. From the river to Ballindaggin, you hardly meet a house, and fallow fields extend on each side.

Father Stafford was asked, rather late in the day, to make a sick call at a cabin that stood among these fields, at a considerable distance from this road,—a cabin from which no lane led either to by-road or public road. He was delayed longer than he expected, and when he was leaving the cabin it was nearly dark. This did not disturb him much. There was a path that led to the road, and he knew he had only to keep a north-easterly direction to come out on it, not far from the village already named. So he went on fearlessly for some time, but complete obscurity soon surrounded him, and he would have been sorely perplexed, had it not been that the path lay for the most part beside the fences.

At last, instead of passing in a line near the fence, it struck across the field; and, open his eyes wide as he might, he could hardly distinguish it from the dry, russet-coloured grass at each side. Well, he kept his eyes steadily fixed in the due direction, and advanced till he was about the middle of the field, which happened to be a large one. There some case of conscience, or other anxious subject, crossed his mind, and he stopped and fidgeted about, walking restlessly this way and that for a few steps, totally forgetting his present circumstances. Coming at last to some solution of his difficulty, full recollection returned, and he was sensible of being thoroughly ignorant of the direction in which his proper route lay. If he could but get a glimpse of Mount Leinster, it would be all well; but, beyond a few perches, all was in the deepest darkness on every side. He then set off in a straight line, which he knew would bring him to some fence, and perhaps he might find stile or gap for his guidance. He went twice round the field, but, in the confusion of his faculties, he could find no trace of path or pass. He at last half resolved to cross the fence, and go straight on, but the dykes were, for the most part, encumbered with briers, and furze-bushes crowned the tops of the steep clay mounds.

While he stood perplexed, he heard the rustle of wings or bodies passing swiftly through the air, and a musical voice was heard :—" You will suffer much if you do not find your way. Give us a favourable answer to a question, and you shall be on the road in a few minutes." The good priest was somewhat awed at the rustle and the voice, but he answered without delay, " Who are you, and what's your question?" The same voice replied, " We are the Chlann Sighe, and wish you to declare that at the last day our lot may not be with Satan. Say that the Saviour died for us as well as for you." " I will give you a favourable answer, if you can make me a hopeful one. Do you adore and love the SON OF GOD?" He received no answer but weak and shrill cries, and the rushing of wings, and at once it seemed as if he had shaken off some oppression. The dark clouds had separated, a weak light was shed round where he stood, and he distinguished the path, and an opening in the bushes on the fence. He crossed into the next field, and, following the path, he was soon on the road. In fifteen minutes he was seated at his comfortable fire, and his little round table, covered with books, was at his side.

The good people, as already mentioned, are not uniformly selfish. They are grateful for food left in their way, and other kindnesses shown them by the human race. The following tale will furnish an illustration. In a modified form, it is well known in Brittany, and is a favourite in Munster. It was the earliest fairy legend known to our boyhood, and is the most popular of those that have been preserved by the people of the south-east of Ireland. Every locality lays the scene in some rath in the neighbourhood. The phraseology in which the legend was so often heard is preserved.

THE PALACE IN THE RATH.

Every one from Bunclody to Enniscorthy knows the rath[1] between Tombrick and Munfin. Well, there was a

[1] A small circular meadow surrounded by a mound overgrown

poor, honest, quiet little creature, that lived just at the pass of Glanamoin, between the hill of Coolgarrow and Kilachdiarmid. His back was broken when he was a child, and he earned his bread by making cradles, and bosses, and chairs, and beehives, out of straw and briers. No one in the barony of Bantry or Scarawalsh could equal him at these. Well, he was a sober little fellow enough, but the best of us may be overtaken. He was coming from the fair of Enniscorthy one fine summer evening, up along the beautiful shady road of Munfin; and when he came near the stream that bounds Tombrick, he turned into the fields to make his road short. He was singing merrily enough, but by degrees he got a little stupefied; and when he was passing the dry, grassy ditch that surrounds the rath, he felt an inclination to sit and rest himself.

It is hard to sit awhile, and have your eyes a little glassy, and the things seeming to turn round you, without falling off asleep; and asleep my poor little man of straw was in a few minutes. Things like droves of cattle, or soldiers marching, or big flakes of foam on a flooded river, were pushing on through his brain, and he thought the drums were playing a march, when up he woke, and there in the face of the steep bank that was overgrown with bushes and blackthorn, a passage was open between nice pillars, and inside was a great vaulted room, with arches crossing each other, a hundred lamps hanging from the vault, and thousands of nice little gentlemen and ladies, with green coats and gowns, and red sugar-loaf caps, curled at the tops like old Irish birredhs, dancing and singing, and nice little pipers and fiddlers, perched up in a little gallery by themselves, and playing music to help out the singing.

He was a little cowed at first, but as he found no one taking notice of him, he stole in, and sat in a corner, and thought he'd never be tired looking at the fine little people figuring, and cutting capers, and singing. But at last he began to find the singing and music a little tedious.

with furze-bushes, the remains of the earthen fort of one of the small chiefs of old days. They are erroneously called "Danes' forts."

It was nothing but two short bars and four words, and this was the style :—

> "Yae Luan, yae Morth—
> Yae Luan, yae Morth."

The longer he looked on, the bolder he grew, and at last he shouted at the end of the verse—

> "Agus Dha Haed-yeen."

Oh, such cries of delight as rose up among the merry little gentry! They began the improved song, and shouted it till the vault rang :—

> "Yae Luan, Yae Morth—
> Yae Luan, yae Morth—
> Yae Luan, yae Morth,
> Agus Dha Haed-yeen."[1]

After a few minutes, they all left off the dance, and gathered round the boss maker, and thanked him for improving their tune. "Now," said the chief, "if you wish for anything, only say the word, and, if it is in our power, it must be done." "I thank you, ladies and gentlemen," says he; "and if you would only remove this hump from my back, I'd be the happiest man in the Duffrey." "Oh, easy done, easy done!" said they. "Go on again with the dance, and you come along with us." So on they went with—

> "Monday, Tuesday—
> Monday, Tuesday—
> Monday, Tuesday,
> And Wednesday too."

One fairy taking their new friend by the heel, shot him in a curve to the very roof, and down he came the other side of the hall. Another gave him a shove, and up he flew back again. He felt as if he had wings; and one time when his back touched the roof, he found a sudden delightful change in himself; and just as he touched the ground, he lost all memory of everything around him.

Next morning he was awakened by the sun shining on

[1] Correctly *Dia Luain, Dia Mairt, Dia Ceadoin* ;—Moon's Day, Mar's Day, Woden's Day (First Fast).

his face from over Slieve Buie, and he had a delightful feel down along his body instead of the disagreeable *cruith* he was accustomed to. He felt as if he could go from that to the other side of the stream at one step, and he burned little daylight till he reached Glanamoin. He had some trouble to persuade the neighbours of the truth of what had happened ; but the wonder held only nine days ; and he had like to lose his health along with his hump, for if he only made his appearance in Ballycarney, Castle-Dockrell, Ballindaggin, Kilmeashil, or Bunclody, ten people would be inviting him to a share of a tumbler of punch, or a quart of mulled beer.

The news of the wonderful cure was talked of high and low, and even went as far as Ballynocrish, in Bantry, where another poor *angashore* of a humpback lived. But he was very unlike the Duffrey man in his disposition : he was as cross as a brier, and almost begrudged his right hand to help his left. His poor old aunt and a neighbour of hers set out one day, along with him, along the Bunclody road, passing by Killanne and the old place of the Colcloughs at Duffrey Hall, till they reached Temple-shambo. Then they kept along the hilly by-road till they reached the little man's house near the pass.

So they up and told their business, and he gave them a kind welcome, and explained all the ins and outs of his adventure ; and the end was, the four went together in the heel of the evening to the rath, and left the little lord in his glory in the dry, brown grass of the round dyke, where the other met his good fortune. The little ounkran never once thanked them for all the trouble they were taking for him. He only whimpered about being left in that lonesome place, and bade them to be sure to be with him at the flight of night, because he did not know what way to take from it.

At last, the poor cross creature fell asleep ; and after dreaming about falling down from rocks, and being held over the sea by his hump, and then that a lion had him by the same hump, and was running away with him, and then that it was put up for a target for soldiers to shoot at, the first volley they gave awoke him, and what was it but the music of the fairies in full career. The melody was the same as it was left them by the hive-maker, and the tune and dancing was twice as good as it was at first. This is the way it went :—

> "Yae Luan, yae Morth—
> Yae Luan, yae Morth—
> Yae Luan, yae Morth,
> Agus Dha Haed-yeen."

But the new visitor had neither taste nor discretion; so when they came about the third time to the last line, he croaked out :—

> "Agus Dha Yærd-yeen,
> Agus Dha Haen-ya."[1]

It was the same as a cross fiddler that finds nobody going to give him anything, and makes a harsh back-screak of his bow along one of the strings. A thousand voices cried out, "Who stops our dance?—who stops our dance?" and all gathered round the poor fellow. He could do nothing but stare at them with his poor, cross, frightened face; and they screamed and laughed till he thought it was all over with him.

But it was *not* over with him.

"Bring down that hump," says the king; and before you could kiss your hand it was clapped on, as fast as the knocker of Newgate, over the other hump. The music was over now, the lights went out, and the poor creature lay till morning in a nightmare; and there the two women found him, at daybreak, more dead than alive. It was a dismal return they had to Ballynocrish; and the moral of my story is, that you should never drive till you first try the virtue of leading.

This fairy legend is certainly one of the most ancient of its kind. Dancing to the tiresome melody was a punishment inflicted on the fairies for their pristine crimes. No wonder that they should have felt grateful for the improvement effected.

[1] Correctly *Diar Daoin, Dia Aoine*, Dies Jovis, Dies Veneris, —Thursday, Friday.

THE BRETON VERSION OF THE PALACE IN THE RATH.

In the Breton mythology the Irish fairies are replaced by the *korils* (night dancers), who assemble on the heaths and execute *rondes* till daybreak. Any inattentive mortal crossing their territory is seized on, and obliged to caper all night, and at sunrise is at the point of death with fatigue. *Benead Guilcher*, the hero of a story similar to the *Lusmore* of the Legends of the South of Ireland, returning with his wife from his labours at the plough, was on the point of being seized on, when they observed his paddle (*fork* in the original) in his hand, and so were obliged to relinquish their prey, singing at the same time,—

> " Lez-hi, lez-hon,
> Bác'h an arér zo gant hon ;
> Lez-hon, lez-hi,
> Bác'h arér zo gant hi."

> " Let him go, let her go,
> Fork of plough has he ;
> Let her go, let him go,
> Fork of plough have they."

But the bold Benead, through curiosity and a wish to get rid of his hump, voluntarily joined the dance on another night, having first made them solemnly promise *on the cross* not to work him beyond his strength. They at once recommenced dance and song,—the whole chant limited to three words—

> " *Di-Lun, Di-Meurs, Di-Mercher.*"
> " Monday, Tuesday, Wednesday."

"With submission to you, gentlemen," said Guilcher, "your song is of the shortest. You stop too soon in the week. I think I could improve it."

" Do so, do so," cried they all, and he chanted—

> " Monday, Tuesday, Wednesday,
> Thursday, Friday, Saturday."

They were so pleased, that when he requested beauty of face and form, they took him up, and pitched him from one to the other; and when he had gone the round, his hump was away, and a handsome face given him.

He did not reveal his adventure in full till he was obliged by another humpback, who exercised the office of usurer, and to whom poor Benead owed eight crowns. He tried his fortune among the little korils, and promised to further improve the melody. But he was a stutterer, and could only get out—

> " Monday, Tuesday, Wednesday,
> Thursday, Friday, Saturday,
> And Su-Su-Sunday too—
> And Su-Sunday too—
> Su-Sunday—
> Su-Sunday too."

They stopped him in vehement anger, and bade him name his wish.

"Gi-gi-give me," said he, "what Guilcher left."

"We will," said they, and down came the additional hump.

Being now most furious with Guilcher, he reduced him to the point of selling off all the little he possessed. So in this strait he once more repaired to the dwarfs.

They went on with the song, enlarged by the Sunday, but Guilcher tiring of the bald melody, added a line, and completed their bliss.

> " Monday, Tuesday, Wednesday,
> Thursday, Friday, Saturday,
> With Sunday, as 'tis meet,
> And so the week's complete."

Guilcher revealing his misery, they all flung their purses to him, and home he went in joy. Alas! when the contents were turned out on the table, they were found to consist of dry leaves, sand, and horse-hair. The frightened wife ran to the *bénitier*, and luckily finding some holy water there, sprinkled it on themselves and the table; and lo, a pile of gold and jewels sparkled before them! In Ireland the reverse would have taken place.

The Breton version is more complete than the Irish one. The korils explained to Guilcher that they had been doomed to perpetual night-dancing, with an imperfect melody, till some mortal should have the courage to join them, and complete the strain. After Guilcher had lengthened it, they were in hopes of the usurer finishing it, and hence their anger with him.

THE FAIRY NURSE.

There was once a little farmer and his wife living near Coolgarrow. They had three children, and my story happened while the youngest was on the breast. The wife was a good wife enough, but her mind was all on her family and her farm, and she hardly ever went to her knees without falling asleep, and she thought the time spent in the chapel was twice as long as it need be. So, begonies, she let her man and her two children go before her one day to Mass, while she called to consult a fairyman about a disorder one of her cows had. She was late at the chapel, and was sorry all the day after, for her husband was in grief about it, and she was very fond of him.

Late that night he was wakened up by the cries of his children calling out, "Mother, mother!" When he sat up and rubbed his eyes, there was no wife by his side, and when he asked the little ones what was become of their mother, they said they saw the room full of nice little men and women, dressed in white, and red, and green, and their mother in the middle of them, going out by the door as if she was walking in her sleep. Out he ran, and searched everywhere round the house, but neither tale nor tidings did he get of her for many a day.

Well, the poor man was miserable enough, for he was as fond of his woman as she was of him. It used to bring the salt tears down his cheeks to see his poor children neglected and dirty, as they often were, and they'd be bad enough only for a kind neighbour that used to look in whenever she could spare time. The infant was out with a wet nurse.

About six weeks after—just as he was going out to his

work one morning—a neighbour, that used to mind women at their lying-in, came up to him, and kept step by step with him to the field, and this is what she told him.

"Just as I was falling asleep last night, I hears a horse's tramp in the bawn, and a knock at the door, and there, when I came out, was a fine-looking dark man, mounted on a black horse, and he told me to get ready in all haste, for a lady was in great want of me. As soon as I put on my cloak and things, he took me by the hand, and I was sitting behind him before I felt myself stirring. 'Where are we going, sir?' says I. 'You'll soon know,' says he; and he drew his fingers across my eyes, and not a *stim* remained in them. I kept a tight grip of him, and the dickens a knew I knew whether he was going backwards or forwards, or how long we were about it, till my hand was taken again, and I felt the ground under me. The fingers went the other way across my eyes, and there we were before a castle door, and in we went through a big hall and great rooms all painted in fine green colours, with red and gold bands and ornaments, and the finest carpets and chairs and tables and window-curtains, and fine ladies and gentlemen walking about. At last we came to a bedroom, with a beautiful lady in bed, and there he left me with her; and, bedad, it was not long till a fine bouncing boy came into the world. The lady clapped her hands, and in came *Fir*[1] *Dhorocha* (Dark man), and kissed her and his son, and praised me, and gave me a bottle of green ointment to rub the child all over.

"Well, the child I rubbed, sure enough; but my right eye began to smart me, and I put up my finger and gave it a rub, and purshuin to me if ever I was so frightened. The beautiful room was a big rough cave, with water oozing over the edges of the stones, and through the clay; and the lady, and the lord, and the child, weazened, poverty-bitten crathurs—nothing but skin and bone, and the rich dresses were old rags. I didn't let on that I found any difference, and after a bit says Fir Dhorocha, 'Go before me to the hall-door, and I will be with you

[1] Correctly, *Fear Doirche*.

in a few moments, and see you safe home.' Well, just as I turned into the outside cave, who should I see watching near the door but poor Molly. She looked round all frightened, and says she to me in a whisper—'I'm brought here to give suck to the child of the king and queen of the fairies; but there is one chance of saving me. All the court will pass the cross near Templeshambo, next Friday night, on a visit to the fairies of Old Ross. If John can catch me by hand or cloak when I ride by, and has courage not to let go his grip, I'll be safe. Here's the king. Don't open your mouth to answer. I saw what happened with the ointment.'

"Fir Dhorocha didn't once cast his eye towards Molly, and he seemed to have no suspicion of me. When we came out I looked about me, and where do you think we were but in the dyke of the Rath of Cromogue. I was on the horse again, which was nothing but a big *boolian bui* (rag-weed), and I was in dread every minute I'd fall off; but nothing happened till I found myself in my own bawn. The king slipped five guineas into my hand as soon as I was on the ground, and thanked me, and bade me good night. I hope I'll never see his face again. I got into bed, and couldn't sleep for a long time; and when I examined my five guineas this morning, that I left in the table-drawer the last thing, I found five withered leaves of oak—bad scran to the giver!"

Well, you may all think the fright, and the joy, and the grief the poor man was in when the woman finished her story. They talked, and they talked, but we needn't mind what they said till Friday night came, when both were standing where the mountain road crosses the one going to Ross.

There they stood looking towards the bridge of Thuar, and I won't keep you waiting, as they were in the dead of the night, with a little moonlight shining from over Kilachdiarmid. At last she gave a start and "By this and by that," says she, "here they come, bridles jingling, and feathers tossing," He looked, but could see nothing; and she stood trembling, and her eyes wide open, looking down the way to the ford of Ballinacoola. "I see your wife," says she, "riding on the outside just so as to rub against us. We'll walk on promiskis-like, as if we suspected nothing, and when we are passing I'll give you a shove. If you don't do *your* duty then, dickens cure you!"

Well, they walked on easy, and the poor hearts beating in both their breasts; and though he could see nothing, he heard a faint jingle, and tramping, and rustling, and at last he got the push that she promised. He spread out his arms, and there was his wife's waist within them, and he could see her plain, but such a hullabulloo rose as if there was an earthquake; and he found himself surrounded by horrible-looking things, roaring at him, and striving to pull his wife away. But he made the sign of the cross, and bid them begone in God's name, and held his wife as if it was iron his arms were made of. Bedad, in one moment everything was as silent as the grave, and the poor woman lying in a faint in the arms of her husband and her good neighbour. Well, all in good time she was minding her family and her business again, and I'll go bail, after the fright she got, she spent more time on her knees, and avoided fairymen all the days of the week, and particularly Sunday.

It is hard to have anything to do with the good people without getting a mark from them. My brave midwife didn't escape no more nor another. She was one Thursday at the market of Enniscorthy, when what did she see walking among the tubs of butter but Fir Dhorocha, very hungry-looking, and taking a scoop out of one tub and out of another. "Oh, sir," says she, very foolish, "I hope your lady is well, and the young heir." "Pretty well, thank you," says he, rather frightened like. "How do I look in this new suit?" says he, getting to one side of her. "I can't see you plain at all, sir," says she. "Well, now," says he, getting round her back to the other side. "Musha, indeed, sir, your coat looks no better nor a withered dock-leaf." "Maybe, then," says he, "it will be different now," and he struck the eye next him with a switch.

Begonies, she never saw a stim after with that one till the day of her death.

This fairy legend is very popular among the branches of the Celtic race. We do not at this moment recollect any variety of it in the Norse or German collections. The leading feature is, however, as old as the heroic ages of Greece. It will remind the classic scholar of the recovery of Alcestis, and the almost recovery of Eurydice. The cavalier treatment of the infernal powers by Hercules and Theseus, finds its counterpart in *Giolla na Chreck an Gour* thrashing the devils. *Labhradh Loingseach* takes after King Midas in the matter of long hairy ears, and *Fionn*, son of *Cumhail*, rivals Apollo and Hercules in the destruction of serpents, wild boars, and birds. The irresistible beauty of Adonis, and his murder by the boar, survive in the legend of *Diarmuidh* with the beauty-spot, and his death by the "green cropped pig." These legends will be given when their turns arrive.

It is only natural in the social condition of the fairies that they should steal human children, and also nurses to give suck to their own puny offspring; but why they should carry off young men and women is not so clear. Such, however, is the fact.

THE RECOVERED BRIDE.

There was a marriage in the townland of Curragraigue. After the usual festivities, and when the guests were left to themselves, and were drinking to the prosperity of the bride and bridegroom, they were startled by the appearance of the man himself rushing into the room with anguish in his looks. "Oh," cried he, "Margaret is carried away by the fairies, I'm sure. The girls were not left the room for half a minute when I went in, and there is no more sign of her there than if she never was born." Great consternation prevailed, great search was made, but no Margaret was to be found. After a night and day spent in misery, the poor brideroom laid down to take some rest. In a while he seemed to himself to wake from a troubled dream, and look out into the room. The moon was shining in through the window, and in the middle of the slanting rays stood Margaret in her white bridal clothes. He thought to speak and leap out of the bed, but his tongue was without utterance, and his limbs unable to move. "Do not be disturbed, dear husband," said the appearance; "I am now in the power of the fairies, but if you only have courage and prudence we may be soon happy with each other again. Next Friday will be May-eve, and the whole court will ride out of the old fort after midnight. I must be there along with the rest. Sprinkle a circle with holy water, and have a black-hafted knife with you. If you have courage to pull me off the horse, and draw me into the ring, all they can do will be useless. You must have some food for me every night on the dresser, for if I taste one mouthful with them, I will be lost to you for ever. The fairies got power over me because I was only thinking of you, and did not prepare myself as I ought for the sacrament. I made a bad confession, and now I am suffering for it. Don't forget what I have said." "Oh, no, my darling," cried he, recovering his speech, but by the time he had slipped out of bed, there was no living soul in the room but himself.

Till Friday night the poor young husband spent a desolate time. The food was left on the dresser over night, and it rejoiced all hearts to find it vanished by morning. A little before midnight he was at the entrance of the old rath. He formed the circle, took his station within it, and kept the black-hafted knife ready for service. At times he was nervously afraid of losing his dear wife, and at others burning with impatience for the struggle. At last the old fort with its dark high bushy fences cutting against the sky, was in a moment replaced by a palace and its court. A thousand lights flashed from the windows and lofty hall entrance, numerous torches were brandished by attendants stationed round the courtyard, and a numerous cavalcade of richly-attired ladies and gentlemen was moving in the direction of the gate where he found himself standing. As they rode by him laughing and jesting, he could not tell whether they were aware of his presence or not. He looked intent at each countenance as it approached, but it was some time before he caught sight of the dear face and figure borne along on a milk-white steed. She recognised him well enough, and her features now broke into a smile—now expressed deep anxiety. She was unable for the throng to guide the animal close to the ring of power; so he suddenly rushed out of his bounds, seized her in his arms, and lifted her off. Cries of rage and fury arose on every side; they were hemmed in, and weapons were directed at his head and breast to terrify him. He seemed to be inspired with superhuman courage and force, and wielding the powerful knife he soon cleared a space round him, all seeming dismayed by the sight of the weapon. He lost no time, but drew his wife within the ring, within which none of the myriads round dared to enter. Shouts of derision and defiance continued to fill the air for some time, but the expedition could not be delayed. As the end of the procession filed past the gate and the circle within which the mortal pair held each other determinedly clasped, darkness and silence fell on the old rath and the fields round it, and the rescued bride and her lover breathed freely. We will not detain the sensitive reader on the happy walk home, on the joy that hailed their arrival, and on all the eager gossip that occupied the townland and the five that surround it for a month after the happy rescue.

A wonderful treasure in the detection of fairy delusions is the four-leaved shamrock! Once at the fair of Enniscorthy, a master of sleight-of-hand, willing to astonish the simple Wexfordians, and extract some money out of their pockets, threw his gamecock up on the roof of a house, and there every one could see him stalk along with a great log of Norway timber in his bill. Every one wondered, and those near the cock as he paced along, got from under the beam as soon as they could.

"Musha," says a young girl who was taking home an armful of fresh grass to her cow, "what are yous gapin' at?" "Gaping at! Do you see the balk the cock is carrying?" "Balk, *inagh!* Purshuin' to the balk within a street of him! All I can see is a good wheaten straw that he has in his *bake*." The showman overheard the discourse, and called out to the girl—"What will you take for that bunch of grass! I'd like to give a mouthful of fresh provender to my horse." The bargain was made, and as soon as the article was handed over to the conjurer, the girl gave a great start and cried, "Oh, the Lord save us! See what the cock is carrying! Some one will be kilt." There was a four-leaved shamrock in the bundle of grass.

We could name the receipt for rendering the "Good People" visible, when a small whirlwind is at work with dust and dry leaves; but much as we wish to diffuse a knowledge of the social economy of Fairy Land, we are not anxious that any of our readers should make personal acquaintance with individuals of that country, or practise any magic rites whatever. You set dangerous machinery in motion, without knowing how to put it at rest again, or whether it may not tear your own person to pieces.

A clannish spirit prevails among the Fairy folk, as well as in that division of the human family amongst whom they delight to dwell. Hurling matches, and even pitched battles, occur between the "Good People" of different provinces. Passing one day along the road that runs near Lough-na-Piastha, in company with an intelligent but visionary neighbour, and talking on the present subject, he pointed out to us a little glen on the side of Mount Leinster, and gave this personal account of a

FACTION-FIGHT AMONG THE FAIRIES.

"I was sitting on the brow of that hill, the other day, and it was so calm you could hear the buzzing of a fly's wing. I was half asleep with the heat and with having nothing to do, when I was aroused by a noise coming down from the mountain along the stream. The road crosses it just above the glen; and at the bridge the sound divided itself, and I heard the beat of wings on one side of the stream and on the other, but I could see nothing. I then seemed to hear the blowing of weak-voiced bugles, and faint shouts, and the sound of blows, as if two winged armies were fighting in the air; and even the firing of shots; but it was as if I was hearing all through a skreen or in a dream. It seemed to me even as if light bodies fell in the water. At last there was greater shouting and work on one side, and hurraing, and then all the noise and rout rose in the air, and everything fell into quiet again. Fairies don't cross streams, you say! How then could the Leinster fairies cross over the Suir and Barrow to have a hurling match with the Munster fairies, or the fairies of Ireland have a battle with the Scotch fairies?"

Mrs. K. was as certain that the following adventure had befallen her father as that she ruled her husband without appeal, and was in turn despotically ruled by his children.

JEMMY DOYLE IN THE FAIRY PALACE.

My father was once coming down Scollagh Gap on a dark night, and all at once he saw, right before him, the lights coming from ever so many windows of a castle, and heard the shouts and laughing of people within. The door was wide open, and in he walked; and there on the spot where he had often drunk a tumbler of bad beer, he found himself in a big hall, and saw the king and queen of the fairies sitting at the head of a long table, and hundreds of people, all grandly dressed, eating and drinking. The clothes they had on them were of an old fashion, and there were harpers and pipers by themselves up in a gallery, and playing the most delightful old Irish airs. There was nothing to be seen but rich silk dresses, and pearls, and diamonds on the gentlemen and ladies and rich hangings on the walls, and lamps blazing.

The queen, as soon as she saw my father, cried out, "Welcome, Mr. Doyle; make room there for Mr. Doyle, and let him have the best at the table. Hand Mr. Doyle a tumbler of punch, that will be strong and sweet. Sit down, Mr. Doyle, and make yourself welcome." So he sat down, and took the tumbler, and just as he was going to taste it, his eye fell on the man next him, and he was an old neighbour that was dead twenty years. Says the old neighbour, "For your life, don't touch bit nor sup." The smell was very nice, but he was frightened by what the dead neighbour said, and he began to notice how ghastly some of the fine people looked when they thought he was not minding them.

So his health was drunk, and he was pressed by the queen to fall to, but he had the sense to take the neighbour's advice, and only spilled the drink down between his coat and waistcoat.

At last the queen called for a song, and one of the guests sang a very indecent one in Irish. He often repeated a verse of it for us, but we didn't know the sense. At last he got sleepy, and recollected nothing more only the rubbing of his legs against the bushes in the knoc (field of gorse) above our place in Cromogue; and we found him asleep next morning in the haggard, with a scent of punch from his mouth. He told us that we would get his knee-buckles on the path at the upper end of the knoc, and there, sure enough, they were found. Heaven be his bed!

THE FAIRY CURE.

We have related the adventures of a woman in the Duffrey, who had been called on at a late hour to assist the lady of a fairy chief in a trying situation. The person about whom we are going to speak was also a *sage-femme* and in that capacity was summoned by a dark rider to aid his lady, who was on the point of adding to the Sighe population of the country.

For nearly a year before that time, Nora's daughter, Judy, had been confined to her bed by a sore leg, which neither she, nor the neighbouring doctor, nor the fairyman,[1] could " make any hand of."

The calling up of the old woman, the ride behind the *Fir Dhorocha*, and the dismounting at the door of an illuminated palace, all took place as mentioned in the tale above alluded to. In the hall she was surprised to see an old neighbour, who had long been spirited away from the haunts of his youth and manhood, to the joyless, though showy life of the Sighe caverns. He at once took an opportunity, when the "Dark man" was not observing him, to impress on Nora the necessity of taking no refreshment of any kind while under the roof of the fairy castle, and of refusing money or any other consideration in any form. The only exception he made was in favour of cures for diseases inflicted by evil spirits or by fairies.

She found the lady of the castle in a bed with pillows and quilts of silk, and in a short time (for Nora was a handy woman) there was a beautiful little girl lying on the breast of the delighted mother. All the fine ladies that were scattered through the large room, now gathered round, and congratulated their queen, and paid many compliments to the lucky-handed Nora. "I am so pleased with you," said the lady, "that I shall be glad to see you take as much gold, and silver, and jewels, out of the next room, as you can carry." Nora stepped in out of curiosity and saw piles of gold and silver coins, and baskets of diamonds and pearls, lying about on every side, but she remembered the caution, and came out empty-handed. "I'm much obleeged to you, my lady," said she, "but if I took them guineas, and crowns, and jewels home, no one would ever call on me again to help his wife, and I'd be sittin' wud me hands acrass,

---

[1] The worthy who possessed skill in curing all maladies inflicted by the "Good People," sympathetic ointments and charmed draughts being the chief articles in his pharmacopœia.

and doin' nothin' but dhrinkin' tay and makin' curtchies (courtesies), an' I'd be dead before a year 'ud be gone by." "Oh dear!" said the lady, "what an odd person you are! At any rate, sit down at that table, and help yourself to food and drink." "Oh, ma'am, is it them jellies, an' custhards, an' pasthry you'd like to see me at? Lord love you! I would'nt know the way to me mouth wud the likes ; an' I swore again dhrinkin' after a time I was overtaken wud the liccor when I ought to be mindin' a poor neighbour's wife." "Well, this is too bad. Will you even condescend to wear this shawl for my sake?" "Ach, me lady, would you have the dirty little gorsoons roaring after me, an' may be pelting me with stones, when I'd be going through the village?" "Well, but what should hinder you from living in this castle all your life with me, eating and drinking, and wearing the best of everything?" "Musha, ma'am, I'd only be the laughin' stock o' the fine ladies and gentlemen. I'd have no ould neighbour to have a shanachus (gossip) wud, and what 'ud the craythurs of women do for me in me own place, when their time 'ud be come?" "Alas! alas! is there any way in which I can show you how grateful I am for your help and your skill?" "Musha, indeed is there, ma'am. My poor girshach, Jude, is lying under a sore leg for a twelvemonth, an' I'm sure that the lord or yourself can make her as sound as a bell if you only say the word." "Ask me anything but that, and you shall have it." "Oh, lady, dear, that's giving me everything but the thing I want." "You don't know the offence your daughter gave to us, I am sure, or you would not ask me to cure her." "Judy offend you, ma'am! Oh, it's impossible!" "Not at all; and this is the way it happened.

"You know that all the fairy court enjoy their lives in the night only, and we frequently go through the country, and hold our feasts where the kitchen, and especially the hearth, is swept up clean. About a twelvemonth ago, myself and my ladies were passing your cabin, and one of the company liked the appearance of the neat thatch, and the whitewashed walls, and the clean pavement outside the door, so much, that she persuaded us all to go in. We found the cheerful turf fire shining on the well-swept hearth and floor, and the clean pewter and delft plates on the dresser, and the white table. We were so well pleased, that we sat down on the hearth, and laid our tea-tray, and began to drink our tea as comfortably as could be. You know we can be any size we please, and there was a score of us settled before the fire.

"We were vexed enough when we saw your daughter come up out of your bedroom, and make towards the fire. Her feet, I acknowledge, were white and clean, but one of them would cover two or three of us, the size we were that night. On she came stalking, and just as I was raising my cup of tea to my lips, down came the soft flat sole on it, and spilled the tea all over me. I was very much annoyed, and I caught the thing that came next to my hand, and hurled it at her. It was the tea-pot, and the point of the spout is in the small of her leg from that night till now." "Oh, lady, darlint! how can you hold spite to the poor slob of a girl, that knew no more of you being there, nor of offending you, that she did of the night she was born?" "Well, well; now that is all past and gone I believe you are right. At all events, you have done so much for me, that I cannot refuse you anything. Take this ointment, and rub it where you will see the purple mark, and I hope that your thoughts of me may be pleasant."

Just then, a messenger came to say that the lord was at the hall door waiting for Nora, for the cocks would be soon a-crowing. So she took leave of the lady, and mounted behind the dark man. The horse's back seemed as hard and as thin as a hazel stick, but it bore her safely to her home. She was in a sleepy state all the time she was returning, but at last she woke up, and found herself standing by her own door. She got into bed as fast as she could, and when she woke next morning, she fancied it was all a dream. She put her hand in her pocket, and there, for a certainty, was the box of ointment. She stripped the clothes off her daughter's leg, rubbed some of the stuff on it, and in a few seconds she saw the skin bursting, and a tiny spout of a tea-pot working itself out. Poor Judy was awake by this, and wondering what ease she felt in her leg. I warrant she was rejoiced at the story her mother told her. She soon received health and strength, and never neglected to leave her kitchen so nice when she was going to bed, that Rich Damer himself might eat his dinner off the floor. She took good care never to let her feet stray over it again after bed-time, for fear of giving offence to her unseen visitors.

THE SEA FAIRIES.

Moruadh, or *Moruach*, is the name given to the mermaids that haunt the shallow waters near our coasts. The word is composed of *Mur*, sea, and *Oich*, maid. The mermen do not seem on the whole to be an attractive or interesting class. Their hair and teeth are green, their noses invariably red, and their eyes resemble those of a pig. Moreover, they have a penchant for brandy, and keep a look-out for cases of that article that go astray in shipwrecks. Some naturalists attribute the hue of their noses to extra indulgence in that liquor. It is little to be wondered at that their young women occasionally prefer marriage with a coast farmer. The wearing of a nice little magic cap (the *Cohuleen Druith*) is essential to their well-being in their country below the waves, and the mortal husband must keep this cap well concealed from his sea-wife. Instances are rife of desolation made in families by the inadvertent finding of it by one of the children, who, of course, shows it to his mother to learn what it is. However strong her affection for husband and children, she is instinctively obliged to seize on it, and clap it on her head. She tenderly embraces her children, but immediately flies to the seabrink, plunges in, and is seen no more. The distracted husband, when he hears the news from the forsaken children, accuses destiny, and calls for aid to the powers of sea and land, but all in vain. Why did he perpetrate an unsuitable marriage?

One man, who lived near Bantry, was blessed with an excellent wife of this class. (As a rule, a Moruach is most desirable as wife, mother, and mistress of a family.) They would have lived comfortably, but many sea-cows, aware of her original condition, would persist in coming up to graze on her husband's meadows, and thus be near their relative. The husband, an unsentimental fellow, would chase and worry the poor sea-cattle, even to wounds and bruises, till the wife, after many useless appeals to his good feelings, poked out her Cohuleen Druith and quitted him. He was sorry when it was too late. His children, and theirs again, were distinguished by a rough scaly skin and a delicate membrane between fingers and toes.

THE BLACK CATTLE OF DURZY ISLAND.

Several centuries since, a family residing on Durzy Island, off Bantry Bay, found a beautiful little coal-black bull and cow on a verdant spot near the beach. The cow furnished sufficient butter and milk for all domestic wants, and next year a calf was added to the number. When this youngster was come to the age of affording additional support to the family, a wicked servant girl, one day milking the parent cow, so far forgot herself as to strike the gentle beast with the spancel, and curse her bitterly. The outraged animal turned round to the other two, who were grazing at some distance, and lowed to them in a sorrowful tone, and immediately the three moved rapidly off to the sea. They plunged in, and forthwith the three rocks, since known as the Bull, Cow, and Calf, arose, and continue to this day to protest against the wickedness and ingratitude of cross-grained servant girls.

We are indebted to Captain F. W. L. Thomas, R.N., for the following legend of the sea-dwellers:—

THE SILKIE WIFE.

Those in Shetland and Orkney Islands who know no better, are persuaded that the seals, or silkies, as they call them, can doff their coverings at times, and disport themselves as men and women. A fisher once turning a ridge of rock, discovered a beautiful bit of green turf adjoining the shingle, sheltered by rocks on the landward side, and over this turf and shingle two beautiful women chasing each other. Just at the man's feet lay two sealskins, one of which he took up to examine it. The women, catching sight of him, screamed out, and ran to get possession of the skins. One seized the article on the ground, donned it in a thrice, and plunged into the sea; the other wrung her hands, cried, and begged the fisher to restore her property; but he wanted a wife, and would not throw away the chance. He wooed her so earnestly and lovingly, that she put on some woman's clothing which he brought her from his cottage, followed him home, and became his wife. Some years later, when their home was enlivened by the presence of two children, the husband awaking one night, heard voices in conversation from the kitchen. Stealing softly to the room door, he heard his wife talking in a low tone with some one outside the window. The interview was just at an end, and he had only time to ensconce himself in bed, when his wife was stealing across the room. He was greatly disturbed, but determined to do or say nothing till he should acquire further knowledge. Next evening, as he was returning home by the strand, he spied a male and female phoca sprawling on a rock a few yards out at sea. The rougher animal, raising himself on his tail and fins, thus addressed the astonished man in the dialect spoken in these islands;—"You deprived me of her whom I was to make my companion; and it was only yesternight that I discovered her outer garment, the loss of which obliged her to be your wife. I bear no malice, as you were kind to her in your own fashion; besides, my heart is too full of joy to hold any malice. Look on your wife for the last time." The other seal glanced at him with all the shyness and sorrow she could force into her now uncouth features; but when the bereaved husband rushed toward the rock to secure his lost treasure, she and her companion were in the water on the other side of it in a moment, and the poor fisherman was obliged to return sadly to his motherless children and desolate home.

The reader will find the character and habits of the

Pooka illustrated in different collections of Irish Legends. The adventure that follows was related by the sufferer to a gentleman, from whose mouth we have it. Our authority felt certain that the man was fully persuaded of the reality of the facts, which he was unable to detail without a feeling of terror.

THE POOKA OF MURROE.

The unfortunate hero of this narrative was returning home one night along an avenue which lay between a hedge and a wood, the trees of which stood so close that the boughs interlaced. He was not naturally subject to superstitious fears, but he could not be otherwise than frightened after advancing some distance, on hearing a rustling in the boughs overhead, keeping pace with his own progress. Looking up, he was terrified by the appearance of a dark object visible through the foliage and boughs where they were not too close, and the outline dimly defined by the obscure light of the sky. The form was that of a goat, and it kept nearly over his head, springing from bough to bough as his shaking limbs carried him forward. The only encouraging idea that occurred to him was, that he would soon be at the border of the wood, and that in all probability the evil thing would trouble him no further. After what seemed a very long time, though it probably occupied but a few minutes, he was under the last tree; but while hoping for the cessation of his torment, the dreadful thing in the full caparison of a he-goat dropped on his shoulders, and bent him down on all fours!

He retained his senses, and merely strength enough to creep on painfully, labouring the while under such a sensation of horror as perhaps none can comprehend except those who have endured the visitation of the nightmare. He could not afterwards form any idea of the time occupied by his staggering home under the fearful burden. His family heard the noise as of a body falling against the door. It was at once opened, and the poor head of the family was found lying across the entrance, insensible. They brought him in, laid him before the fire, had his hands chafed, water thrown on his face, &c., till he recovered consciousness. He was confined to his bed for two or three weeks with pains and stiffness in his bones and joints, as if he was suffering under a severe attack of rheumatism. As there was no intentional deception on the victim's side, perhaps the delusion and illness may be accounted for by his lying insensible for some time in a damp place, and being called on while in that state by that dreadful visitant the nightmare.

The Pooka's head-quarters in Ireland are Carrig-a-Phooka, west of Macroom, Castle Pooka, near Doneraile, and the island of Melaan, at the mouth of the Kenmare river, a locality dreaded by sailors and fishers at night, or in bad weather, the most frightful noises being heard there at these times.

The Lubber fiend, Lubberkin, or Lurdane, of the old English poets, seems to be related to our Celtic Lurigadan, by name at least; but our variety is not noted for household duty, unless making a beast of himself in the cellar pass for such. The *Fear Dearg* (Red Man) is indeed fond of a comfortable hearth in winter, and using the tobacco-pipe left on the hob for his need. He occasionally shows himself to members of the family, but does not like to be looked at too curiously. He likewise takes food, which is thoughtfully left aside for him, and his continued presence in a house brings good fortune with it. Croker says that this little red-capped and red-coated power heads the native forces against the fairies of foreign parts; and if any mortals come in their direct course, they will for the nonce bridle and saddle them, and convert them into special war-horses, rewarding them by "hands" of tobacco or other delicacies when the fight is done.

The supernatural agent of the next legend will not fit comfortably in any of the divisions of the spiritual world made by Grimm, Croker, Keightley, and others. He would be the Lubber-Fiend of Milton, or the Brownie of

Scotland, or the Kobold of the North, but for once having been a "christened man." Every one up to the mere alphabet of fairy lore, knows that the pooka does not condescend to household drudgery, but his townsfolk would give the sprite in question no other name; and in consequence, the present editor of the tale does not feel entitled to take any liberties with it. A girl of Kilcock thus related the story to us.

THE KILDARE POOKA.

Mr. H―― R――, when he was alive, used to live a good deal in Dublin, and he was once a great while out of the country on account of the "Ninety-eight" business. But the servants kept on in the big house at Rath――, all the same as if the family was at home. Well, they used to be frightened out of their lives after going to their beds, with the banging of the kitchen door and the clattering of the fire-irons, and the pots, and plates, and dishes. One evening they sat up ever so long, keeping one another in heart with telling stories about ghosts and fetches and that when—what would you have of it?—the little scullery boy that used to be sleeping over the horses, and couldn't get room at the fire, crept into the hot hearth, and when he got tired listening to the stories, sorra fear him but he fell dead asleep.

Well and good, after they were all gone, and the fire raked up, he was woke with the noise of the kitchen door opening, and the trampling of an ass on the kitchen floor. He peeped out, and what should he see but a big grey ass, sure enough, sitting on his currabingo, and yawning before the fire. After a little, he looked about him, and began scratching his ears as if he was quite tired, and says he, "I may as well begin first as last." The poor boy's teeth began to chatter in his head, for says he, "Now he's goin' to ate me;" but the fellow with the long ears and tail on him, had something else to do. He stirred up the fire, and then he brought in a pail of water from the pump, and filled a big pot, that he put on the fire before he went out. He then put in his hand—foot, I mean—into the hot hearth, and pulled out the little boy. He let a roar out of him with the fright, but the pooka only looked at him, and thrust out his lower lip to show how little he valued him, and then he pitched him into his pew again.

Well, he then lay down before the fire till he heard the boil coming on the water, and maybe there wasn't a plate, or a dish, or a spoon on the dresser, that he didn't fetch and put into the pot, and wash and dry the whole bilin' of 'em as well as e'er a kitchenmaid from that to Dublin town. He then put all of them up in their places on the shelves, and, if he didn't give a good sweepin' to the kitchen after all, leave it till again. Then he comes and sits fornent the boy, let down one of his ears and cocked up the other, and gave a grin. The poor fellow strove to roar out, but not a dheeg 'ud come out of his throat. The last thing the pooka done was to rake up the fire, and walk out, giving such a slap o' the door that the boy thought the house couldn't help tumbling down.

Well, to be sure, if there wasn't a hullabulloo next morning, when the poor fellow told his story! They could talk of nothing else the whole day. One said one thing, another said another, but a fat, lazy scullery girl said the wittiest thing of all. "Musha!" says she, "if the pooka does be cleaning up everything that way when we're asleep, what should we be slaving ourselves for, doing his work?" "*Sha gu dheine,*" says another : "them's the wisest words you ever said, Kauth : it's meself won't contradict you."

So said so done. Not a bit of a plate or dish saw a drop of water that evening, and not a besom was laid on the floor, and every one went to bed soon after sundown. Next morning everything was as fine as fire in the kitchen, and the lord mayor might eat his dinner off the flags. It was great ease to the lazy servants, you may depend, and everything went on well till a foolhardy gag of a boy said he would stay up one night and have a chat with the pooka.

He was a little daunted when the door was thrown open, and the ass marched up to the fire. He didn't open his mouth till the pot was filled, and the pooka lying snug and sausty before the fire.

"Ah then, sir!" says he, at last, picking up courage, "if it isn't taking a liberty, might I ax who you are, and why are you so kind as to do half of the day's work for the girls every night?" "No liberty at all," says the pooka, says he: "I'll tell you, and welcome. I was a servant here in the time of Squire R.'s father, and was the laziest rogue that ever was clothed and fed, and done nothing for it. When my time came for the other world, this is the punishment was laid on me—to come here, and do all this labour every night, and then go out in the cold. It isn't so bad in the fine weather, but if you only knew what it is to stand with your head between your legs, facing the storm, from midnight to sunrise on a bleak winter night!" "And could we do anything for your comfort, my poor fellow?" says the boy. "Musha, I don't know," says the pooka; "but I think a good quilted frieze coat would help to keep the life in me, them long nights." "Why then, in throth, we'd be the ungratefulest of people if we didn't feel for you."

To make a long story short, the next night but two the boy was there again; and if he didn't delight the poor pooka, holding up a fine warm coat before him, it's no matter! Betune the pooka and the man, his legs were got into the four arms of it, and it was buttoned down his breast and his belly, and he was so pleased, he walked up to the glass to see how he looked. "Well," says he, "it's a long lane that has no turning. I am much obliged to yourself and your fellow-servants. Yous have made me happy at last: good-night to you."

So he was walking out, but the other cried, "Och! sure you're going too soon: what about the washing and sweeping?" "Ah, you may tell the girls that they must now get their turn. My punishment was to last till I was thought worthy of a reward for the way I done my duty. You'll see me no more." And no more they did, and right sorry they were for being in such a hurry to reward the ungrateful pooka.

Our notice of the Cluricawn, Leprechaun, or Lurikeen, shall be brief, as he is one of the best known of all the fairy tribe. Keightley and Croker have given us a surfeit of the deceitful old rogue. With some trouble, a relationship might be established between himself and the industrous little mine-workers of the North, but the return would not be equal to the outlay.

THE KILDARE LURIKEEN.

A young girl that lived in sight of Castle Carberry, near Edenderry, was going for a pitcher of water to the neighbouring well one summer morning, when who should she see sitting in a sheltery nook under an old thorn, but the Lurikeen, working like vengeance at a little old brogue only fit for the foot of a fairy like himself. There he was, boring his holes, and jerking his waxed ends, with his little three-cornered hat with gold lace, his knee-breeches, his jug of beer by his side, and his pipe in his mouth. He was so busy at his work, and so taken up with an old ballad he was singing in Irish, that he did not mind Breedheen till she had him by the scruff o' the neck, as if he was in a vice. "Ah, what are you doin'?" says he, turning his head round as well as he could. "Dear, dear! to think of such a purty colleen ketchin' a body, as if he was afther robbin' a hen roost! What did I do to be thrated in such an undecent manner? The very vulgarest young ruffin in the townland could do no worse. Come, come, Miss Bridget, take your hands off, sit down, and us have a chat, like two respectable people." "Ah, Mr. Lurikeen, I don't care a wisp of borrach[1] for your politeness. It's your money I want, and I won't take hand or eye from you till you put me in possession of a fine lob of it." "Money, indeed! Ah! where would a poor cobbler like me get it? Anyhow there's no money hereabouts, and if you'll only let go my arms, I'll turn my pockets inside out, and open the drawer of my seat, and give you

[1] Coarse tow. The mere English reader will in vain attempt the horrible sound of this word. Let him apply to a native to pronounce it for him.

leave to keep every halfpenny you'll find." "That won't do; my eyes'll keep going through you like darning needles till I have the gold. Begonies, if you don't make haste, I'll carry you, head and pluck, into the village, and there you'll have thirty pair of eyes on you instead of one." "Well, well! was ever a poor cobbler so circumvented! and if it was an ignorant, ugly bosthoon that done it, I would not wonder; but a decent, comely girl, that can read her *Poor Man's Manual* at the chapel, and——" "You may throw your compliments on the stream there; they won't do for me, I tell you. The gold, the gold, the gold! Don't take up my time with your blarney." "Well, if there's any to be got, it's undher the ould castle it is; we must have a walk for it. Just put me down and we'll get on." "Put you down indeed! I know a trick worth two of that; I'll carry you." "Well, how suspicious we are! Do you see the castle from this?" Bridget was about turning her eyes from the little man to where she knew the castle stood, but she bethought herself in time.

They went up a little hill-side, and the Lurikeen was quite reconciled, and laughed and joked; but just as they got to the brow, he looked up over the ditch, gave a great screetch, and shouted just as if a bugle horn was blew at her ears—"Oh, murdher! Castle Carberry is afire." Poor Biddy gave a great start, and looked up towards the castle. The same moment she missed the weight of the Lurikeen, and when her eyes fell where he was a moment before, there was no more sign of him than if everything that passed was a dream.

This passage in the natural history of the Lurikeen is furnished by the chronicler of the "Rath C.-Pooka." The only instance of a Wexford Lurikeen that we can recall, differs only slightly from this. Wexford Molly was as vigilant as Kildare Biddy, and never took eye or hand off him till he pointed out the very stalk of booliaun bui under which the treasure lay. There was no other weed of the kind within half the field of it at the moment, but when Molly returned in half an hour, attended by father and brothers with spades and picks, all round the spot, to a considerable distance, was as thick with booliauns as a plantation with young trees.

The next tale cannot boast of a very remote origin in its present form, having been written in the beginning of the last century, but it is an adaptation of one as old as the times of paganism. These ancient fictions, when thoroughly abandoned to a traditional existence, passing from the mouths of one generation of story-tellers to the ears of their successors, or even left to the mercy of careless and ignorant scribes, suffered considerable damage. We find in those that have been preserved by the peasantry passages in the worst taste, grotesque, extravagant, and unintentionally ludicrous, which never were uttered by the educated and really gifted bards, who found a welcome in the hall of chief or king, or at the public assembly.

We do not make this remark in a fault-finding spirit with our peasantry. They have saved a great number of legends peculiar to themselves, as well as the fairy and household stories, which are the common property of most of the countries of Europe.

We conclude the present section with

THE ADVENTURES OF THE "SON OF BAD COUNSEL."

The tale, of which the following is an abridgment, was composed in mixed prose and verse by Brian Dhu O'Reilly,[1] who was living in Cavan about the year 1725. The original title is *Eachtra mhic na Miochomhairle*. Our plan allows admission but to a few of the adventures. The hero tells the tale in his own person, and it must be owned that his is a very rambling mode of fixing his hearer's interest. You would suppose at first that his

[1] Some give the credit of it to that loose fish, Carroll O'Daly.

meeting with a lovely fairy and their subsequent courtship would be the central group of his fortunes; but after singing her glorious form and features, and the splendour of the surrounding landscape, in the most florid Irish poesy, night comes on, and he is obliged to seek for shelter in the castle of a Gruagach (giant, enchanter; *Breton*, groac'h). Here is a taste of the original, literally translated :—

> " On the sun going to his bed I knew not what place, what land,
> What district I was in, on the earth or above.
> My eyes to the four quarters of the sky I cast round,
> And by the roadside I there saw the beautiful Sighe.
>
> " I approached her, though arduous and bold was the deed :
> Seated on the bank, like an angel she seemed.
> Her silky sweet shape not bony nor angular,
> Like the blossoms of the berry her fair-coloured breasts."

The "Son of Bad Counsel" was evidently very whimsical and fickle-minded; he turned from the lovely fairy beauty at once to sing the glory of the landscape.

> " The like of that land I've not seen nor heard of,
> For amenity, for goodness, for its clear flowing streams;
> Dew-drops of honey on all the tree branches,
> And the bee's humming music was heard without pause."

Dark stormy night came on the landscape. No more is heard of the fairy belle, and the Son of Bad Counsel somehow found himself before a castle, the beauties of which he described in poetic language. Entering, he found the Gruagach master, "strong, truly powerful, ruddy in countenance, and clad in silken robes." And on the right hand of the Gruagach, on a chair of burnished gold, was his lady daughter, beauteous, gentle, *honest*, unexceptionable in her attire, musical in voice and compassionate, young, glorious, sweet-spoken, lightsome, like a shining diamond, a harvest moon, a morning sun, a heavenly angel. Her eyes were gray and thoughtful, like the gleaming sparkling stars of a hard frosty night. Her golden, curling hair was divided, and hung on each side like bunches of clustering grapes. Her robe was of silk, gracefully covering her beautiful figure, and an ornamented brooch glittered on her bosom, and on her knee was a hand-harp (Cruith), from which she was drawing sweet sounds.[1]

The hero of the story was an arrant coward, as well as a poet; but he plucked up courage to address the host, who, after all, was not very formidable in appearance :—

"King of the globe, fair is this place which I have come to—
A royal fort, white-boarded, erected as the abode of Maev;
Like unto the Dun Aileach, it is similar to Paradise,
And I am not certain that it is not in a court I am truly.

"More delightful is this sight than Tara and Naas together,
And than the three branches in Emania,[2] once held by the hero Dairg,
My journey I arrest till I know who dwells here."

The richly dressed Gruagach made a suitable reply :—
"Long it is since we saw a person or people before you, who could afford us joy or pleasure" (they were apparently not aware of his cowardice and general worthlessness), "and long were we expecting you, for we have neither children nor heirs, but that daughter you see before you; and we have nursed and nobly reared her from her infancy for you to be your wife and companion." "By your hand," was the ready answer, "if I had known so much—but how could I? It is I that would have searched the four quarters of the globe for her sweet self, even to the loss of my life."

Then the Gruagach arose, and bade the guest take his golden chair; and then he began his own particular grievances, and the service he required at the hands of his future son-in-law before the silken-attired lady could become his wife.

It seemed that Trom Ceo Draochta (Heavy Enchanted Fog), the fairy chief residing at Din Aoilig, had stolen the two sons of the King of the *Isle of the Living*, as he

---

[1] A profusion of epithets nearly synonymous often occurs in Irish poetry and romance. It arises from the richness of the language in words of the same or nearly the same meaning, and the temptation thrown in the way of the poet by alliteration.

[2] *Maev*, the Semiramis of the Royal Court of Conacht. *Aileach*, the Great Stone Fortress in the north-east of Donegal. *Naas*, once the residence of the kings of Leinster. *Emania*, the Court of Ulster, whose ruins are yet to be seen near Armagh. *Red Branch*, an order of knighthood there established.

had no heirs to enjoy his power. Ruan Luimneach, a powerful Sighe chief, a neighbour of him of the Isle of the Living, on hearing of this wrong, summoned all his subjects of the Western World to assemble, and attack the Fog-chief in his stronghold, and rescue the sons of his friend. *Heavy Magic Fog*, on hearing of the projected attack on Din Aoilig, summoned his confederates to his aid. Among these were Donn Ceiv Fionn from Magh Hi in Conacht, Donn Feiriné O'Conail from Knocfierna, and Donn Binné Eachla labhra (The Lord of the Hill of the Speaking Horse[1]), Gilla Brighid O'Faolan, a *Sighe gaoithe* (Fairy Blast) from the Decies, and Gilla Fiamach O'Doran, Chief of Ceibhfion.[2]

"I was also summoned among these chiefs," continued the master, "and my footmen and my horsemen departed yesterday to Din Aoilig, and I myself will follow to-morrow. I did not go with my people, for I expected you; and if your feats of valour deserve the hand of my daughter, my daughter shall be your wife on our return. If you fall, a mighty mound shall cover your remains, your caoine shall be said by eloquent and very famous fileas, and your name, and your ancestors, and your deeds engraved on the Oghuim stone."

Fair was the daughter of the Gruagach, but she was to be won with risk of life; and a shivering seized on the limbs of the young man, and his teeth chattered. The master seemed to know that trouble had come on his spirit, and he asked his wife to bring in the golden, gem-incrusted goblet of comfort and forgetful-

[1] Scholars who insist on beast-worship among the pagan Irish, adduce this tradition in support of their views. At every midsummer festival of the sun, this Each Labhra would issue from his mound, and give full and true answers to all who consulted him on the occurrences that would take place up to the next summer festival.

[2] As in our country parts, Cæsar, Pincher, Juno, and other favourite dogs enjoy the surnames of the families whom they serve, so we find here the fairy chiefs called by the names of the old families whose districts they frequented, and whose deceases they marked by their lamentations. The O'Dorans were Brehons to the kings of South Leinster. Gilla Brighid O'Faolan, St. Bridgid's servant (now Kilbride), would otherwise have been a strange name for a fairy chief.

ness. It was brought, and this was the quality of that goblet, that every one drinking from it should forget their cares and troubles as if they had never been; and if a thousand persons drank their fill from it, never was the wine a hair's breadth lower.

Mac drank, and great courage came into his heart. "Deep is my gratitude to you, O powerful chief," said he; "and I would be glad to know your name, and the name of the Bhan Tiernach (Woman-chief), your wife, and how your castle is called." "*Gruagach Tiré gan Taithige* (Giant[1] of the Unfrequented Land) is my name," said he, "and my wife is daughter of the King of the Lonesome Land, and *Dun Tochluaiste* (Uncertain Castle) is the name of this castle; and it is as easy for me to be at the end of Erinn at any hour as to be here."

Then the master of the house and his guest sat down at *Taibleish Mhor* (backgammon, large table), and the fashion of the tables was this. Fine elephant (ivory) were the dice, and fine carved wood, and emerald, and gold, and white silver, and carbuncle were the tables; and a blind man could see to play with them, and people with their sight could play with them on the darkest night. But if the body of the *Mac na*, &c. was at the table with the Gruagach, his "intellect, his desire, his sight, and his reason, were at the other side of the hall, where sat the Gruagach's daughter, with her golden curling hair and her silken robe."

So the unfortunate youth lost the game, but the Gruagach made him a present of the tables that he might learn to play. Very grateful was he, but he feared he should pay for all to-morrow before Din Aoilig. Then came supper time, and the youth sat opposite the magician, with the fair beauty on his right hand, and better food or better liquor was not consumed that night at Tara of the Kings.

But when the time of rest was come, and the Grua-

[1] Gruagach has for root, *Gruach*, hair,—giants and magicians being usually furnished with a large provision of that appendage. A favourite song (even in its English dress) with the dying out generation, was the *Bouchal 'na Gruaga Dhouna,* "The Boy with the Brown Hair."

gach bade the Mac, &c. sleep soundly, as the flight of night was to see them on their way to Aoilig, "great fear, and discomfort, and hate, and loathing," fell on the heart of the Son of Bad Counsel, and said he to himself, "I wish I had the dressed skin of a white sheep, that I might leave my last thoughts to my friends."

> "Long it is to tell how I first saw the maid.
> When she came in my sight I lit up full of her love.
> My heart is sad that I see no more her fair face,
> Her neck like the snow, and her bosom like two fair hills;
> And by the king's hand I'm sorry she is not mine."

Then they prepared his state bed, and the Gruagach and his wife went to their own apartment, after first giving him a token of life and health (wishing him good-night). He was thinking more of the morning than the night; but the maid of the flowing hair, and the mild gray eyes, and the sweet smile, told him not to fear for his life, for that it was not in the power of all the fairy hosts within the four seas of Erinn to bring the end of life on him that had received baptism. They might pierce him with sighe-darts that would disable arm or leg, or cause him to pine, but perhaps they would not. And she also "gave him a token of life and health," and went to her couch in the next chamber.

Bad it was to lose life and the maid of the silk robe together, and but little better was it to be stretched on rushes with sighe-darts in the leg. So the Son of Bad Counsel, while lying on the wolf-skin, felt a shivering all over him, and then all the blood in his body rushed up to his head, and his skin seemed on fire, and at last despair put it into his mind to persuade the lady that had won his heart to fly with him where neither Gruagach, nor Heavy Magic Fog, nor Ruan Luimneach, King of all the Fairies of the West, could find them out. So he arose, with his heart in his mouth, and his legs trembling under him: he opened her door, and he found himself in a wild lonesome place, and then he knew that it was *Aimsighthe* and *Aimgeoireach'd* (*qu.* ambushes and temptations) were on him; and he heard the *bonanaich* and the *boconaigh* (*qu.* wild boars or wild bulls, and he-goats), and the other forest dwellers, hideous, terrible, loud-voiced, sharp, inflamed. And he became like a madman, and he flew like a wild cat from its nest in the tree, or a stag from his lair. And when he cleared the wood he found himself in a plain, wide-spread and grassy, and in the middle a high green hill, where neither boars nor goats could easily catch him.

When he was on the hill he found a great rim round its summit, and within, a boiling, boisterous, noisy, foamy, very tempestuous sea, with no path round it. By the harbour was an old boat, which the unfortunate, ill-advised youth strove to repair; but hearing the wild piercing cries of the beasts or devils of the woods at his back, he put to sea. This was all that the fierce, incessant, spiteful, threatening, very destructive winds waited for. They blew as if to scoop out the sea from its hollow, and the earth belched out from its caverns the restless waters. The boatman flying up to the clouds at this side of the wave, and descending into the dark caverns of the earth on the other, bellowed to heaven for help; and the Gruagach, hearing the outcry, bade his daughter light a candle!

In the cellar they found the son of ill-luck as well as of ill-counsel, seated on a cullender that was covering a vat of strongly-working new beer. These were the high-rimmed mound and the sea. The roaring of the he-goats, the boars, and the bulls, and the wolves, was the cry of two cats which the sleep-walker had disturbed, and the howling of the storm, a breeze blowing through the cellar window.

The Gruagach and his daughter, seeing the youth crouched in the cullender over the great beer vat, burst out a laughing, and, said the master of the house, "Very fond of sailoring you must be to get into so small a vessel; and if it was in search of my daughter you were, better it would be to seek her on dry land." The misguided boy, descending from his damaged boat, hastened to his state bed to hide his confusion and great shame. Lying on his back, he composed a strain of lamentation over his hard fate; and when he fell asleep, all the ugly dreams that float between the moon and the earth passed through his mind. At last he awoke, and the fear of death came upon him when he remembered the gathering of Din Aoilig next day.

He arose, and opened the door of the maiden's chamber, intending to persuade her to fly with him; and great was his terror when he found himself in a wide field without track of man or beast. He recollected the roaring of the wild devils, and his heart turned into water when he saw a beast, black, devilish, hideous-coloured, heavy-headed, dull-buzzing, approaching him. A great plum or a small apple would fit on every one of his coarse hairs. Two dead eyes were locked in his head, an empty long-falling snout he had, and rough white teeth.

When the doomed boy saw this hellish beast rushing right on him to devour him, he felt it full time to seek an escape. So with swift, mighty springs he made to the edge of that large field, and at its bounds he found himself stopped by a stormy, dangerous, coarse-waved, light-leaping, strongly-diffused, streamy, troublesome river; and thought within himself whether it would be better to try to swim across it, not knowing anything of the art, or face the cursed-of-form, diabolical, odious-coloured, hideous-countenanced, amazingly-hateful, and malicious beast. He had heard of persons ignorant of swimming, who crossed wide streams under terror, and was sure that he would do the deed if ever fear, surprise, terror, timidity, fright, or loss of reason helped any one.

But, while he was considering what he should do, he looked back, and the big animal, with his gluttonous mouth open, was just behind. It was not a courageous look of defiance he gave him, but he took a high, powerful, very light spring into the slowly-flowing river, and struck out vigorously with his arms for life. But deep and thick with mud was that pool, and choked with reeds, and no boat with sail or oar could work its way out. It was then he considered indeed that it was to the suffocating sea he had come, and that he should not leave it till he had been permanently drowned, and unworlded, and till the ravenous birds, open-beaked, should have taken away his skin, his flesh, and his blood. In that state he gave out a wondrous, hard, slender, complaining, frightened cry. The waters were oozing into his open mouth, and cold death was creeping up his limbs, when he heard the voices of the Gruagach and his daughter over him. He was lying in a large trough filled with water and grains, his face downwards, his mouth full of the contents of the trough, and his arms striking out. "If you wished for a bath," said the master, "better would a vessel of clean water be than where the pigs take their food."

He cleared his mouth and his eyes, and sorrow was upon him to be seen by the maiden; and, when he turned away his eyes in shame, he discovered the fierce, ravenous, life-seeking wild beast of the big, lonesome field, grunting and rummaging in the litter, and it was as small and as tame as the rest of the enchanter's pigs.

With bitter grief he again betook himself to his rest, his soul divided between love for the maid of the sweet eyes and lips, and dread of the battle.[1] The Gruagach told him to sleep soundly till he should be called, as he himself was then going to gird the horses in their battle harness for the morrow. The blood rushed again to his head, while a shivering fit seized on his limbs. In the middle of his despair a raw gray light fell on his eyes; and his bed was the dry grass of a moat; and little wonder it was that he should be shivering, for his clothes were the pillow that supported his head.

But the love of the sighe-maid was still strong in his soul, and he vowed he would never lie two nights in the same bed till he had discovered her. For a year and a day he searched through the length and breadth of Erinn, and his resting-place at night was a sheltered grassy nook near a Sighe-Brugheen or a Danish fort. At the end of a year and a day, he was again at the spot where he had discovered the Castle of Uncertainty; and in his sleep that night he had a vision of his fairy love, who told him to give over his pursuit of her, as she had been obliged by her father to take a husband. Next morning he found the charm gone, and his soul freed from the sighe-spell. He reformed his ways, and became the

[1] There is a third adventure, of course, but it does not possess much novelty or interest.

"Son of Good Counsel," and these are the verses he made about it :—

> "Farewell, sweet and false dreams of my fancy!
> The happiness you give is like the gold of the Clurichaun.
> By the light of the moon the weight and the colour are there;
> Withered leaves only remain in our hands at the dawn.
> My course I'll change as the feathers fall from the birds;
> I'll keep my hands busy, and take the sogarth's [1] advice;
> And surely in Erinn of chaste and beautiful women,
> I'll find some fair angel to come and sit on my hearth,
> With smiles on her face when wearied I come from the fields;
> She'll make evening happy, and lie all night at my side."

Among the old fireside romances were more than one or two of this deceptional character. Thor's visit to Jotunheim was the reverse in the order of things. What to him and his companions seemed of a mean and trifling character, were in reality of awful dimensions. The vessel from which he drank, but could scarcely see any way diminished of its contents, was the bed of ocean. The cat which he found it impossible to raise from the ground, was in reality the wolf Fenris, and so on.

The knights in quest of the San Graal also suffered in body and mind from being led aside by one of the three chief enemies of the human soul.

The general belief of the peasantry is that the existing fairies are those angels who, without openly joining Satan in his rebellion, gave it no opposition. Their future destiny will be determined at the Day of Judgment.

Some archæologists fancy that the tales of mortals abiding with the fays in their Sighe palaces are founded on the tender preferences shown by the Druidic priestesses of old to favourite worshippers of the Celtic Divinities.

[1] The Irish construction of *sacerdos*, one of the many words introduced with Christianity.

PART III

WITCHCRAFT, SORCERY, GHOSTS, AND FETCHES

WITCHCRAFT, SORCERY, GHOSTS, AND FETCHES

It is probable that the first tradition is to be met outside the Pale, and even as far as Connemara, but the writer has heard or read it nowhere since he learned it in his youth from Mrs. K., our already quoted authority.

THE LONG SPOON.

The devil and the hearth-money collector for Bantry set out one summer morning to decide a bet they made the night before over a jug of punch. They wanted to see which would have the best load at sunset, and neither was to pick up anything that wasn't offered with the goodwill of the giver. They passed by a house, and they heard the poor vanithee cry out to her lazy daughter, "O musha, —— take you for a lazy sthronshuch of a girl! do you intend to get up to-day?" "Oh, oh!" says the tax-man, "there is a lob for you, Nick." "Ovoch!" says the other, "it wasn't from her heart she said it: we must pass on." The next cabin they were passing, the woman was on the bawn-ditch crying out to her husband, that was mending one of his brogues inside: "Oh, tattheration to you, Mick! you never rung them pigs, and there they are in the potato drills rootin' away; the —— run to Lusk with them!" "Another windfall for you," says the man of the inkhorn, but the old thief only shook his horns and wagged his tail. So they went on, and ever so many prizes offered to the black fellow without him taking one. Here it was a gorsoon playing *marvels* when he should be using his clappers in the corn-field ; and there it was a lazy drone of a servant asleep with his face to the sod, when he ought to be weeding. No one thought of offering the hearth-money man even a drink of buttermilk, and at last the sun was within half a foot of the edge of Cooliagh. They were just then passing thro' Monamolin, and a poor woman that was straining her supper in a skeeoge outside her cabin door, seeing the two standing at the bawn gate, bawled out, " Oh, here's the hearth-money man,—— run away wid 'im ! " " Got a bite at last," says Nick. " Oh, no, no ! it wasn't from her heart she said it," says the collector. " Indeed an' it was from the very foundation stone of her heart it came. No help for misfortunes ; in with you," says he, opening the mouth of his big black bag ; and whether the devil was ever after seen taking the same walk or not, no one ever laid eyes on his fellow-traveller again.

The Cooliagh, or White Mountain, forms part of the north-west boundary of Wexford. The mere English reader is informed that the skeeoge or flattish wicker basket, having received the potatoes and boiling water on the pavement, lets the liquid off to the pool at the bottom of the yard. The shields of the ancient Irish, consisting of strong leather, or plates over a wicker framework, were called skiaghs.

At some period of the troubles in Munster a small tribe emigrated to the north-east portion of the county Wexford. The following legend connected with the family was current among the descendants who lived, and loved, and sinned, and fought the battle of life half a century since.

THE PROPHET BEFORE HIS TIME.

About a hundred years ago lived Mr. Diarmuidh K., a strong gentleman-farmer of this family. His place was not far from *Slieve Buie* (Yellow Hill). He was much addicted to the study of astrology, and the occult works of Cornelius Agrippa. When his only son was about a month old, one of his servant boys ran into the parlour one day to tell him a circumstance that had greatly astonished himself: "Oh, master," said he, "the black cow was just while ago under the old thorn-tree in the meadow, and all of a sudden a fog came round herself and the tree, while all the rest of the field was in the sunshine. I was going over to try what was the matter, when what should I see but a big sea-gull flying into the fog, and making ever so much noise with his wings. For fear he'd pick out the poor beast's eyes I ran over, but just as I got to the edge of the fog it all cleared as if there was some magic in it, and Blacky was walking away on the other side." "Oh, ho!" said the master; "what I have been long wishing for has happened at last. Now, Pat, attend to what I say. Watch that cow close; and when she calves, be sure to bring me some of the first beestings, and I'll give you more money than you have ever seen at once in your own possession."

The boy did his duty, such as it was. He brought the first beestings to his master, and received 10*l.* for his pains; and Mr. K. ordering the child to be brought to him, made it take a spoonful or two of this first milk of the black cow. When the child began to speak intelligibly, the master of the house called all the family together one day, and charged them as they valued his favour, or dreaded his resentment, never to ask his son a question till he was full fourteen years of age. "The questions, I mean," said he, "are such as he could not answer without being a prophet. He is gifted with a spirit of prophecy, and when he reaches his fifteenth birthday, you will be at liberty to get all the information you please from him, concerning anything that is passing anywhere in any part of the world at the moment, or to ask about things lost or stolen, or your own future destiny. But attend to what I say. If you ask a question of him before he is full fourteen years of age, something terrible shall happen to him and you; take timely warning."

The boy had a wonderful capacity for science and language, but seldom spoke to those about him. He was very amiable, however, and every one anxious for some favour from his father always got him to be their spokesman. Strange to say, he reached to within a few days of the fatal time without being asked an improper question by any one.

He would occasionally when in company start and begin to talk of what was passing at the moment in the town of Wexford, or the cities of Dublin or London, as if the people about him were aware of these matters as well as himself. Finding, however, by their looks and expressions of surprise, that they had not the same faculty, he began to grow very silent and reserved.

About this time a grand-daughter of the famous Blacky was about to calve; and Mr. K., who set a great value on the breed, recommended her particularly to the care of a young servant boy, a favourite of his. While he was looking after her and some others in a pasture near the house, a young girl to whom he was under promise of marriage was passing *by chance* along the path that bordered the fence. He asked her to stop, but "she was in a hurry to the big house." Stop she did, however, and full twenty minutes passed unmarked while they stood and conversed on very interesting nullities.

At the end of the twenty minutes he gave a sudden start, and examined the different groups of cattle with his eyes, but no Blacky was to be seen. He searched, and his betrothed assisted, but in vain; and the poor girl burst out a crying for the blame he would be sure to get through her folly. She went forward at last on her message to the big house, and passing by the kitchen garden, whom should she see, looking at the operations of the bees, but the young master. Let her not be blamed too much: she forgot everything but her lover's mishap; and so, after making her curtsey, she cried out across the hedge—"Ah! Master Anthony, alanna, do you know where the black cow has hid herself?" "Black cow!" said he, "she is lying dead in the byre." At the moment his eyes opened wide as if about to start from his head, an expression of terror took possession of his features, he gave one wild cry, fell powerless on his face, and when his wretched father came running to the spot, on hearing of the circumstance, he found an idiot in the place of his fine intelligent son.

The following event, said to have occurred near Scarawalsh, was told by a certain Owen Jourdan, on a winter night, in a farm-house of Cromogue, some seven miles away from the scene of action, the locality of such stories being never in the neighbourhood of their exposition.

THE BEWITCHED CHURN.

Near the townland mentioned there lived an old woman in bad repute with her neighbours. She was seen, one May eve, skimming a well that lay in a neighbouring farm; and when that was done, she went into the adjoining meadow, and skimmed the dew off the grass. One person said he heard her muttering, "Come all to me, and none to he." In a day or two, the owner of the farm, coming in from the fields about noon, found the family still at the churn, and no sign of butter. He was a little frightened, and looked here and there, and, at last, spied a bit of stale butter fastened to the mantel beam of the open fire-place.

"Oh, you may as well stop," said he; "look what's there!" "Oh, the witch's butter," said one of the girls; "cut it off the mantel-piece." "No use," said another; "it must be a charmed knife, or nothing. Go and consult the fairy man, in the old ruined house at ——; if he doesn't advise you, nobody can." The master of the house took the advice; and, when they had milk enough for another churning, this is what they did:—

They twisted twigs of the mountain ash round their cows' necks; they made a big fire, and thrust into it the sock and coulter of the plough; they fastened the ash twigs round the churn, and connected them to the chain of the plough-irons; shut door and windows, so that they could not be opened from without; and merrily began the churning.

Just as the plough-irons were becoming red-hot, some one tried the latch of the door, and immediately they saw the face of the witch outside the window. "What do you want, good woman?" "The seed of the fire, and I want to help you at the churning. I heard what happened to you, and I'm rather lucky." Here she roared out; for the burning plough-irons were scorching her inside. "What ails you, poor woman?" "Oh, I have a terrible colic! let me into the fire for mercy's sake, and give me a warm drink." "Oh, musha, but it's ourselves are sorry for you; but we could not open door or window now for St. Mogue himself; for 'fraid the witch 'ud come in and cut our quicken gads, or pull out the plough-irons, or even touch the churn-staff. She got a bit of butter out of the fresh churning the other day, and took a sod out of our fire; and till she brings back the butter and the sod we must labour away. Have patience, poor woman; when we see a sign of the butter we'll open the door for you, and give you such a warm tumbler of punch, with caraways in it, as would bring you back from death's door. Put more turf on, and keep the irons at a red heat." Another roar ensued, and then she ejaculated, "Oh, purshuin' to all hard-hearted *naygurs*, that 'ud see a fellow-creature dying in misery outside of their door! Sure, I was coming to yous with relief, and this is the sort of relief you'd give me. Throw up the window a bit, and take those things I made out for yous. Throw the bit of butter you'll find in this sheet of white paper into the churn, and this sod of turf into the fire, and cut away the bit of butter on the mantel beam with this knife, and give it back to me, till I return it to the knowledgeable woman I begged it from for yous."

The direction being followed, the butter began to appear in heaps in the churn. There was great joy and huzzaing, and they even opened the door to show hospitality to the old rogue. But she departed in rage, giving them her blessing in these words—"I won't take bit nor sup from yez. Yez have thrated me like a Hussian or a Cromwellian, and not like an honest neighbour, and so I lave my curse, and the curse of Cromwell on yez all!"

There is a counterpart to the next legend in Campbell's *West Highland Tales;* we have met nothing similar in other collections. It would seem to have first been told long after the time of St. Patrick. In the stories found among the native Irish and Highlanders there is always evident more of the Christian element than among the Norse or German collections, yet even in this respect there is a peculiarity worth noticing. The Blessed Virgin is personally introduced two or three times in Dasent's Norse collection, and we cannot recollect a single instance of such a liberty being taken in our Leinster recitals.

THE GHOSTS AND THE GAME OF FOOTBALL.

There was once a poor widow woman's son that was going to look for service, and one winter's evening he came to a strong farmer's house, and this house was very near an old castle. "God save all here," says he, when he got inside the door. "God save you kindly," says the farmer. "Come to the fire." "Could you give me a night's lodging?" says the boy. "That we will, and welcome, if you will only sleep in a comfortable room in the old castle above there; and you must have a fire and candlelight, and whatever you like to drink; and if you're alive in the morning I'll give you ten guineas." "Sure I'll be 'live enough if you send no one to kill me." "I'll send no one to kill you, you may depend. The place is haunted ever since my father died, and three or four people that slept in the same room were found dead next morning. If you can banish the spirits I'll give you a good farm and my daughter, so that you like one another well enough to be married." "Never say't twice. I've a middling safe conscience, and don't fear any evil spirit that ever smelled of brimstone."

Well and good, the boy got his supper, and then they went up with him to the old castle, and showed him into a large kitchen, with a roaring fire in the grate, and a table, with a bottle and glass, and tumbler on it, and the kettle ready on the hob. They bade him good-night and

God speed, and went off as if they didn't think their heels were half swift enough.

"Well," says he to himself, "if there's any danger, this prayer-book will be usefuller than either the glass or tumbler." So he kneeled down and read a good many prayers, and then sat by the fire, and waited to see what would happen. In about a quarter of an hour, he heard something bumping along the floor overhead till it came to a hole in the ceiling. There it stopped, and cried out, "I'll fall, I'll fall." "Fall away," says Jack, and down came a pair of legs on the kitchen floor. They walked to one end of the room, and there they stood, and Jack's hair had like to stand upright on his head along with them. Then another crackling and whacking came to the hole, and the same words passed between the thing above and Jack, and down came a man's body and went and stood upon the legs. Then comes the head and shoulders, till the whole man, with buckles in his shoes and knee-breeches, and a big flapped waistcoat and a three-cocked hat, was standing in one corner of the room. Not to take up your time for nothing, two more men, more old-fashioned dressed than the first, were soon standing in two other corners. Jack was a little cowed at first; but found his courage growing stronger every moment, and what would you have of it, the three old gentlemen began to kick a *puckeen* (football) as fast as they could, the man in the three-cocked hat playing again' the other two.

"Fair play is bonny play," says Jack, as bold as he could; but the terror was on him, and the words came out as if he was frightened in his sleep; "so I'll help *you*, sir." Well and good, he joined the sport, and kicked away till his shirt was wringing wet, savin' your presence, and the ball flying from one end of the room to the other like thunder, and still not a word was exchanged. At last the day began to break, and poor Jack was dead beat, and he thought, by the way the three ghosts began to look at himself and themselves, that they wished him to speak.

So, says he, "Gentlemen, as the sport is nearly over, and I done my best to please you, would you tell a body what is the reason of yous coming here night after night, and how could I give you rest, if it is rest you want?" "Them is the wisest words," says the ghost with the three-cocked hat, "you ever said in your life. Some of those that came before you found courage enough to take a part in our game, but no one had *misnach* (energy) enough to speak to us. I am the father of the good man of next house, that man in the left corner is *my* father, and the man on my right is my grandfather. From father to son we were too fond of money. We lent it at ten times the honest interest it was worth ; we never paid a debt we could get over, and almost starved our tenants and labourers.

"Here," says he, lugging a large drawer out of the wall ; "here is the gold and notes that we put together, and we were not honestly entitled to the one-half of it ; and here," says he, opening another drawer, "are bills and memorandums that'll show who were wronged, and who are entitled to get a great deal paid back to them. Tell my son to saddle two of his best horses for himself and yourself, and keep riding day and night, till every man and woman we ever wronged be rightified. When that is done, come here again some night ; and if you don't hear or see anything, we'll be at rest, and you may marry my grand-daughter as soon as you please."

Just as he said these words, Jack could see the wall through his body, and when he winked to clear his sight, the kitchen was as empty as a noggin turned upside down. At the very moment the farmer and his daughter lifted the latch, and both fell on their knees when they saw Jack alive. He soon told them everything that happened, and for three days and nights did the farmer and himself ride about, till there wasn't a single wronged person left without being paid to the last farthing.

The next night Jack spent in the kitchen he fell asleep before he was after sitting a quarter of an hour at the fire, and in his sleep he thought he saw three white birds flying up to heaven from the steeple of the next church.

Jack got the daughter for his wife, and they lived comfortably in the old castle ; and if ever he was tempted to hoard up gold, or keep for a minute a guinea or a shilling from the man that earned it through the nose, he bethought him of the ghosts and the game of football.

The peculiar style of conversation adopted by cats in their nightly reunions, and other odd fashions of theirs, have invested them in the eyes of our people with an eerie character.

In the Norse tales, a young hillman was banished from his tribe by the influence of an old chief, whose lady was suspected to be rather partial to him. He took refuge with a farmer, and did service in the form of a house cat. After some time, the farmer's servant coming by the enchanted mound, heard a shrill voice repeating—

> "Go bid Tom Platt,
> To tell his cat
> That Knurre Murre's dead."

When the servant entered the kitchen, he repeated the verse; and the moment the exile heard it from his seat by the fire, he gave a wild mew of delight, spouted out in feline language, "Knurre Murre's dead," cleared the yard-fence at a leap, and was off to his hill to bring comfort to the widow. Now hear the impotent conclusion to which this tale has come in Leinster :—

THE CAT OF THE CARMAN'S STAGE.

A carman was leaving Bunclody one morning for Dublin, when what should he see but a neighbour's cat galloping along the side of the road, and crying out every moment, "Tell Moll Browne, Tom Dunne is dead; tell Moll Browne, Tom Dunne is dead." At last he got tired of this ditty, and took up a stone and flung it at the cat, bidding himself, and Tom Browne, and Moll Dunne, to go to Halifax, and not to be botherin' him. When he got to Luke Byrne's in Francis Street, where all the Wicklow and Wexford carmen used to stop, he was taking a pot of beer in the tap-room, and began to tell the quare thing that happened on the road. There was a comfortable-looking gray cat sitting by the fire, and the moment he mentioned what the Bunclody cat was saying, she cried out, "That's my husband! that's my husband!" She made only one leap out through the door, and no one ever saw her at Luke Byrne's again

The narrator of the following travelling sketch was a half-witted woman, who, although she had heard it from some one else, was under the impression that she had undergone part of the adventures in some form or other. She was a very honest, inoffensive creature, and would do any work assigned to her carefully enough; but she had a certain district of the country under her supervision, and it was essential to her well-being that she should perambulate (*serenade* was her term) this portion about once in the year. She went by the name of Cauth (Catherine) Morrisy, and this is the style in which she related her juvenile experience:—

CAUTH MORRISY LOOKING FOR SERVICE.

Well, neighbours, when I was a *thuckeen* (young girl) about fifteen years of age, and it was time to be doing something for myself, I set off one fine day in spring along the yalla high-road; and if anybody axed me where I was goin' I'd make a joke about it, and say I was goin' out of Ireland to live in the Roer.[1] Well, I travelled all day, and dickens a bit o' me was the nearer to get a sarvice; and when the dark hour come I got a lodging in a little house by the side of the road, where they were drying flax over a roaring turf fire. I'll never belie the vanithee her goodness. She give me a good quarter of well-baked barley bread, with butter on it, and

[1] A district in Kilkenny, not far from the bridge of Ferry Mountgarret. Consequential Wexford folk regarded it in matters of learning and politeness, as the Athenians did Bœotia in ancient times.

made me sit on the big griddle over the ash-pit in the corner; but what would you have of it? I held the bread to the fire to melt the butter, and bedad the butter fell on the lighted turf, and there it blazed up like vengeance, and set the flax afire, and the flax set the *tatch* afire, and maybe they didn't get a fright. "Oh, musha, vanithee," says they, "wasn't it the divel bewitched you to let that *omadhān* of a girl burn us out of house and home this way? Be off, you torment, and purshuin' to you!" Well, if they didn't hunt me out, and throw potsticks, and tongses, and sods o' fire after me, lave it till again; and I run, and I run, till I run head foremost into a cabin by the side of the road.

The woman o' the house was sitting at the fire, and she got frightened to see me run in that way. "Oh, musha, ma'am," says I, "will you give me shelter?" and so I up and told her my misfortunes. "Poor colleen," says she, "my husband is out, and if he catches a stranger here he'll go mad and break things. But I'll let you get up on the hurdle over the room, and for your life don't budge." "I won't," says I, "and thank you, ma'am." Well, I was hardly in bed when her crooked disciple of a man kem in with a sheep on his back he was afther stealing. "Is everything ready?" says he. "It is," says she. So with that he skinned the sheep, and popped a piece down into the biling pot, and went out and hid the skin, and buried the rest o' the mate in a hole in the flure, and covered it with the griddle, and covered the griddle again with some o' the clay he removed from the flure. Well, when he made his supper on the mutton he says to his wife, "I hope no one got lodging while I was away." "Arrah, who'd get it?" says she. "That's not the answer I want," says he. "Who did you give shelter to?" "Och, it was only to a little slip of a girl that's as fast as the knocker of Newgate since eleven o'clock, on the hurdle." "Molly," says he, "I'll hang for you some day, so I will. But first and foremost I'll put the stranger out o' pain." When I hear him talk I slip down, and was out o' the door in a jiffy; but he was as stiff as I was stout, and he fling the hatchet after me, and cut off a piece of my heel. "Them is the tricks of a clown,"

WITCHCRAFT, SORCERY, GHOSTS, AND FETCHES

says I to myself, and I making away at the ling of my life; but as luck would have it, I got shelter in another cabin, where a nice old man was sitting over the fire, reading a book. "What's the matter, poor girl?" says he, and I up and told him what happened me. "Never fear," says he; "the man o' the mutton won't follow you here. I suppose you'd like your supper." Well, sure enough, the fright, and the run, and the cut heel, and that, made me hungry, and I didn't refuse a good plate o' stirabout.

"Colleen," says the man, "I can't go to sleep early in the night; maybe you'd tell a body a story." "Musha, an the dickens a story meself has," says I. "That's bad," says he; "the fire is getting low: take that *booran*[1] out to the clamp, and bring in the full of it of turf." "I will, sir," says I. But when I took a turf out of the end of the clamp 500 sods tumbled down on me, head and pluck; and I thought the breath was squeezed out of me. "If that's the way," says I, "let the old gentleman himself come out, and bring in his firing."

So I went in, and had like to faint when I came to the fire. "What ails you, little girl?" says he. "The clamp that fell on me," says I. "Oh, but it's meself that's sorry," says he. "Did you think of e'er another story while you were at the clamp?" "Indeed an I didn't." "Well, it can't be helped. I suppose you're tired. Take that rushlight into the barn, but don't set it on fire. You'll find plenty of dry straw for a bed, and come into your breakfast early." Well, I bade him good-night, and when I came into the barn, sure enough, there was no scarcity of straw. I said my prayers, but the first bundle I took out of the heap I thought all the straw in the barn was down on my poor bones. "O vuya, vuya, Cauth," says I to myself, "if your poor father and mother knew the state you're in, wouldn't they have the heart-scald." But I crept out and sat down on a bundle, and began to cry.

I wasn't after cryin' a second *dhrass* when I heard steps outside the door, and I hid myself again under the straw, leaving a little peep-hole. In came three as ugly-looking

[1] A domestic article, shaped like an overgrown tambourine.

fellows as you'd find in a kish o' brogues, with a coffin on their shoulders. They wondered at the candle, but they said nothing till they put the coffin down, and began to play cards on it with the dirtiest *deck* (pack) I ever see before or since. Well, they cheated, and scolded, and whacked one another, and in two minutes they were as great as pickpockets [1] again.

At last says one, "It's time to be goin'; lift the corpse." "It's easy say lift," says another. "You two have the front, and I must bear up all the hind part—I won't put a hand to it." "Won't you?" says the others; "sure there's little Cauth Morrisy under the straw to help you." "Oh, Lord, gentlemen, I'm not in it at all," says myself; but it was all no use. I had to get under one corner, and there we trudged on in the dark, through knocs, and ploughed fields, and bogs, till I thought the life would leave me.

At last at the flight of night, one of them says, "Stop here, and Cauth Morrisy will mind the corpse till we come back. Cauth, if you let anything happen to the honest man inside you'll sup sorrow—mind what I say." So they left me, and lonesome and frightened I was, you may depend.

But wasn't I frightened in earnest when I heard the corpse's knuckles tapping inside o' the *led*. "O, sir, honey," says I, "what's troubling you?" "It's air I want," says he; "lift up the led a little." I lifted up a corner. "That won't do," says he; "I'm stifling. Throw off the led, body and bones." I did so, and there was a wicked-looking old fellow inside, with a beard on him a week old. "Thankee, ma'am," says he; "I think I'll be the easier for that. This is a lonesome place them thieves left me in. Would you please to join me in a game of spoil-five?" "Oh, musha, sir," says I, "isn't it thinking of making your sowl you ought to be?" "I don't want your advice," says he; "maybe I haven't a soul at all. There's the cards. I deal—you cut."

Well, I was so afeard that I took a hand with him; but the dirty divel, he done nothing the whole time but cursin', and swearin', and cheatin'. At last says I to my-

---

[1] On the most friendly terms.

self, "I can't be safe in such company." So I threw down the cards, though I was within three of the game, and walked off. "Come back and finish the game, Cauth Morrisy," says he, shouting out, "or I'll make it the bad game for you." But I didn't let on to hear him, and walked away. "Won't you come back, Cauth?" says he; "then here goes." Well, the life had like to leave me, for I heard him tearing after me in his coffin, every bounce it gave striking terror into my heart. I run, and I bawled, and he bawling after me, and the coffin smashing against the stones. At last, where did I find myself but at the old gentleman's door, and if I didn't spring in and fasten the bolt, leave it till again.

"Ah, is that you, my little colleen? I thought you were asleep. Maybe you have a story for me now." "Indeed an' I have, sir," says I, an' I told him all that happen me since I saw him last. "You suffered a good deal," says he. "If you told me that story before, all your trouble i'd be spared to you." "But how could I tell it, sir," says I, "before it happened?" "That's true," says he, and he began to scratch his wig. I was getting drowsy, and I didn't remember anything more till I woke next morning in the dry gripe of the ditch with a *bochyeen* (dried cow-dung), under my head. So—

"There was a tree at the end of the house, and it was bending, bending,
And my story is ending, ending."

A dream romance of the same kind will be found in Crofton Croker's collection. Our authorities are Owen Jourdan of the Duffrey, as well as the woman called here Cauth Morrisy. O. J.'s version differed a little from that given, as he had to adapt the adventures to a male character. All are slightly related to the *Story Teller at Fault* of Gerald Griffin.

The following piece of diablerie is probably unknown out of Ireland. At least, we do not recollect having found it in the collections of Grimm or Dasent. It bears the usual marks of pagan origin. In the system of natural magic of a celebrated living writer, the adept, availing himself of the chemical and magnetic virtues inherent in some substances, and even those belonging to mere figures, such as the pentacle, can not only subject intelligent and sensitive beings to his will, but even insensible chairs and stools. When his critics twit him with the unsoundness of his theory, and its unsuitableness to the present state of physical and social science, he may appeal to its antiquity. The pagan magicians handed it to their quasi-Christian successors, and when these worthies departed to some world more worthy of them, their system exploded in fragments, and fell under the wise control of our story-tellers.

BLACK STAIRS ON FIRE.

On the top of the hill of *Cnoc-na-Cro'* (Gallows Hill) in Bantry, just in full view of the White Mountain, Cahir Rua's Den, and Black Stairs, there lived a poor widow, with a grandchild, about fifteen years old. It was *All-Holland Eve*, and the two were about going to bed when they heard four taps at the door, and a screaming voice crying out. "Where are you, feet-water?" and the feet-water answered, "Here in the tub." "Where are you, band of the spinning wheel?" and it answered, "Here, fast round the rim, as if it was spinning." "Besom, where are you?" "Here, with my handle in the ash-pit." "Turf-coal, where are you?" "Here, blazing over the ashes." Then the voice screamed louder, "Feet-water, wheel-band, besom, and turf-coal, let us in, let us in:" and they all made to the door.

Open it flew, and in rushed frightful old hags, wicked, shameless young ones, and the *old boy* himself, with red horns and a green tail. They began to tear and tatter round the house, and to curse and swear, and roar and bawl, and say such things as almost made the poor women sink through the hearthstone. They had strength enough however, to make the sign of the cross, and call on the Holy Trinity, and then all the witches and their master yowled with pain. After a little the girl strove to creep over to the holy water croft that was hanging at the bed's head, but the whole bilin' of the wicked creatures kep' in a crowd between her and it. The poor grandmother fell in a faint, but the little girl kep' her senses.

The old fellow made frightful music for the rest, stretching out his nose and playing the horriblest noise on it you ever heard, just as if it was a German flute. "Oh!" says the poor child, "if Granny should die or lose her senses what'll I do? and if they can stay till cockcrow, she'll never see another day." So after about half an hour, when the hullabullo was worse than ever, she stole out without being noticed or stopped, and then she gave a great scream, and ran in, and shouted, "Granny, granny! come out, come out, Black Stairs is a-fire!" Out pelted both the devil and the witches, some by the windows, some by the door; and the moment the last of them was out, she clapped the handle of the besom where the door-bolt ought to be, turned the button in the window, spilled the feet-water into the channel under the door, loosed the band of the spinning-wheel, and raked up the blazing coal under the ashes.

Well, the poor woman was now come to herself, and both heard the most frightful roar out in the bawn, where all the company were standing very *lewd*[1] of themselves for being so easily taken in. The noise fell immediately, and the same voice was heard. "Feet-water, let me in." "I can't," says feet-water; "I am here under your feet." "Wheel-band, let me in." "I can't—I am lying loose on the wheel-seat." "Besom let me in." "I can't—I am put here to bolt the door." "Turf-coal, let me in." I can't—my head is under the greeshach." "Then let yourselves and them that owns you have our curse for ever and a day." The poor women were now on their knees, and cared little for their curses. But every Holy

---

[1] "Regretful, ashamed," the root being *leiden*, to suffer. Many words and expressions among our folk of the Pale are looked on as abuses or perversions, when they are in truth but old forms still carefully preserved.

Eve during their lives they threw the water out as soon as their feet were washed, unbanded the wheel, swept up the house, and covered the big coal to have the seed of the fire next morning.

We have not in Ireland many traditional or legendary records of our wise women meeting the devil at such abominable sabats as he delighted to hold in German and Flemish forests, being conveyed thither on any article that came to hand. The utmost atrocity of which Irish witches were, in times past, proved guilty in their excursions, was the taking of an airy ride on a *booliaun bui* to the cellar of some English castle, and making themselves glorious with the wine and strong waters found there. The following adventure has been differently treated by fairy historians; so we confine ourselves to the principal facts, adhering to the Leinster version:—

THE WITCHES' EXCURSION.

Shemus Rua (Red James) was awakened from his sleep one night by noises in his kitchen. Stealing to the door, he saw half-a-dozen old women, sitting round the fire, jesting, and laughing, his own old housekeeper, Madge, quite frisky and gay, helping her sister crones to cheering glasses of punch. He began to admire the impudence and imprudence of Madge, displayed in the invitation and the riot, but recollected on the instant her officiousness in urging him to take a comfortable posset, which she had brought to his bedside just before he fell asleep. Had he drunk it he would have been just now deaf to the witches' glee. He heard and saw them drink his health in such a mocking style as nearly to tempt him to charge them, besom in hand, but he restrained himself. The jug being emptied, one of them cried out, "It is time to be gone," and at the same moment, putting on a red cap, she added—

> "By yarrow and rue,
> And my red cap too,
> Hie over to England."

Making use of a twig which she held in her hand as a steed, she gracefully soared up the chimney, and was rapidly followed by the rest. But when it came to the housekeeper's turn, Shemus interposed. "By your leave, ma'am!" said he, snatching twig and cap. "Ah, you desateful ould crocodile! If I find you here on my return, there'll be wigs on the green.

> "By yarrow and rue,
> And my red cap too,
> Hie over to England."[1]

The words were not out of his mouth when he was soaring above the ridge-pole, and swiftly ploughing the air. He was careful to speak no word (being somewhat conversant in witch lore), as the result would be a tumble, and the immediate return of the expedition. In a very short time they had crossed the Wicklow hills, the Irish Sea, and the Welsh mountains, and were charging at whirlwind speed the hall-door of a castle. Shemus, only for the company in which he found himself, would have cried out for pardon, expecting to be *mummy* against the hard oak door in a moment; but all bewildered he found himself passing through the key-hole, along a passage, down a flight of steps, and through a cellar-door key-hole, before he could form any clear idea of his situation.

Waking to the full consciousness of his position, he found himself sitting on a stillion, plenty of lights glimmering round, and he and his companions, with full tumblers of frothing wine in hand, hob-nobbing and drinking healths as jovially and recklessly as if the liquor was honestly come by, and they were sitting in Shemus's own kitchen. The red birredh had assimilated Shemus's nature for the time being to that of his unholy companions. The heady liquors soon got in their brains, and a period of unconsciousness succeeded the ecstasy, the head-ache, the turning round of the barrels, and the

---

[1] For the above formulary the words Borraun, Borraun, Borraun! are sometimes substituted. *Borran* is anger, *booraun* a domestic article mentioned already; the reader is at liberty to fashion a theory on these data.

"scattered sight" of poor Shemus. He woke up under the impression of being roughly seized, and shaken, and dragged upstairs, and subjected to a disagreeable examination by the lord of the castle, in his state parlour. There was much derision and laughter among the whole company, gentle and simple, on hearing Shemus's explanation; and as the thing occurred in the dark ages, the unlucky Leinster-man was sentenced to be hung as soon as the gallows could be prepared for the occasion.

The poor Hibernian was in the cart proceeding on his last journey, with a label upon his back, and another on his breast, announcing him as the remorseless villain who for the last month had been draining the casks in my lord's vault every night. He was striving to say a prayer, when he was surprised to hear himself addressed by his name, and in his native tongue, by an old woman in the crowd. "Ach, Shemus, alanna! is it going to die you are in a strange place, without your *cappeen dearg!*" These words infused hope and courage into the victim's heart. He turned to the lord, and humbly asked leave to die in his red cap, which he supposed had dropped from his head in the vault. A servant was sent for the head-piece, and Shemus felt lively hope warming his heart while placing it on his head. On the platform he was graciously allowed to address the spectators, which he proceeded to do in the usual formula composed for the benefit of flying stationers:—" Good people all, a warning take by me;" but when he had finished the line, "My parients rared me tenderly," he unexpectedly added—" By yarrow and rue," &c. and the disappointed spectators saw him shoot up obliquely through the air in the style of a sky-rocket that had missed its aim. It is said that the lord took the circumstance much to heart, and never afterwards hung a man for twenty-four hours after his offence.

THE CROCK FOUND IN THE RATH.

If any of our English readers are unfortunately ignorant of the social position of tailors in the remote districts of this country, let them hereby learn that Brian

Neill, the unlucky hero of this narrative, when he arose on Monday morning, betook himself to the farmer's house where his services were required, took the measures of his clients, sat on the large kitchen table, kept his goose in the turf fire, mended and made clothes, chatted with the women, and there remained till his business was finished. He then repaired to some other farmstead where his presence was desirable, and thus his life glided on.

Brian was employed as mentioned one afternoon on Mrs. Rooney's great table. He had been remarked all the day for an unwonted silence, and now began to acquaint Mrs. Rooney with the subject on which his thoughts were employed. "Be this and be that, ma'am, it's very strange that I should have the same dream for the last three nights. There it was, in the rath of Knocmōr, I saw, as plain as I see you now, a big grey stone, and an old thorn tree, and the hole between them, and the crock at the bottom of it. I declare to you I can't stand it any longer. I'll take a spade and shovel, and try my fortune, and have it off my mind. You needn't tell anybody where I'm gone."

About three hours afterwards he returned in a very dismantled condition, his hair in moist flakes, his eyes glassy, and his whole appearance betokening one who would drop in pieces if some strong power were not keeping him together. "Oh, ma'am, honey!" he faltered out, "let me lie down somewhere; I think I'll die." Mrs. Rooney had put him into the bed belonging to the servant boy, and good-naturedly brought him a warm drink of whey in a quarter of an hour or so. She then sat down by the bed; and when he had refreshed himself, and seemed somewhat restored, she requested to know how he fared after he had left the house. This is the account he rather reluctantly gave after some pressing :—

"When I got to the rath, ma'am, I wondered to find the stone and the old thorn just as I dreamed they were. Bedad I took off my coat, and fell to, and dug and shovelled, and shovelled and dug till my poor arms were tired. I rested myself for a little while, and then fell to again. Well, I think I was down between three and four feet, when I felt something hard against the spade. I cleared away the clay carefully from about it, and what was it but a heavy crock, just like the very one I saw in the dreams. I lifted it out on the heap of clay I threw up, and was going to get the cover off when I felt myself getting as weak as water. I was trembling indeed, and my heart fluttering from the first touch I gave it with the spade. Well, what would you have of it! I fell down in a *stugue*, and don't know how long I was in it; and when I came to myself the very sight of the crock brought my heart to my mouth. I done nothing after that but crawled back as well as I could. I suppose all happened to me because I did not say e'er a prayer, or take any holy-water with me to sprinkle a ring round the place. I think I'll go asleep now; I can't keep my eyes open."

So he slept soundly, and never woke till next morning, and the first thing he was conscious of was a strong inclination to go to the rath again, and recover the crock, if it still remained there. He went in all haste, found the spade and shovel, the heap of clay, and the pit, but no sign of the crock or its cover. He came back overpowered with vexation at the silly way in which he had behaved the day before, and begged Mrs. Rooney to give him his crock, and promised to give her a good handful of its contents. "Crock!" said she; "what are you talking about?" "Sure I am talking about the crock I dug up in the rath of Knoc-mōr yesterday, and that I told you about after you gave me the drink of whey in the bed." "Oh, my poor man, you are raving! I gave you a drink, sure enough, but this is the first time you opened your mouth about a crock." "But sure, if you come you can see the hole and the clay, and here is the spade and shovel that I used." "And if they are, is that a reason I should have your crock, that I never heard of till this blessed hour?"

There was great commotion in the neighbourhood. Several people, including Mr. and Mrs. Rooney, went to the rath, and saw the hole and the clay, but that did not prove that Mrs. Rooney got the money. All that the sharpest neighbour could make out was the absence of the farmer and his wife from their house for about an hour on the evening in question. It all resulted in poor Brian losing his reason, and coming to vituperate Mrs. Rooney about once a week at her own door. We will say of her that she always gave him something to eat on these occasions, and a coat or breeches when his need was sore for good clothing. By degrees the farm was improved, and more land taken. Her children were well provided for, and so are such of her grandchildren as are now living. Ill-got money does not in general produce such comfortable results.

In the *Leadbeater Papers* will be found another version of the next legend. What we heard from Mrs. K. in 1816, or thereabouts, is here given to the reader most conscientiously. It is a curious instance of old circumstances being attached to the fortunes of a new man, such as Earl Garrett must be considered when thought of in comparison with Holger the Dane or King Arthur.

Such legends belong to a race which has been obliged to give way to a less imaginative people. James IV. of Scotland, survived Flodden, and will appear when his country wants him. Don Sebastian of Portugal did not perish in Africa. Holger the Dane remained watching in his cavern long after the period—

> "When Roland brave, and Olivier,
> And every paladin and peer,
> On Roncesvalles died."

King Arthur is still waiting in the Isle of Avalon; and some old Welsh king can scarcely disengage his beard from the stone table into which it has grown, as he has slept till his coming forth can be of no manner of use.

THE ENCHANTMENT OF GEARHOIDH IARLA.

In old times in Ireland there was a great man of the Fitzgeralds. The name on him was Gerald, but the

Irish, that always had a great liking for the family, called him *Gearoidh Iarla* (Earl Gerald). He had a great castle or rath at Mullaghmast, and whenever the English government were striving to put some wrong on the country, he was always the man that stood up for it. Along with being a great leader in a fight, and very skilful at all weapons, he was deep in the *black art*, and could change himself into whatever shape he pleased. His lady knew that he had this power, and often asked him to let her into some of his secrets, but he never would gratify her.

She wanted particularly to see him in some strange shape, but he put her off and off on one pretence or other. But she wouldn't be a woman if she hadn't perseverance; and so at last he let her know that if she took the least fright while he'd be out of his natural form, he would never recover it till many generations of men would be under the mould. "Oh! she wouldn't be a fit wife for Gearoidh Iarla if she could be easily frightened. Let him but gratify her in this whim, and he'd see what a *hero* she was!" So one beautiful summer evening, as they were sitting in their grand drawing-room, he turned his face away from her, and muttered some words, and while you'd wink he was clever and clean out of sight, and a lovely *goldfinch* was flying about the room.

The lady, as courageous as she thought herself, was a little startled, but she held her own pretty well, especially when he came and perched on her shoulder, and shook his wings, and put his little beak to her lips, and whistled the delightfullest tune you ever heard. Well, he flew in circles round the room, and played *hide and go seek* with his lady, and flew out into the garden, and flew back again, and lay down in her lap as if he was asleep, and jumped up again.

Well, when the thing had lasted long enough to satisfy both, he took one flight more into the open air; but by my word he was soon on his return. He flew right into his lady's bosom, and the next moment a fierce hawk was after him. The wife gave one loud scream, though there was no need, for the wild bird came in like an arrow, and struck against a table with such force that the life was dashed out of him. She turned her eyes from his quivering body to where she saw the goldfinch an instant before, but neither goldfinch nor Earl Garrett did she ever lay eyes on again.

Once every seven years the Earl rides round the Curragh of Kildare on a steed, whose silver shoes were half an inch thick the time he disappeared; and when these shoes are worn as thin as a cat's ear, he will be restored to the society of living men, fight a great battle with the English, and reign King of Ireland for two score years.

Himself and his warriors are now sleeping in a long cavern under the Rath of Mullaghmast. There is a table running along through the middle of the cave. The Earl is sitting at the head, and his troopers down along in complete armour both sides of the table, and their heads resting on it. Their horses, saddled and bridled, are standing behind their masters in their stalls at each side; and when the day comes, the miller's son that's to be born with six fingers on each hand will blow his trumpet, and the horses will stamp and whinny, and the knights awake and mount their steeds, and go forth to battle.

Some night that happens once in every seven years, while the Earl is riding round the Curragh, the entrance may be seen by any one chancing to pass by. About a hundred years ago, a horse-dealer that was late abroad and a little drunk, saw the lighted cavern, and went in. The lights, and the stillness, and the sight of the men in armour cowed him a good deal, and he became sober. His hands began to tremble, and he let fall a bridle on the pavement. The sound of the bit echoed through the long cave, and one of the warriors that was next him lifted his head a little, and said in a deep hoarse voice, "Is it time yet?" He had the wit to say, "Not yet, but soon will," and the heavy helmet sunk down on the table. The horse-dealer made the best of his way out, and I never heard of any other one getting the same opportunity.

The terrible superstition of the *Lianan Sighe* dates, as we here find, from an early period.

It was the fate of those mortals who loved, and were beloved by, women of the Sighe people, that they could not be freed from the connexion unless with the entire consent of their wayward mistresses. In illustration of the system, we subjoin the very old legend of

ILLAN EACHTACH AND THE LIANAN.

Illan was a friend of Fion, and was willing to become more intimately connected with him by marrying his aunt Tuirrean. It had come to Fion's ears that Illan was already provided with a sighe-love, so he secured the fate of his aunt in this wise. He put her hand into that of Oisin, who intrusted her to Caoilté, who intrusted her to Mac Luacha, &c.; and thus she passed under the guardianship of Diarmaid, Goll Mac Morna, another Luacha, and so into the arms of Illan. Her married life was happy for a while, but it did not please the Sighe, *Uchtdealbh* (Fair Bosom) that her mortal lover should be happy in any society but her own. So she paid her a visit in the absence of her husband, and invited her out, as she wished to give her an important message from Fion, relative to a feast he wanted to have prepared. Being safe from the eyes of the household, she muttered some words, and drawing a druidic wand from under her mantle, she struck her with it, and changed her into the most beautiful wolf-hound that eyes ever beheld. She then took her to the house of Feargus Fionnliath, on the shore of the bay of Galway. Illan, hearing on his return that his wife had gone out with a strange woman, and had not since been seen, guessed that Fair Bosom had disposed of her in some way, and began to tremble for the result. It was not long arriving. Fion missing his aunt, demanded her safe in life and limb at the hands of Oisin, who demanded her from Caoilté, who demanded her from Mac Luacha, &c. till Luacha the second demanded from Illan the person of his wife in good health, or his own head. Illan acknowledged the justice of the request, and merely demanded a few days' grace.

He at once set forward to the palace-cavern of his

sighe, and obtained his wish, but on the pure condition of being faithful to her till his death, and never more seeking mortal mistress or wife. She then sought out Tuirrean, and bringing her to some distance from Fergus's rath, restored her to her pristine shape, and then delivered her over to her nephew. Luacha the second, the last of the sureties, represented to the great chief, that the least recompense he could make him for the terror he had experienced, was the hand of the restored beauty, and Fion gave his gracious consent to this second espousals of his aunt.

During the lady's transformation she brought to the world the two celebrated hounds *Brann* and *Sceoluing*. Fair Bosom was willing to give them the human shape when she restored it to their mother, but Fion preferred them to remain as they were.

When Paganism prevailed, such connexions were not looked on as *very* baneful or unnatural. Under the Christian dispensation the unhappy person is strictly bound to the unholy being, is always sensible of its presence, and cannot be freed from the alliance without finding a substitute to take his or her place. It is said that the Lianan is nourished by the food received by its companion. Whatever were the circumstances attending the beginning of the connexion, the wretched mortal suffers at a later period such misery allied to horror, that he or she would welcome death, were it not for the torments to be looked for after it.

The person possessed can make the Lianan confer riches and other worldly goods on friends or favourites, but is not in a position to receive or enjoy such things in his or her own person. While the contract is not broken on the mortal side the familiar is the slave, otherwise unendurable misery and slavery is his or her portion. In the tale of *Zanoni* and in the *Lianan Shie*, by Carleton, are obscurely figured the indescribable wretchedness of the too rash and too curious mortals who would tear asunder the veil that divides the visible from the invisible world.[1]

An ancient Ossianic story is the original on which Carroll O'Daly or Hugh Duff O'Reilly founded the tale of the "Son of Evil Counsel." Such legends passed from the mouths of the professed bards and story-tellers to those of a lower rank and less talent; and again descended from their keeping to the care of uneducated peasants. We cite the last degraded form of this old fiction, as told by a *scealuidhe* of the lowest rank.

THE MISFORTUNES OF BARRETT THE PIPER.

Barrett the Piper, you see, lost his skill, and was advised to go to the Black North to recover it (Barrett was a Munster man). Well, he took his little boy with him and they walked and they walked till the dark came, and they went into a cabin by the roadside to look for lodging. "God save all here!" says they. "Save you kindly!" says the man of the house, but he left out the HOLY NAME. "How are you, Jack Barrett?" "Musha, pure and hearty, sir; many thanks for the axing, but how did you know me?" "Och, I knew you before you were weaned. Sit down and make yourself at home; here you stay till morning." Well, faith, they got a good supper of pytatees and milk, and a good bed of straw was made for them by the wall up near the fire, and they lay down quite comfortable to get a good sleep. But some bad thoughts came over Jack Barrett in the dead of the night, and he got up and went out of the bed, and it's in the fields he found himself, and a couple of mad dogs running after him. There was a big tree near him with ever so many crows' nests in the top, and he run and climbed up in it from the dogs, and if he missed the

---

[1] Classic scholars will find the memory of the Incubi, and Succubi, and Nympholepts of the Pagan system, preserved in these Lianans and the persons possessed by them.

dogs he found the crows, and didn't they fall on him to tear his eyes out! He bawled, and he roared, and the man of the house came into the kitchen, and stirred the fire, and there was Jack Barrett on the hen-roost, and the cocks and hens cackling about him. "Musha, the sorra's on you for a Jack Barrett! How did you get up there among the fowl?" "The goodness knows; it's not their company I want. Will you help me down, honest man?"

Well, he got into bed again, and if he did he was not long there when a bad thought come into his head, and up he got. He was going into the next room, when where did he find himself but by the bank of a big river, and the same two dogs tearing along like vengeance to make gibbets of him. There was a tree there, and its boughs were out over the river. Up climbs Jack, and up after him with the dogs; and to get out of their clutches he scrambled out on a long bough. The dogs were soon feeling after him, and he going out farther and farther, till he was afraid it would break. At last he felt it cracking, and he gave a roar out of him that you'd hear a mile off, and the man of the house came into the kitchen, and stirred the fire, and there was Jack sthraddle-leg on the pot-rack. "Musha, Jack, but you're the devil's quare youth at your time o' life to be makin' a horse of my pot-rack. Come down, you onshuch, and go to bed."

Well, the third time, where did the divel guide him but to a bed in the next room, and when he flopped into it, he let such a yowl out of him that you'd think it was heaven and earth was coming together. "What's in the win' now, Jack?" says the man o' the house. "Oh, it's in the pains of labour I am," says the unfortunate piper. "Will we send for the midwife for you?" says the other. "Oh, the curse o' Cromwell on yourself an' the midwife!" says the poor man; "it wasn't God had a hand in us the hour we darkened your door. Oh, tattheration to you, you ould thief! won't you give us some aise?" "Father honey," says the boy, "it's pishrogues is an you. A drop of holy water will do you more good nor the master o' the house, God bless him!"

"I'll tear you limb from limb," says the ould villain when he heard the HOLY NAME, "if you say that again." "Well, anyhow," says the boy, "make the sign of the cross on yourself, father, and say the Lord's Prayer." The poor ould piper did so, and at the blessed words and the sign, his pains left him. There was no sight of the man of the house on the spot then; maybe he was in the lower room.

When the piper and his son woke next morning, they were lying in the dry moat of an ould rath that lay by the high road.

Having never enjoyed the undesirable privilege of a foregathering with an unearthly appearance, though in our youth we had passed, many many times, at the dead hour through haunted *glounthaans* (glens), and across the haunted fords of *Ath-na-Capail*,[1] *Ochnanayear*, *Ochayolthachawn*, and many other eery *aths* and *thubbers* (fords and wells), we yet can bring to mind many of the true narratives we have heard at rustic firesides.

Of those we are about to relate, we are as sure of the good faith of the tellers as of any ordinary truth or fact that has occurred to us, but are yet of opinion that, could all circumstances connected with the occurrences be ascertained, everything related might probably be referred to natural causes. The narratives are not classified: we give them as they occur to memory, vouching for the thorough sincerity of the original reciters.

THE WOMAN IN WHITE.

Pat Gill, of the county of Kildare, was driving towards Dublin, with a load of country produce. He

[1] The first of these names is pronounced by the people round Castleboro, Och-na-goppal; the others are pronounced as here phonetically spelled. The English equivalents are—the "Ford of the Horse," the "Ford of the Evil Spirits," and the "Ford of the Naked Man."

had made a comfortable seat for himself on the car, and had plenty of hay about him and under him. He was pleasantly employed thinking of nothing in particular, dozing and giving an eye to the proceedings of his beast. He was between the mill of Baltracy and the cross roads of Borraheen, when he was startled by the appearance of a woman dressed in long white clothes, crossing the fence, and advancing into the road. She came up to the horse, and walked on with him, close by his neck. The driver chucked the beast's head to the opposite side, for fear he should tread on her feet or long robes, but she still kept as close to him as before, and sometimes he thought he could see the lower part of the horse's fore leg through her dress. The matter had now become very serious. He could not keep his eyes off the apparition; and he felt his whole frame covered with a cold perspiration. He became bewildered, and could not determine either on going on or stopping. So, the horse, finding matters left to himself jogged on apparently unconscious of his fellow-wayfarer. The centre of the cross-roads of Borraheen is or was occupied by a patch of green turf; and when they came to its edge, the white figure stood still, while a portion of the shaft of the car on that side seemed to pass through her. Gill, observing this, drew the beast at once to the other side, crying in a voice made tremulous by terror, "By your leave, ma'am!" On went horse and car, the edges of the load preventing him from seeing the white form. Having advanced two or three yards, he looked back, fearing to see a mangled body on the road behind him, but he saw, instead, the white appearance standing in the centre of the plot of grass, her hand seeming to shade her eyes, as she looked earnestly after him. Terrified as he was, he never turned his gaze till a bend in the road cut off the view.

The neighbourhood of Borraheen, Baltracy, and Rathcoffey was blessed, or the contrary, in times past, by a fortune-teller and charm-concocter, Molly Anthony by name. So unedifying was her life and conversation, that the priest refused to have any religious services performed for her after death. She left a son, who had acquired some skill in curing cattle by herbs, and did not pretend to any supernatural gifts. A farmer, Pat Behan, at whose house he had remained about a fortnight, and who was well pleased with his performances, was passing near the green hills in his jaunting car, accompanied by Jack Anthony, the doctor, when, on a sudden, an old woman in a red cloak appeared to them between the bushes on the road-fence, and cried, "Jack, it's time for you to come." "Sir," said Jack to his patron, "will you excuse me for a minute, while I go to say a word to this neighbour of mine?" "Oh, to be sure!" Jack got on the fence, and passed through the bushes, but the farmer was surprised at not subsequently hearing the sound of his or her voice. He waited for about the space of a minute, and then bade his servant climb the fence, and see if Jack was about to return. The servant did as he was told, and the master observed him look along the inner side of the *ditch*, now to the left, and then to the right, and then straight before him, with a perplexed expression of face. The master sprung down, joined his servant, and found he had a long range of vision right and left, and up the sloping side of the green hill, and no bushes or rocks to afford concealment. Neither Jack nor the red-cloaked women were in view. It was months before the doctor presented himself before his patron, and even then his account of his disappearance was not consistent in all its parts. Our informant was acquainted with Pat Behan and Jack Anthony, and heard the former relate the adventure.

Mrs. FitzPatrick, a native of Queen's County, has furnished us with the next tale.

THE QUEEN'S COUNTY GHOST.

Squire Garret (let us say), whose seat lay near Kilcavan, was not a pattern for faith or morals while above mould, and afterwards caused considerable annoyance to his surviving friends and dependents. No night passed without the noises usual in such cases being heard. Doors would be flung open, keys heard turning in locks, plates and dishes hurled down from the dresser on the kitchen floor, tables overturned, and chairs flung about, yet in the morning nothing would be found out of its place. The family at last removed to another manor-house at some distance, but the steward, and old coachman, and a few hangers-on, remained behind. None suffered more from the ghostly and ghastly freaks of the late master than the coachman. When once the night came he could not reckon on a moment's rest. If he attempted to take a nap in the great chair, his wig would be plucked off, or the chair pulled from under him, and he would occasionally find himself pinched and bruised black and blue. At last, he seemed utterly callous and indifferent to these marks of interest in him evinced by the old Squire. Perhaps he was more obnoxious to this persecution for having aided the defunct in his designs upon the innocence of sundry young women during his reign on earth. There was one peculiarity in his visitations; he never made himself visible to more than one person in a company; and, though he adopted the appearance of black dog, or boar, or bull on these occasions, the individual singled out always knew the old Squire under his disguises.

The wives, sons, and daughters of the neighbouring farmers once took it in head to club and have a ball in the big house, for which they readily got permission. All was as merry as music, and drink, and an assemblage of young boys and girls could make it, when in the height of the festivity, the old gentleman took it into his head to become visible in a hideous shape to the aunt (then a young woman) of Mrs. FitzPatrick. She shrieked out, and fainted, and the universal mirth and jollity came to an abrupt conclusion. When she was brought to herself, and related what had occurred, there was a general dispersion, and that was the last attempt at a ball in the big house.

THE GHOST IN GRAIGUE.

A lady in the neighbourhood of that old town, much celebrated for her charities, died, and great sorrow was felt for her loss. Many masses were celebrated, and many prayers offered up for the repose of her soul, and there was a moral certainty of her salvation among her acquaintance. One evening, after the family had retired to rest, a servant girl in the house, a great favourite with her late mistress, was sitting beside the fire, enjoying the dreamy comfort of a hard-worked person after the day's fatigues, and just before the utter forgetfulness of sleep. Her mind was wandering to her late loved mistress, when she was startled by a sensation in her instep, as if it were trodden upon. "Bad manners to you for a dog," said she, suspecting the "coley" of the house to be the offender. But to her great terror, when she looked down and round the hearth, she could see no living thing. "Who's that?" she cried out, with the teeth chattering in her head. "It is I," was the answer, and the dead lady became visible to her. "Oh, mistress darling!" said she, "What is disturbing you, and can I do anything for you?" "You can do a little," said the spirit, "and that is the reason I have appeared to you. Every day and every hour some one of my friends are lamenting me, and speaking of my goodness, and that is tormenting me in the other world. All my charities were done only for the pleasure of having myself spoken well of, and they are now prolonging my punishment. The only real good I ever did was to give, once, half-a crown to a poor scholar that was studying to be a priest, and charging him to say nothing about it. That was the only good act that followed me into the other world. And now you must tell my husband and my children to speak well of my past life no more, or I will haunt you night after night." The appearance, the next moment, was no longer there, and the poor girl fainted the moment it vanished. When she recovered, she hastened into her settle-bed, and covered herself up, head and all, and cried and sobbed till morning.

Every one wondered the next day to see such a troubled countenance. But she went through her business one way or other, though she could not make up her mind to tell her master what she had seen and heard. She dreaded the quiet hour of rest; and well she might, for the displeased lady visited her again at the same hour, and reproached her for her neglect. Three times she endured the dread visits before she made the required revelation.

Some readers will give us no thanks for the next two sketches; of course we feel all suitable sorrow.

DROOCHAN'S GHOST.

A townland north of Mount Leinster is infested by the above-named evil spirit. Within a few years, sundry people returning from a cross-roads' dance, on a Sunday evening, just as night had set in, were greatly terrified. Their road lay along the side of a tolerably steep hill, and as they were coming on, and chatting, they heard the most dreadful cries above them, and a noise as of rocks tumbling down directly to crush them. They ran away at their best speed, and still heard the unearthly yells higher up, and the dreadful sounds, as if half the rocks and loose stones on the heights were sweeping down, crossing the road behind them, and plunging headlong into the stream at the bottom of the hill. Terror and dismay ruled the neighbourhood that night, and for a week longer, when the fright of the Sabbath-breakers was turned to anger and shame. The wag of the next village had carried an empty cask to the summit of the hill, supplied the inside with some stones, fastened the end securely, and just as the gossipers came below, he let slip the engine.

Droochan, the bugbear of the district, had been a man of evil life, and consequently entitled after his death, to annoy all peaceable subjects that had the ill-luck to live in his neighbourhood.

A small family in that blighted vicinity were taking their evening meal in their little parlour, when they were alarmed by their servant-girl rushing across the hall from the kitchen, and crying out, "Oh, masther, masther, Droochan's ghost! He's in the kitchen." After fifteen minutes spent in exclamations, hasty questions, confused answers, and researches, the following dialogue took place :—" What shape did he appear to you in?" "Oh, I didn't see him at all!" "Who saw him?" "The cats." "How do you know?" "Ah, sure there wasn't a breath stirrin', when them two craythurs cocked their ears, stood up on their hind legs, wud their eyes stanin' in their heads, and sparred at one another with their hands—I mean their fore paws. Then they let a yowl, as if heaven and earth was coming together, and run off into the coal shed. And what ghost could they be seeing only Droochan's?"

About four miles east of Baltinglass stands the hill of Bally Carrigeen (rocky pass), and on its top a large ring of rounded flags about nine yards in diameter, and called *Fan-a-Cool's griddle stones.* On the side of the neighbouring eminence are two long strips of turf, much greener than that by which they are surrounded. These are the marks of the resting-places of Fion Mac Cuil and his wife, who, when they rose early in the morning, descended the slope, washed their faces in the stream, and baked the cakes for their breakfast on a griddle supported by these flags. However, we have not much to say of them on this occasion. In their neighbourhood, on the crest of another hill, is the churchyard of Kilranelagh, where no corpse of Protestant man or woman has ever been allowed to rest. The boundary-wall is formed of loose stones, and the top is very narrow in comparison with its base. Every man attending a funeral brings a stone picked up on its way, and throws it on the circular fence, and so the mighty ring has grown. Outside this boundary is a deep, round well, and a tall curved recess in the wall just above it. This recess is furnished with ledges, which are plentifully provided with wooden cups—every one interring in the graveyard the corpse of a child under five years of age providing one of these vessels. The spirit of the latest interred is obliged to supply every one of its predecessors with a cup of water and to keep watch and ward over the sacred inclosure till the next funeral; and so, when two convoys are approaching at the same time, there sometimes occur unseemly races and struggles. Having sketched our scenery, we proceed with the legend of

THE KILRANELAGH SPIRIT.

Two men repairing to their homes just in the twilight, were obliged to pass through this churchyard, or take a considerable circuit. They had come up the hill, and were beginning to proceed through the cemetery, when they heard, just on their left, and apparently proceeding from a tomb, the most awful groans and frightful outcries, and a shower of red-hot cinders fell on them. They retreated down hill in great dismay; yet, after getting to some distance, they plucked up courage and returned. They were received in a more fearful fashion this time, and once again fled in terror. Unaccountable as it may appear, they made a third attempt; but this time the noise was more appalling than ever, and a terrible being, with a wild outcry, sprang up from behind the monument, and rushed on them. Down the hill they flew like deer, and, after a wild flight, took refuge in the first cabin they reached. This was their version. We supply another from the mouth of the fiend, then a young stripling, and now a plodding citizen of Dublin, and proprietor of a farm near this extensive and ancient cemetery.

He was seated on the stony enclosure, when he saw, in the gloom, the two men approaching up hill. He at once conceived the design of frightening them, and for this purpose ensconced himself behind a tomb with a provision of small stones. All the ghostly machinery consisted in the groans and howlings he contrived to make, and the showers of pebbles he discharged on the adventurers. At the third attempt he himself was startled by a rustling among the dry weeds and stones behind, and his headlong charge was the result of his panic. Of course he managed not to come up with the fugitives.

We must not omit mention of the Fetch (qu. *Feach*, to see). But the readers of *Chambers's Journal*, and the works of German physiologists, and *Harold* and the *Strange Story* will comprehend (if the matter be comprehensible) how the human being under *un*happy circumstances can (involuntarily in most cases) project some outer casing, or emanation, or larva, or *Scin Læca* (horrible name). If this phantom be seen in the morning it betokens good fortune and long life to its prototype; if in the evening a near death awaits him. This superstition was known and felt in England even in the reign of Elizabeth. We quote a passage from Miss Strickland's account of her last illness:—

"As her mortal illness drew towards its close, the superstitious fears of her simple ladies were excited almost to mania, even to conjuring up a spectral apparition of the Queen while she was yet alive. Lady Guildford, then in waiting on the Queen, leaving her in an almost breathless sleep in her privy chamber, went out to take a little air, and met her Majesty, as she thought, three or four chambers off. Alarmed at the thought of being discovered in the act of leaving the royal patient alone, she hurried forward in some trepidation, in order to excuse herself, when the apparition vanished away. She returned terrified to the chamber, but there lay the Queen still in the same lethargic slumber in which she left her."

Within a few days an unexplained mystery has been communicated to us. It is here given without any further commentary than our assurance of the good faith of our informant, who equally vouched for the veracity of her authorities, one of them being the principal witness of the apparition.

THE DOCTOR'S FETCH.

In one of our Irish cities, and in a room where the mild moonbeams of a summer night were resting on the carpet and on a table near the window, Mrs. B——, wife of a doctor in good practice and general esteem, looking towards this window from her pillow, was startled by the appearance of her husband, standing near the table just mentioned, and seeming to look with attention on a book that was lying open on it. Now the living and breathing man was lying by her side, apparently asleep; and greatly as she was surprised and affected, she had sufficient command of herself to remain without movement, lest she should expose him to the terror which she herself at the moment experienced. After gazing at the apparition for a few seconds, she bent her eyes on her husband, to ascertain if his looks were turned in the direction of the window, but his eyes were closed. She turned round again, though dreading the sight of what she now felt certain to be her husband's fetch, but it was no longer there. She lay sleepless throughout the remainder of the night, but still bravely refrained from disturbing her partner.

Next morning Mr. B—— seeing signs of disquiet in his wife's countenance while at breakfast, made some affectionate inquiries, but she concealed her trouble; and at his ordinary hour he sallied forth to make his calls. Meeting Dr. C—— in the street, and falling into conversation with him, he asked his opinion on the subject of fetches. "I think" was the answer, "and so I am sure do you, that they are mere illusions, produced by a disturbed stomach acting upon the excitable brain of a highly imaginative or superstitious person." "Then," said Dr. B—— " I am highly imaginative or superstitious, for I distinctly saw my own outward man last night, standing at the table in the bedroom, and clearly distinguishable in the moonlight. I am afraid my wife saw it too, but I have been afraid to speak to her on the subject." "You have acted like a sensible man; but now be off to your patients, as I must run to mine."

About the same hour on the ensuing night the poor lady was again roused, but by a more painful circumstance. She felt her husband moving convulsively, and immediately after he cried to her in low and interrupted accents, "Ellen, dear, I am suffocating; send for Dr. C——" She sprang up, huddled on some clothes, and, without waiting for the slow movements of the servant, she ran to his house. He came with all speed, but his efforts for his friend were useless. He had burst a large blood-vessel in the lungs, and was soon beyond human aid.

In the passionate lamentations which the bereaved wife could not restrain in the presence of the physician, she frequently cried out, "Oh! the fetch, the fetch!" At a later period she told him of the appearance the night before her husband's death; and as he thoroughly believed her statement, it involved the theory he henceforth entertained on the subject of Fetches in considerable confusion.

It is not a difficult matter to a person of finely strung nerves to conjure up the eidolon of one in whom he or she is deeply interested.

A few accidental instances of deaths speedily following on such manifestations were sufficient to establish the existence of fetches.

THE APPARITION IN OLD ROSS.

An instance came under our own notice of the almost establishing of a ghost story that would have braved investigation and contradiction. A gentleman farmer, Mr. J—— of Old Ross, was returning home in company with his daughter, about eleven o'clock at night, from a visit paid in their neighbourhood. They were going up a steep hill, with a stiff breeze at their backs, and as they advanced they saw on the top of the ascent a headless man, perfectly motionless. The poor young woman was terribly frightened, and held convulsively by her father's arm. He was also terrified not a little, but his habitual piety came to his aid. "Don't fear, child," said he; "we are in God's presence, and under His protection. This thing, if it be evil, cannot harm us without His permission." So, though his heart beat violently, he advanced, supporting his daughter; and when they were at the proper distance, their apparition changed into a poor ass, who had selected that spot to face the wind, with legs firmly planted and head lowered. The poor young lady nearly fainted, but they managed to get home without further adventure. Had they turned on one side at the first glimpse of the dreadful sight, the hill would have been a haunted one to this day.

PART IV

OSSIANIC AND OTHER EARLY LEGENDS

OSSIANIC AND OTHER EARLY LEGENDS

IT never entered the head of the glorious author of the *Iliad*, or his separate rhapsodies, to publish his work by subscription, or sell his copyright to the Longmans, or the Murray, or the Macmillan of Ephesus or Athens : such literary patrons did not exist in his day. He recited it in the Theatre of the Agora, and was well or ill requited. So no Irish *Bolg an Dana* (wallet of poems) in the good old times, with a new work ready for issue, would walk into Luimneach, or Portlairge, or Baile-atha-cliath,[1] with his manuscript in his scrip, and make arrangement for its publication. He betook himself to the hall of king or chief, or to the fair of Tailtean, and recited his production to an excitable crowd. If the subject was a fine-spun treatise in narrative, *à la Balzac*, on the physiology of marriage, or the long-enduring woes of a lady not appreciated by her coarsely-moulded husband, or the tortures of a man of fashion who longs for a divorce, he would soon detect a portion of his constituents yawning, and the rest striving to escape from the uninteresting lecture.

But our sixth or ninth century-man knew better. He was a poet or story-teller of the first or second order ; and if he had lately invented nothing new, he rattled on with a siege, a burning, a battle, an adventure in a cavern,

[1] Limerick, Waterford, or Dublin.

a search over land and sea for some priceless commodity, a love-chase, a war between the Ard-Righ at Teamor and one of his petty kings, or an adventure of the Fianna in some stronghold of the Danaan Druids, where they underwent spells, and at last found an unexpected deliverance. Sometimes it was a coward-hero, who endured troubles and terrors for a whole night in a strange castle, and in the morning found himself uncomfortably shivering in a ditch. Occasionally a wife was false, and the strife waged by the wronged husband against faithless spouse and lover furnished a theme. But the poet chiefly dwelt on the hairbreadth escapes of the false fair, and the wonderful adventures that befell all parties, and made no attempt to prove marriage an unjust and tyrannical institution, or to show the blessings that would hallow a cheap system of divorce.

The *filea* or *scealuidhe* addressed, even as a modern playwright, a mingled audience, including all ranks between chieftain and horse-boy, and sought the qualities of a composition that would interest all. He studied the motives, and passions, and conditions that interest or sway humanity—suspense, surprise, love, hatred, rest, action, fear, horror, love of country, of tribe, of family, clanship, supernatural awe, &c. ; and within the frame of his story he introduced more or less skilfully all these passions or sentiments, intimately combined with his facts. Above all, as the modern scene is never to be left unoccupied, and philosophical speculations or poetical descriptions to be of brief continuance, so the story-teller of ancient days admitted but few quiet intervals in his narrative. Heroic or superhuman action, quick succession of wild events, intercourse with spiritual beings, &c. were all managed so as to surprise and keep the interest of the assembly on the alert and tightly strung, till it was his pleasure to bring his story to a close.

There is no pressing need of pity or contempt for the childish taste possessed by the kings, and chiefs, and franklins of old in common with their wives and daughters. There was no such thing as learned leisure for any of the conditions of humanity mentioned, no sitting in comfortably furnished libraries, reading the last quarterly, monthly, or weekly. The king was leading his troops to battle, heading them in the strife, or devising measures with his Ollamhs or Fileas for the better or worse government of his province. The chief had a less extent of land and fewer individuals to attend to, but his life also was fully occupied at the proper business of his chieftaincy, or in the battle or chase. The grazier had his land and his cattle to look after, and queens, chieftainesses, and graziers' wives found the hours too short for the well administering of their households. A late dinner or early supper put an end to the daily cares, and the poets in the early times, and the prose story-teller later on, helped men and women to forget their own cares for two or three hours by their wondrous recitals. Would it have been a wise measure on the part of the story-teller to relate a narrative having the same relation to the state of existing society as the modern novel has to our own? Not at all. If he drew a faithful picture of the common life of the time, he would find his noble audience yawning or going to sleep.

Every one had come to be interested or electrified; every one's expectations were enhanced by those of his neighbours. So the grand, the terrible, the deeply affecting, and -occasionally the ludicrous, must be presented. The earliest subjects of our old bards were the real events of days then ancient, the exploits of the ancestors of the noble chiefs or kings before them, all of course magnified by the glowing medium of romance and poetry through which they were presented.

When the stories lost their first poetic garb, they were not left to the greater or less skill of the prose storyteller. Some of the ancient alliterations, pleasant combinations of sounds, and happy formulas were kept in memory, and story-telling retained its prestige as an art even to the close of last century. Joseph Cooper Walker, in his *History of the Irish Bards*, presented the engraved portrait of one of the latest, Cormac Coman, who used to delight the Connaught households in the long winter evenings with his old-world tales of Oisin and Osgur, and the rest.

Our fair readers, part of whose every-day occupation is the perusal of the sentimental woes or the terrible machinations of the heroes and heroines of the circulating library, will doubtlessly pity the condition of the daughters or young wife of Irish or Highland chief, who had nothing more soothing or exciting or higher in quality than such stories as these to occupy their leisure hours in their boudoirs, called by themselves *Grianans*, sunny chambers. They will, perhaps, bestow an extra portion of that blessed quality on them when they learn that even these were not accessible unless they wished to peruse them closely written on vellum, in small, cramped characters, no punctuation, no breaks, and very small margins. But household duties, attendance on sick or wounded followers, an occasional ride after hounds or hawks, and embroidery with the needle, occupied their fifteen or sixteen hours of waking, and novel reading was unknown.

Of the beautiful work in metals, and of the delicate illuminations of gospels and missa's, we have abundance of specimens rescued from time's ravages. Of the labours of the fair Celtic wives and daughters we have, alas! no relics; the frail materials on which their care was expended have long since been the prey of the moth, and of neglect—still more destructive.

Thus the Celtic ladies of former days, having no conveniences or comfortable opportunities for indulging in the luxury of fictional woe and terror, were obliged to have recourse to the occupations we have mentioned to employ their hours. They listened to the recitations that succeeded the evening meal, and, having no criterion at hand to determine their quality, were thoroughly satisfied with them. If our readers are not equally pleased, we regret the circumstance, but can offer no comfort.

Sir William Temple relates an instance of an Irish north-country gentleman of his day employing a professional story-teller, night after night, to put him to sleep. This he always managed to do by reciting one of the wild magical tales in which Fion and his knights had to contend with gruagachs and hags, who by their potent spells could reduce robust and active warriors to the condition of weaklings of a year old. The Rev. Matthew Horgan, the intimate friend and zealous fellow-labourer of the late John Windele in the fields of Celtic archæology, was during his later years obliged to have recourse to a similar auxiliary. This *scealuidhe* was Tim or Thigue O'Sullivan, a man without education, but rich in the second stage of Ossianic lore, in which all the original poetic form is lost, with the exception of some remarkable quatrains appearing here and there through the prose.

He, taking his station near the good clergyman's bed, would commence, and conduct his mighty men of old through their trials; and by dint of the soft, guttural, gliding sounds of the Gaelic, uniform pitch of voice, and frequent repetitions, such as may be found even in Homer, would at last bring the thick folds of slumber down on the priest's eyes. He was very careful, however, not to cease his monotonous lay on the first appearance of sleep, nor for several minutes afterwards; for he had found by experience that the change from the uniform hum to absolute silence would rouse his patient, and reimpose his own tiresome task.

Even when story-telling was a national institution, the highest professors were not expected to have in their mental storehouse more than seven times fifty separate tales: the ordinary professors had by no means so many. So the patient had probably already heard all in the possession of his literary retainer.

The readers of the tales here collected are necessarily unconscious of the pleasure which the recitals of the originals gave the Irish-speaking listeners of former days. For this there is no remedy. The tales are given, not so much for their intrinsic merit as for their value as literary curiosities,—relics of the social usages of a people whose circumstances, aspirations, and tastes were as different as they well could be from those of their living descendants. An archæological artist may have it in his power to present us with a good idea of the outer man of an ancient Celt. If it were given to us to overhear the conversation of the same Celt and a few of his neighbours on some phases of their ordinary life, we should obtain a glimpse of his character, his likings, his dislikings and his tastes. As this is out of the question, we must content ourselves with such knowledge as the stories to which he listened in his hours of relaxation can afford. Let the reader indulgently reflect on these circumstances when scanning the qualities of these Gaelic remains.

Most welcome to the audiences of kings or chiefs' halls were the wild stories of the *Fianna Eirionn*, or Heroes of Ireland, some of whom really flourished in the third century of the Christian era.

Of the numerous Ossianic legends found among the Irish-speaking people of the west and south, there were but two or three current in the north-west part of Wexford in the early part of this century, though the elders of families among the farmers and peasants all spoke, or at least understood Irish.

Jemmy Reddy, the authority for the adventures of *Gilla na Chreck an Gour*, is our warrant for these also.

FANN MAC CUIL AND THE SCOTCH GIANT.

The great Irish *joiant*, Fann Mac Cuil, lived to be a middle-aged man, without ever meeting his match, and so he was as proud as a paycock. He had a great fort in the Bog of Allen, and there himself and his warriors would be playing soord and pot-lid, or shootin' bowarras, or pitchin' big stones twenty or thirty miles off, to make a quay for the harbour of Dublin. One day he was quite down in the mouth, for his men were scattered here and there, and he had no one to wrestle or hurl, or go hunt along with him. So he was walking about very lonesome, when he sees a foot-messenger he had, coming hot-foot across the bog. "What's in the *win'* (wind)?" says he. "It's the great Scotch giant, *Far Rua*, that's in it," says the other. "He's coming over the big stepping stones that lead from Ireland to Scotland,[1] and you will have him here in less than no time. He heard of the great Fann Mac Cuil, and he wants to see which is the best man." "Oh, ho!" says Fann, "I hear that the Far Rua is three foot taller nor me, and I'm three foot taller nor the tallest man in Ireland. I must speak to Grainne about it."

[1] The Giant's Causeway, of which there are now visible only some slices at the two extremities. Those trustworthy chroniclers, the ancient bards, affirm that it is the work of the ancient Irish and Scotch men of might, laid down to facilitate their mutual visits.

Well, it wasn't long till the terrible Scotch fellow was getting along the stony road that led across the bog, with a sword as big as three scythe blades, and a spear the *lenth* of the house. "Is the great Irish giant at home?" says he. "He is not," says Fann's messenger: "he is huntin' stags at Killarney; but the vanithee is within, and will be glad to see you, Follow me if you please." In the hall they see a long *deal* (fir) tree, with an iron head on it, and a round block of wood, with an iron rim, as big as four cart wheels. "Them is the shield and spear of Fann," says the messenger. "Ubbabow!" says the giant to himself.

"You're welcome, Far Rua," says Grainne, as mild as the moon. "Sit down, and take such fare as God sends." So she put before him a great big griddle cake, with the griddle itself inside, that had a round piece cut out at one part of the rim; and for a beefsteak, she gave him a piece of a red deal plank, with a *skrimshin* of hard meat outside. The first bite the giant give the cake, he broke three of his teeth; and when he tried the beef the other ones stuck so fast in the deal, he could not draw them out. "By me soord, ma'am," says he, "this is hard diet you give your company." "Oh, Lord love you!" says she, "the children here think nothing of it. Let us see if the infant would object." So she takes the cake over where Fann was lying in the cradle, and offers him the part where the piece was taken out of the griddle. Well, he bit off the bread with the greatest ease, chawed it, and swallyed it, and smacked his lips after it, and then he winked one eye at Far Rua. "Be the laws!" says the Scotchman to himself, "these is wonderful people."

Well, they didn't *stent* him in the drink any way. The jug of beer they laid before him would hold four gallons, and he emptied it out of spite at one offer, as he didn't get fair play at the bread and mate. "I think," says he, after his drink, "I'd like to see how Fann and his men amuses themselves after dinner." "You must see that," says the messenger. "Step out into the bawn, if it is agreeable to you." Well, when they wor outside, the messenger pointed to four or five stones, the size and shape of a gate post. "Them is their finger stones, that they do be casting to see who'll throw them farthest. It is a good throw when one of them reaches Dublin. But Fann does *mooroon* (more than enough) sometimes; and you'll see some of them sticking up out o' the say where they light after a great fling. Maybe you'd like to try your hand." He did try his hand, and after winding it round and round his head he let fly, and it went half a mile whistling through the air, and broke in a hundred smithereens on a big stone in the bog. "You'll do well," says the boy, when you come to your full growth, and get a year's practice or so with Fann." "To the d—— I pitch Fann and his finger stones!" says the big Red Man to himself.

"Well, is there any other way they divart themselves?" says the stranger. "Oh, yes," says the boy. "Fann and his men does be throwing that handball (the ball was a round stone that 'ud fill this hearth up to the mantel beam) from the bawn here over the house, and running round and catching it before it comes to the ground. Every miss counts one lost." "Wonderful quare people is the Irish," said the big man. "Maybe if it wouldn't go over with me at the first offer, it might break down the roof, and that 'ud annoy the vanithee. I'll pitch it up in the air here, and you can mark." So he gave a heave. "How high is it gone?" "Up to the window sill." "Now?" "Up to the eaves." "Dickens take it! Now where is it!" "Oh, sir, it is on your head." And indeed so it was, and levelled him also, and only he had a reasonable hard noggin of his own, it would be cracked in two with the souse the big stone gave it again' the ground.

He got up, and rubbed his poor skull, and looked very cross. "I suppose Fann won't be home to-night." "Sir, he's not expected for a week." "Well, give the vanithee my compliments, and tell her I must go back without bidding her good bye, for fear the tide would overtake me crossing the Causeway."

HOW FANN MAC CUIL AND HIS MEN WERE BEWITCHED.

The King of *Greek's* daughter had a great spite to Fann Mac Cuil, and Goll, one of his great heroes, and Oscur his grandson. So she came one day and appeared like a white doe before him; and bedad he chased her with his two hounds, Brann and another, till she led them away to the bottom of the black North. She *vanquished* from them at the edge of a lake, and while they were looking about for her, a beautiful lady appeared sitting on the bank, tearing her hair, and crying. "What ails you, lady?" says Fann. "My ring is dropped into the water," says she, "and my father and mother will murder me if I go home without it." "I'll get it for you," says he, and he dived three times one after another for it. The third time he felt the chill of death on him, and when he was handing the ring to her, he was a *decripid*, weak, gray-haired old man. "Now," says she, "maybe you'll remember the King of Greek's daughter, and how you killed her husband and her two sons." "If I did," says he, "it was on the battle-field, fighting man to man." She left him there as helpless as the child two days old, and went away with herself.

There was great sorrow and trouble that night at Fann's house, and the next day all his warriors, except Oscur, set out after him. Well, they travelled and they travelled, till they were tired and hungry, and at last they entered an old fort, and what did they see but a fine table laid out, and seven stone seats around it. They were too hungry to make much ceremony; so they sat down, and ate and drank; and just as they were done, in walks the lady, and says she—"Sith ye merry, gentlemen; I hope your meal agreed with you. Fann is at the edge of that lake you see down there; if you like, you may come with me to pay him a visit." They gave a shout of joy, but bedad, when they offered to get up they found themselves glued to their stone seats. Oh, weren't they miserable! and they could see poor Fann lying on a bank by the loch not able to stir hand or foot.

There they stayed in grief for a day and a night, and at last they saw Oscur following Brann that was after going a hundred miles in quest of him. Brann found Oscur lying asleep by the Lake of Killarney, and he barked so loud that the wolves, and *deers*, and foxes, and hares, run fifty miles away; the eagles, and kites, and hawks, flew five miles up in the sky, and the fishes jumped out on dry land. Never a wake did Oscur wake, and then Brann bit his little finger to the bone. "Tattheration to you for an Oscur!" says poor Brann, and then he was so mad he seized him by the nose. Very few can stand to have any liberty taken with the handle of their face—no more did Oscur. He opened his eyes, and was going to make gibbets of the dog, but he put up his muzzle, and began to *caoin*, and then trotted off, looking round at Oscur. "Oh ho!" says he, "Fann or Goll is in danger," and he followed him hot-foot to the North. He came up to Fann, but could hardly hear what he was striving to tell him. So Oscur put Fann's thumb to his lips, for himself wasn't able to stir hand or foot. "And now, Fann," says he, "by the virtue of your thumb, tell me how I'm to get this *pishrogue* removed." "Go," says he, in a whisper that had hardly anything between it and dead silence, "go to the fairy hill, and make the enchanter that lives there give you the drink of youth."

When he came to the hill, the thief of a fairy man sunk down seven perches into the ground, but Oscur was not to be circumvented. He dug after him till the clay and stones made a new hill, and when they came to the solid rock he pinned him, and brought him up to the light of the sun. His face was as gray as ashes, and as shrivelled as a *russidan* apple, and very unwilling he was to give up the cup. But he was forced to do so, and it wasn't long till Oscur was by Fann's side, and spilling a little, drop by drop, down his throat. Up he sprung five yards in the air, and shouted till the rocks rung; and it wasn't long till himself, and Oscur, and Brann were in the middle of the enchanted men. Well, they were nearly ashamed of themselves pinned to their seats, but Oscur didn't leave them long in grief. He spilled some of the cup down by every man's thigh, and freed he was; but, be the laws, there wasn't hardly a drop in the cup when he come to the ounkran of a make-game, foul-mouthed, bald Cunyán (Conan). He could only free a part of one thigh, and at last Oscur, getting onpatient, took him body and sleeves, and pulled him off the stone. What a roar he let out of him! his breeches—if it's breeches they wore in them ould times—stuck to the seat, and a trifle of Cunyán's skin along with it. "Whist!" says Oscur, "we'll get a sheep-skin sewed on you, and you'll be as comfortable as any May-boy after it."

Well, when all were free, they gave three shouts that were heard as far as the Isle of Man; and for a week after they got home they done nothing but eating the *vengeance* of goats and deers, and drinking wine, and *meadh*, and beer that the Danes larned them to make from heath; and gentle and simple might go in and out, and eat and drink, and no one was there to say—"Who asked you to visit us?"

The admirers of our Ossianic relics will give anything but a hearty welcome to these disfigurations of the brave old bard. But let them not blame poor Reddy too much. He understood Irish, for his father and mother spoke it pretty fluently, but they would not suffer their children to speak it. They got them taught to spell and read English, and would not allow of anything that might tend to counteract their studies. Some few of the native poetic beauties would flash out here and there, but they were stifled in the colloquial style natural to the story-teller.

QUALIFICATIONS AND DUTIES OF THE FIANNA EIRIONN.

With the name and opinions of modern Fenians every one's ears have been dinned. For the sake of that portion of our readers who have not devoted much attention to Gaelic archæology, we devote a few pages to the subject of that body of ancient militia whose title they have appropriated.

As to the derivation of the word we are not so much embarrassed by the poverty as the abundance of the materials. *Fine* means tribe, family, kindred, nation, soldier, vineyard; *Finne*, whiteness, fairness; *Fion*, wine, truth, ancient; *Fionn*, a head, chief, troops, sincere, true, fine, fair, pleasant. The term *Fianna*, giants or soldiers, was applied to the warriors of Albanach (Scotland) and Britain, as well as to those of Ireland.

This standing army, if the bardic chronicles are reliable, consisted of men of good birth, and what would in later times be called knightly rank. They were not distinguished by any name of the same signification as *Knight*, which in its parent language, the Teutonic, simply meant *Valet*. They were *Luuchs*, heroes (the German *Helden*), and when associated to a military order they were *Curai*, companions. A postulant for admission among the Fians should be a free man in every respect, and so expert that, merely armed with a stick and shield, he could defend his otherwise unguarded body from half a dozen men darting spears at him from a distance of nine ridges. If he escaped unwounded, he was required to run through a tangled wood with his long hair hanging loose, and get out at the other side, uncaught by the same or another half dozen warriors. If an ill-conditioned bough as low as his knee crossed his path, he should run under it; if it were no higher than his shoulder, he should bound over it. Having passed this bodily ordeal he was obliged to swear fealty to the *Ard Righ* (head king), to promise on his word as Curadh to be charitable to the poor and to respect women. His near relations were also engaged never to seek *eric* (blood-fine) for his death, but to leave that care and the defence of his honour to his brothers-in-arms.

During the winter half year, the Fians were entertained at the expense of the kings and chiefs. In the other they spent most of their time fishing and hunting, when not watching for invaders. They took their principal meal in the evening, and this was the programme of mealtime and bedtime :—Through the forest, and on the plains, and on the hillsides, were small circular cavities, paved with stones, and surrounded with low stone walls. A party of hunters arriving here in the afternoon made a strong fire of brushwood in this pit, and disposed therein several loose stones, of which there was a large provision lying about. The fire having burned down, and the embers being cleared away, a layer of venison or wild boar's flesh, as it might be, wrapped in grass or rushes, was laid on the hot bottom, and a layer of the red-hot stones on this. Then succeeded another layer of meat similarly garnished, and crowned by hot stones No. 2, the process being again repeated if necessary.

Near these "Ovens of the Feine,"[1] as they are still called by the peasantry, was a bathing tank supplied by some neighbouring stream, and here, while the dinner was cooking, the warlike hunters bathed. A large bothy, built of sods, stones, scraws, and branches, served for dining-hall, and thither the savoury joints were conveyed, and consumed by the men just risen from their refreshing bath. The beds of the Fians were composed of withered grass and heath, with the flowered tops uppermost. The coverlets were the cloaks of the sleepers, or stag and wolf skins.

[1] The final *e* is always heard in Celtic words.

Remains of these primitive ovens are still extant, the soil about them being distinguished by its dark colour. They are also met with in the Scottish Highlands.

The institution was not long-lived. No records are left of it of longer extent than three generations. Portions of the troops were always in the neighbourhood of harbours; and if the approaching foe was strong in men and barques, signals sped from hill to hill until a sufficient band of defenders was collected.

If the following event happened to be as true as it was remarkable, it would finely illustrate the great services rendered to their country by these brave militia men, who, when they were not employed in hunting or watching the coasts, occupied themselves in directing their corrachs to the coasts of Britain or Gaul, and returning with such nuggets of gold or silver, or cattle or slaves, as they could appropriate at the expense of wounds and bruises.

THE BATTLE OF VENTRY HARBOUR.

On one occasion, while their chief, Fion, and his friends, were enjoying existence, swimming and fishing in the Sionan, word was brought to him from the warder stationed at the harbour of *Finntraighe* (White Strand, Ventry), that Daire Donn, King of Rome and all the world, except Erinn, had been conducted by a recreant member of the Fianna to Glas Carraig (Skellig Rocks), and was now with his mighty fleet lying in the harbour mentioned, ready to land, and make his domain and the entire surface of the earth one and the same.

Fleet runners now carried the news to the separate corps throughout the island, including a remnant of the Danaan race settled at Conal Gavra, in the present county of Limerick. The warriors nearest the post of danger hastened thither, and for a year and a day there was a terrible diurnal fight on the strand between a detachment landing from the ships and an equal number of Fenian heroes, one great warrior generally slaying a couple of hundred of the opposing party, and securing a portion of the tale to himself, just as Agamemnon, or Diomede, or Patroclus, had a book of the *Iliad* which he might call his own. It all ended, as it should, in favour of native valour and patriotism, few of the captains of the King of the World surviving the year and day's war. The brave young Gall, Prince of Ulster, worked himself into such a state of fury in the fight, that he lost his senses, and fled to the lonely Glenn na-n-Gealt, in Kerry. And there all the lunatics in Ireland must repair before or after they pay the great debt.

Spenser had a great dislike to the custom prevalent in his day, which sent up in summer-time the inhabitants of the plains and valleys to the hills, where they lived, in imitation of the *Fianna*, on game and the produce of their cattle, till their instinct warned sheep and cows of the suitable moment to seek the shelter of the lowlands. He complained that this usage afforded the disaffected means of shelter and of support among these dwellers in the "scraw-covered" shielings, and opportunities of concocting designs unfriendly to the authority of his beloved Gloriana.

It must be acknowledged that our information as to the institution of the national militia is given by our romantic historians alone, who have invested a real personage of military fame—Fion, son of Cumhail—with the title of their commander in the days of King Cairbre. This hero was slain at the Boyne, A.D. 283, and the *Fianna* stood in such a defiant attitude towards the monarch some twelve years later, that he assailed them, with the assistance of the Connaught portion of the body, in the memorable battle of *Gavra* (Garris-town, in Meath), where most of their chiefs were slain, and an end put to the institution. This battle is sung in a poem ascribed to Oisin, son of Fion, preserved in the Book of Leinster, a manuscript of Finn M'Gorman, Bishop of Kildare, who died 1160.

The following quatrains are not from this version, but will give a good idea of the style of the old heroic poetry, when divested of the peculiar aids of alliteration, position, and rhyme. Oisin, who alone of all the Fenian heroes survived the fight, remained in life in Tir-na-n-Oge till the arrival of St. Patrick, to whom he related the strife where he lost all his loved comrades, together with his son, Oscur the Invincible, whom he mentions as treachously slain by King Cairbre.

> "My son urged his course
> Through the battalions of Tara,
> Like a hawk through a flight of birds,
> Or a rock rushing down a steep.
>
> *　　　*　　　*　　　*
>
> "As many as two score shields
> In each fierce onset,
> Mac Garraidh, the pure, and my own son,
> Broke in the fight of Gavra.
>
> "Until the grass of the plain is numbered,
> And every grain of sand on the seashore,
> All who fell by my son
> Cannot be counted.
>
> "Many a mail of noble warriors—
> Many a fair head-piece
> And shields lay on the plain,
> With chiefs bereft of life.
>
> *　　　*　　　*　　　*
>
> "I found my son lying down
> On his left side, by his shield,
> The sword clutched in his right hand,
> And the red blood pouring through his mail.
>
> *　　　*　　　*　　　*
>
> "We raised the manly Oscur
> Aloft on the shafts of our spears,
> Bearing him to another pure mound,
> To remove his bloody harness.
>
> *　　　*　　　*　　　*

"We buried Oscur of the red weapons
On the north side of Gabhra,
With Oscur Mac Garraidh of great deeds,
And Oscur, son of the King of Lochlann."

Of Fion, the man honourably mentioned in the Book of Leinster, and by the Four Masters, there was never related more than that he was a redoubted champion; but the poets and romancers seized on him, and his sons and grandson, and elevated them and their immediate friends into heroes of surpassing might, round whom moved at a greater or less distance other heroes—friends and foes—and all fertile in exploits and adventures sufficient to fill libraries entire. And while the people, generation after generation, took comparatively slight interest in the deeds and renown of living chiefs, and soon forgot the notables of the age just past, they carefully retained the exploits of heroes, some altogether fabulous, and others of whom nothing was authentic but their names and their existence in the third century. Fion and his heroes were to the Irish romancers what Diedrich of Berne, Charlemagne, and King Arthur, with their respective knights, were to the bards of Germany, France, and Brittany.

THE FIGHT OF CASTLE KNOC.

Cumhail, father of Fion, King of Leinster, and head of the Clan Baoisne, ruled the Fianna in the reign of Con of the Hundred Battles. While in Alba (the Highlands), checking the attempts of the Romans and other unprincipled marauders, *circa* A.D. 154, the Ard-Righ Con transferred his honours and dignities to his own *Daltha* (foster-father), Crimthan. Hearing this, Cumhail sped back in the "high-cornered, big-bellied, broad-sailed barque," landed at Inver Colpa (Drogheda), dispossessed Crimthan, and made raids on *Breʒia* (the level plain from the Boyne to the Dublin hills), and on to Meath, and took spoils of cattle and slaves, male and female, and cloaks and bucklers, and well tempered glaives (*Cloidhimh*, pron. *Chloive*) and coats of mail, and chessboards and chessmen. Loudly complained the graziers, and farmers, and small chiefs to the king, and, in consequence, he sent swift messengers to Naas of the Kings, then the capital of North Leinster, ordering Cumhail to attend a national meeting at Tara, and answer for his outrages. On his refusal, Con summoned to his aid Goll Mac Morna, the best warrior in Connaught, along with the Ulster chiefs, Achy of the Red Neck, Iomchy of the Red Arm, and the terrible warrior Liath Luachra (Grey Rushes), a chief disgraced by Cumhail. Coil was promised the command of the Fianna, and Liath Luachra the magic Corrbolg (Body Defence) of Cumhail, and the fisherman of the Boyne, who was accustomed to take in three draughts at the mouth of that "yellow-valed, ever-beautiful river, as many fishes as sufficed for a meal to all the forces of Cumhail."

So defiance was made, and a pitched battle appointed on the grassy plain on the east side of Cnucha (Castle Knoc). While the preparations were making, Cumhail met in one of his hunting excursions the fair Muirrean, daughter of the powerful Druid, "Tadg of the Luminous Side," whose abode was the fortress of Almuin (Hill of Allen). Evil fate at the time gathering thick round the path of the warrior, he forgot his knightly vows, and that reverence for female purity so deeply inherent in the Celtic disposition.

Deep and torturing remorse seized on him when too late; but her incensed and powerful father vowed by his gods to devote him to irrevocable defeat and death. When the day of strife approached, he sent the swift-footed Balar to the fairy hill of Maev the Sighe-Queen, who abode in the enchanted hill at Carmain (Wexford), for the impenetrable coat of mail the Corrbolg, and the accompanying resistless, jewel-hilted glaive and spear. But the revengeful Tadg spread such a thick druidic fog on his path, that he was unable to find the enchanted mound. So Cumhail was obliged to content himself with the inferior arms furnished by *Aoiné* (Venus), the presiding Sighe-Queen of Naas.

Warnings were given to Cumhail's confederates that for his forgetfulness of his vow, which in common with all the Fianna he had made, never to do wrong to woman, defeat and death awaited him at Cnucha. Most of them had scattered homewards before the day of battle dawned. With a strong presentiment of his ill-fortune full upon him, on the eve of the battle he called before him Boghmin, his female runner, and thus addressed her :—

"My fleet and faithful Boghmin, the night of the grave is gathering fast round me, and I address you for the last time. Speed to the rath at Almuin. Seek the golden-haired Muirrean, and tell her my chief sorrow on quitting life arises from the wrong she has suffered at my hands. Attend her diligently, and when my son is born flee away with him, and let him be brought up in the most secret places you can find. Otherwise the wrathful Tadg will destroy him. The wise Conmean, the Druid, has foretold his fortune, and that under his rule the fame of the Fianna of Erinn shall much exceed what it enjoys under mine. Entreat the forgiveness of the golden-haired Muirrean for me. Farewell!"

When the next morning sun was shining pleasantly over the gorse-sprinkled plain (now the western portion of Phœnix Park), the clans of Leinster, and those of the noble Eogan of Munster, a small but compact force, rushed among the multitudinous hosts of Ulster, Conacht, and Meath, even as a score of noble and fierce dogs would among a pack of desperate and ravenous wolves. They overturned them, they pierced their masses; they levelled, and slew, and scattered their foes, who were still replaced by fresh and strong fighting men, till their tired arms could scarce wield the sword or fling the spear. Hundreds and hundreds perished that day by the resistless arms of Cumhail; and when he and Goll, son of Morna, engaged, it was like the meeting of two hawks on a rock, two furious bulls, or two raging lions. Deep was the hard brown skin of Goll gashed by the keen blade of Cumhail; but when they were separated by the press of struggling warriors, the heavy ash-shafted and keen-pointed spear of the Conacht hero darted with mighty force, tore the lorica, the silken shirt, and the heart of the mighty son of Trenmor asunder, and the green sod was reddened with his life's blood.

Again and again did the ear-piercing war-bugle of Eogan gather the Leinster and Munster troops to the waning fight; and when all hope was lost they retired in close array, and still kept their furious foemen in check. Thus ended the memorable fight of Cnucha, in the account of which no mention is made of sling, arrow, bow, mace, or battle-axe. The bronze leaf-shaped, double-edged glaive, and the spears and javelins flung over hand, were the same as those sung by Homer as doing the work of death on the plain before Troy.

THE YOUTH OF FION.

The faithful Boghmin lovingly executed her trust, and, assisted by the sage woman Fiecal, reared up the son of Cumhail in a cavern on the side of Slieve Bloom (*Blama*). She called him Deimne, and he gave evidence of his noble race at an early age. When a youth, his foster-mother ventured with him as far as Tara, at the celebration of games by youths not yet qualified for the rank of Curai. He so distinguished himself, that the King cried out in admiration, "What is the name of this *Paustha Fion* (fine youth)?" "I thank you, O Con of the Hundred Fights," answered his nurse, "for having conferred a name on him. Fion he is, and Fion he shall remain." "By your royal hand," said one of the Conacht laochs, "that is the son of Cumhail, son of Trenmor: let him be secured." But the word was too late. Boghmin, seizing her boy, and flinging him on her shoulders, had passed through the assembly before anything could be done, and the fleet runner, not yet having lost the cunning of her limbs, soon put sufficient distance between her charge and his enemies.

The next exploit performed by our youth was the acquisition of supernatural knowledge, by tasting the salmon that was intended for the Druid Fion.

This sage, not content with his own acquired wisdom, was determined on securing the "salmon of knowledge," whose taste would make him cognizant of everything passing in Erinn at any time. He stationed himself at a ford on the Boyne, and employed all his pupils, among whom was Fion (then called Deimne) catching salmon, broiling them, and serving them up. They had strict charge not to let any of the cooked fish touch their tongues or lips. One day Fion, seeing a blister on the side of the fish that was then in the pan, pressed it down with his thumb, and getting a smart burn, he applied it (the thumb) to his lips, and at once found himself aware of what was passing in the courts of Tara, of Naas, and Emania. He at once ran to the Druid and told him what had happened.

"How can this be?" said the disappointed Druid. "I know by my art that the salmon of knowledge was to be tasted by a Fion. I am Fion, and you are Deimne." "Ay, but I am Fion also, thus named by Con of the Hundred Battles himself." "Well, well, I see fate is against me. Keep yourself out of the power of the Ard-Righ for a time. When the opportunity arrives, acquaint him with your newly-acquired faculty, and he will be only too happy to make you chief commander of the Fianna."

FION'S FIRST MARRIAGE.

The only other adventure of Fion's youth for which we can find space could only be suitably told in the language of the old story-tellers. See *Ossianic Transactions*, vol. ii. Fion thus relates the exploit:—

"I lost my way, and strayed to Lughar Diega in the south. I saw two different assemblies met on two high cairns opposite each other. One was an assembly of comely men; the other, beautiful, blooming women. There was a high, terrific precipice on either side, and a windy formidable valley between. I inquired the reason why they assumed that separate position. They informed me that Shane M'Carroll, son of Crovan, King of Kerry Luachra, was seized by a current of affection and a torrent of deep love towards Donæ, daughter of Daire, and that the condition she required of him was that he should leap (over the valley) every year, but that when he came to the brink of the precipice he balked the leap. I inquired if she would marry any other man who would achieve it. She replied that she never saw a man with worse clothing than myself (this dress consisted of the skins of the animals lately slain by him for food; hence his title at the time, '*Giolla na Chroicean*'—the fellow in the skins), but that she found no fault with my personal appearance, and that she would accept me if I succeeded. I thereupon tucked myself up in my skins, took my race to the margin of the precipice, and sprang over in a truly swift, scientific manner to the opposite side. I then with a high, light, airy bound, sprang back, and the princess gave me fit clothing, and became my wife, binding me by solemn geasach to perform the same feat every year."

Fion always succeeded—one unlucky day excepted, on the morning of which he had met a hare or a red-haired woman as he approached the chasm.

As the Druid of Boyne had predicted, Fion, after making some demonstrations in Conacht, and punishing some of the foes of his family, and obtaining the favour of the King of Munster, began to engross the attention of King Cormac. He appreciated the advantage it would be to the general weal to secure the services of a chief distinguished by heroism, and endowed with such supernatural qualities as Fion possessed. So he summoned Goll to his presence, and so wrought on him by his persuasive powers (Goll was more dogged than ambitious), that he consented to hold second rank in the national militia. In the Ossianic rhapsodies he aids his chief merely through a principle of loyalty. When imminent danger approaches, he fearlessly meets it, but is never forward to undertake any of the chivalrous enterprises so frequent in the history of the body; he finds it impossible to forget that Fion's father perished by his hand. He is more redoubtable in fight than Fion himself, being only excelled by Diarmuid and the peerless Oscur. Diarmuid bears a certain resemblance, in character and fortune, to Sir Launcelot and Sir Tristrem; Fion himself to King Arthur and Agamemnon. The bald Conan is Thersites, not altogether devoid of animal courage; Goll himself is an amalgamation of Ajax and Diomed, and the rest are amiable and noble-minded as Don Quixote himself, but destitute of any striking characteristics, except in the article of fleetness possessed by Caeilte Mac Ronan, poetic inspiration by Oisin, Fergus, &c.

HOW FION SELECTED A WIFE.

This great chief had more than one bosom-partner in his time; but as we do not hear much of the institution of polygamy among the ancient Celts, it is to be hoped that he did not marry any one of them during the life of another. In his first years of fame, he found himself an object of general censure for indulging in the freedom of a single life, so he was forced by public opinion to change his state. But here arose an inconvenience. He could only ally himself to the family of one king or chief; consequently he would obtain the ill-will of many others. However, he showed himself equal to the occasion. He let it be generally understood that as his object in selecting a wife was the greater glory of the Fianna, in his becoming the father of future courageous, robust heroes, he would take his stand on a certain high hill in Munster on such a day, and he respectfully invited every lady who desired to be a mother of heroes to take her station at the base of the said hill, and at a given signal start for the summit, where he would be ready with open heart and arms to receive the fair competitor of healthy constitution and fleet limbs, who would first bless him with her presence. The invitation was not neglected. Many beauteous and active ladies sped upwards through rocks, grass, and heath at the signal, and, according to common report, Grainne, daughter of King Cormac, outstripped her rivals. As the nuptials of Fion and Grainne are differently related in one of the best of the Ossianic romances, we are inclined to think that Grainne's predecessor, the fair and fleet Maghneiss, was the successful aspirant on that day. However that may be, the hill thenceforward was called *Sliabh na Bhan Fionn* (the Hill of the Fair Women), the *Slienamon* of the vulgar tongue.

In time the Lady Maghneiss died, and he obtained the hand of the daughter of King Cormac. This marriage was unfortunate for all parties. Grainne on her wedding-day laid geasa on Diarmuid to bear her away, and the flight and pursuit form the subject of the third volume of the *Ossianic Transactions*.

PURSUIT OF DIARMUID AND GRAINNE.

Diarmuid was unhappily gifted with a *ball seirce* (beauty spot) on his shoulder, and Grainne, catching sight of it while sitting at the window of her Grianan (sunny chamber) while looking at him hurling, could no more avoid loving him than hapless Phædra, her stepson Hippolytus. When she laid geasa on him to take her away, it was with much grief he obeyed her. It was deeply wronging his chief, but to disobey a lady's injunctions was out of the question. The close pursuit and the hairbreadth escapes were what might be expected, but Diarmuid's brother warriors, Oisin, Oscur, Caeilte the swift, MacLuacha, Fergus the poet, and the others carried out Fion's revengeful intents in a way very displeasing to the wrathful chief. They gave the fugitives every opportunity of escaping, for they were fully aware of Diarmuid's unwillingness at the outset. The peasants still point out their resting-places, marked by standing stones, and still called the "Beds of Diarmuid and Grainne." Of the hero's reception of Fion's auxiliaries here is a sample taken from the *Ossianic Transactions*, vol. iii. :—

"He drew near the warriors and began to slaughter them heroically and with swift valour. He went under them, over them, and through them as a hawk would go through small birds, or a wolf through a flock of weak sheep. Even thus it was that Diarmuid hewed crossways the glittering, very beautiful mail of the men of Lochlann, so that there went not from that spot a man to tell tidings without having the grievousness of death executed upon him."

Fion was at last obliged to make peace, and on one occasion he and Diarmuid went to hunt on Ben Gulban in Sligo in company. A youth slain several years before by Donn, Diarmuid's father, was changed at the moment of his death into a Druidic boar, and appointed to slay at some future time the son of his murderer, but Diarmuid had got warning at the same time not to give chase to the magic beast. While Fion and he were conversing, the fatal animal came charging like thunder up the hill.

Diarmuid was at the time unprovided except with an inferior blade, but with this he struck the savage a mighty blow, which smashed the ill-tempered bronze in two, and his foot slipping, the beast tore his side open with his tusk. At the returning charge of the enchanted animal down hill, Diarmuid broke his skull with a strong cast of the hilt of the treacherous sword. His own life was now fast ebbing away, but it was in Fion's power to prevent his death by giving him, from a spring nine ridges away, a draught of water brought in the hollow of his joined palms. Oscur, Oisin, Caeilte, Fergus, and MacLuacha, had hurriedly arrived at the spot, and loudly and earnestly did the heroes urge Fion to haste, but he went about the unwelcome work so leisurely that when the water touched Diarmuid's lips, life had departed. Three shouts of indignation were raised by Oscur and the rest, and only for their binding vows of loyalty they would have slain their chief on the spot. In memory of the tragic deed, the place was thenceforward called the "Mound of the Sword hilt." Archæologists find a similarity between this and the legend of Venus, Adonis, and the boar.

In such importance were held fictional narrations in old times, that they were carefully classified. The following were the chief varieties :—Tales of battles, of voyages, of the taking of forts, of sieges, of deaths of heroes, of cattle-raids, of courtships, of adventures in caverns, of land and sea expeditions, of banquets, and of elopements. Then there were the mere imaginative tales in prose or verse, of which Fion or some of his friends were the heroes. The one that follows is a specimen of the class of stories relative to flights and pursuits; it is called

THE FLIGHT OF THE SLUGGARD.

After a great feast held at the palace of Almhuin, the Fianna betook themselves to Knockany, in Limerick. There Fion, setting up his tent, despatched his warriors to search the mountains that lie on the borders of Limerick, Cork, and Kerry, for game. As he was sitting in his tent playing chess, the scout placed on the brow of the hill entered to apprise him of the approach of a huge unwieldy man, leading, or rather dragging, a wretched horse after him. Coming out they beheld this worthy approaching in a most lazy mode, each step being achieved apparently by some complicated and painful operation. When he was within speaking distance, Fion accosted him. "What is your name—whence come you —and what do you seek?" "*Giolla Deacair* (slothful fellow) is the name I am called. The spot I came from is not worthy a place in your memory. No one will employ me, I'm so lazy, and so I come to seek service with the hospitable chief of the Fianna Eirionn." "And why do you bring this garran with you?" "To carry me when I go of messages, I am so lazy."

Fion, and those with him, laughed so loud that the wild game within a mile fled to their lairs. He told the lazy fellow he might stay among his giollas. "May the King of Lochlann live in fear of you a hundred years. Go, my poor garran, and graze with the noble beasts on that meadow: Fion allows you."

But Fion was scarcely set at his chess-board again, with Bald Conan opposite him, when he heard such squealing and galloping from the pasture that he was outside the tent in a moment; and there was the bony garran biting and kicking the war steeds of Oisin, of Oscur, of Fergus, and of Caeilte, and scattering them in all directions. "Dog of a sluggard," said Fion, "hasten to the pasture and secure your cursed beast, and let me not set eyes on either of you again." "Chief of the men of Erinn, the swift-footed Caeilte would be at Finntraighe, before your servant could reach that meadow. Let Conan rush and catch him by the mane, and I'll be warrant for his quiet." No sooner said than done. Conan seized the mane of the brute, and at once he stood still as if changed to stone. In vain did twigs and leather-braces sound on his ribs. With set feet he held his ground. "Bestride him, O Conan of the sharp tongue," said Slothful Fellow, "and perhaps he'll move." Up flew Conan, and strokes from his rod fell like hail on the sluggard's beast, but his legs remained as if rooted to the soil. "Ah! where has my memory fled?" said Giolla Deacair. "He will not move without feeling the weight of six men such as Conan *Maol* (the bald)."

Six of Fion's stoutest followers now mounted the steed of ill condition, and at a touch of the sluggard's rod of metal he was off to the ocean, like the arrow that cuts the air. It required the swift limbs of the chief to keep within view; and when they gained the white strand, horse and sluggard footed the waves as if they were a rolled meadow. They were Druids of the Tuath de Danaan people; and Fion, seeing the strange sight, stayed his course, sounded the *Bar Buadh*, and collected the Fianna to council.

For the pursuit of the captors and their prey over the Atlantic by Fion and a chosen band, the imprisonment of the heroes in a strong tower, and the disenchantment of the Druidic spells, we have not space.[1]

BEANRIOGAIN NA SCIANA BREACA.[2]

Fion son of Cumhail was one day separated from his knights as they were engaged at the chase, and came out on a wide grassy plain that stretched along the sea strand.

---

[1] The Fianna were disturbed by the Danaan Druids, much in the style adopted by the giants to plague Odin and his court.
[2] The MS. from which this story is extracted is distinguished by very careless spelling. The title means "the Queen with the Speckled Dagger," or with a slight alteration in the letters, "the Queen of the Many-Coloured Bed-Chamber." The principal word is pronounced *vanreen*.

There he saw the twelve sons of Bawr Sculloge playing at *comán* (hurling), and wonderful were the strokes they gave the ball, and fleeter than the wind their racing after it. As Fion approached they ceased their sport, and all coming forward hailed him as the protector of the wronged, and the defender of the island against the white strangers. "If you like to amuse yourself, Fion son of Cumhail," said the chief of one party, "take my coman, and pull down the vanity of our opponents." "I would do your party no honour with this toy," said Fion, taking the coman between his finger and thumb. "Let that not disturb you," said the hurling chief. So he pulled up a *neanthog* (nettle), and muttering a charm over it, and changing it thrice from one hand to the other, it became a weapon fitting for the hand of the son of Cumhail. It was worth a year of idle life to see the blows struck by the chief, and hear the terrible heavy sound as the coman met the ball, and drove it out of sight. And there was *Cosh Lua* (fleet foot) to pursue the flying globe and bring it back. "My hand to you," said the eldest boy, "I never saw hurling till now." Fion's party won the first game, and while they were resting for the second a boat neared the land, and a man sprung out and approached the party. "Hail, very noble and courageous chief!" said he, addressing Fion. "My lady, the Queen of *Sciana Breaca*, lays on you geasa, binding on every Curadh, that you come forthwith to visit her in her island. She is persecuted by the powerful witch *Chluas Haistig* (flat ear), and she has been advised to call on you for help." "Perhaps in vain," said Fion. "I can find out from the gift of the Salmon of Wisdom what is passing in any part of the island, but I am unprovided with charms against witchcraft." "Let not that be a hindrance," said the eldest boy of Bawr Sculloge, *Grune Ceanavaltha* (young bearded man): "my two brothers, *Bechunach* (thief) and *Chluas Guillin*[1] (Guillin's ears), and myself will go with you. We were not born yesterday."

He took two hazel twigs in his hand; and when they

[1] Guillin, the Celtic Vulcan. Several mountains have his name attached to them. One of the devil's titles is "Giolla Guillin."

came to the edge of the water, one became a boat and the other a mast. He steered; one brother managed the sail, the other baled out the water, and so they sailed till they came to the harbour of the island, and there the helmsman secured the boat to a post with a year's security.[1]

They visited the Queen, and were hospitably treated, and after they were refreshed with the best of food and liquor she explained her trouble. "I had two fair children, and when each was a year old it fell sick, and on the third night was carried away by the wicked sorceress Cluas Haistig. My youngest, now a twelve-month old has spent two sick nights. This night she will surely carry him away unless you or your young friends prevent her."

When the darkness came, Fion and the three brothers took their station in the room of the sick child; Grunne and Bechunah played at chess, Cluas Guillin watched, and Fion reclined on a couch. Vessels full of Spanish wine, Greek honey (mead), and Danish beer, were laid on the table. The two chess players were intent on their game, the watcher kept his senses on the strain, and a druidic sleep seized on the son of Cumhail. Three times he made mighty efforts to keep awake, and thrice he was overcome by powerful weariness. The brothers smiled at his defeat, but left him to repose. Soon the watcher felt a chill shiver run over him, and the infant began to moan. A feeling of horror seized on the three boys, and a thin, long hairy arm was seen stealing down the opening above the fire. Though the teeth of Cluas Guillin were chattering with terror, he sprung forward, seized the hand, and held it firm. A violent effort was made by the powerful witch sprawling on the roof to draw it away, but in vain. Another, and then another, and down it came across the body of Cluas Guillin. A deadly faintness came over him, the chess players ran to his aid, and when his senses returned, neither child nor arm was to be seen. They looked at each other in dismay, but in a moment Cluas cried, "Grunne, take your

[1] No stranger was to unmoor it for a twelvemonth. After that it became the property of the chief who owned the harbour.

arrows, you, Bechunah, your cord, and let us pursue the cursed Druidess." In a few minutes they were at the mooring post, and away in their boat they went as fleet as the driving gale till the enchanted tower of the witch came in sight. It seemed built with strong upright bars of iron with the spaces between them filled by iron plates. A pale blue flame went out from it on every side, and it kept turning, turning, and never stood at rest. As soon as the boat approached, Cluas began to mutter charms in verse, and to raise and sink his arms with the palms downwards. He called on his gods to bring a mighty sleep on the evil dweller within, and cause the tower to cease its motion. It was done according to his incantation, and Bechunah taking his cord-ladder and giving it an accurate and very powerful heave, it caught on the pike of the steep circular roof, and up he sprung fleeter than the wild cat of the woods. Looking in through the opening, he beheld the dread woman lying on the floor weighed down with the magic sleep, the floor stained with the blood which was still flowing from her torn shoulder, and the three children crying, and striving to keep their feet out of it. Descending into the room he soothed them, and one by one he conveyed them through the opening, down the knotted cords, and so into the boat. The power of the spell ceasing as soon as the boat began to shoot homewards, the tower began again to whirl, and the witch's shriek came over the waves. It was so terrible that if Cluas had not covered the heads of the children with a thick mantle, their souls would have left their bodies with terror. A dark form was seen gliding down the building, and the dash of an oar was heard from the witch's corrach, which was soon in swift pursuit. "Draw your bowstring to your ear, O Grunne," said Cluas, "and preserve your renown." He waved his arms and said his spells, and light proceeding from his finger-ends, illumined the rough, dark, foam-crested waves for many a fathom behind them. The hellish woman and her corrach were coming fleet as thought behind, but the light had not rested on the fearful figure and face a second moment when were heard the shrill twang of the bowstring, and the dull stroke of the arrow in her breast. Corrach and rower sunk in the waters; the magic light from Cluas's hands vanished, but a purple-red flame played over the spot where the witch had gone down till the boat was miles ahead.

As they approached the harbour, the landing-place and all around were lighted up with numberless torches held in the hands of the anxious people; the sight of the three children and their three deliverers made the sky ring with cheers of gladness.

At the entrance of the fort they met the mother and her attendants, and the joy the sight of the recovered children gave them is not to be told. Fion had awakened at the moment of the witch's destruction, and was found walking to and fro in high resentment against himself. He knew by his druidic knowledge that the children were safe on their return, and cheered the Queen with the glad news, and thus the people had been waiting at the mooring point.

Three months did Fion and the three boys remain with the Queen of Sciana Breaca, and every year a boat laden with gold and silver, and precious stones, and well-wrought helmets, shields, and loricas, and chess tables, and rich cloaks, arrived for the sons of Bawr Sculloge at the point of the shore where the Queen's messenger had laid geasa on the famous son of Cumhail.

To any one conversant with the spirit of the Ossianic stories, the MacPherson imposture was self-evident. In hardly a single instance is Fion found superior to any of his curais in personal prowess. He is their chief in generosity, and kindliness,[1] and wisdom; but when the terrible foreign adventurers, male or female, attack the Fianna, he shares the general doom of defeat, the " Beam of Battle " still declining on their side till set straight by " Diarmuid of the Beauty-spot," or Goll Mac Morna, or chief of all in might, invincible Oscur.

The same thing takes place in the cycles of which

[1] A saddening exception is to be found in the tale of the " Pursuit of Diarmuid and Grainne."

King Arthur, Charlemagne, and Robin Hood were the centres. But in the "Temora" and "Fingal" of MacPherson, Fion is always kept in reserve till Cuchullain and the other chiefs are put beyond fighting, and then he comes clothed in terror and gloom, and crushes the ruthless invaders—Kings of Lochlin and elsewhere.

CONAN'S DELUSIONS IN CEASH.

As Fion and some of his curai were one day employed in the chase, a druidic dwarf observing that they were tired, invited them to his hut. However much they distrusted him, they would have deemed it unworthy of their fame to shun anything that promised an adventure. They followed him home, and ate and drank, and were then accommodated with beds. They slept each in a separate apartment on beds of heath, with the flowers upwards, covered with wolf-skins. The following adventure happened to each in succession:—The room in which Fion slept was lighted up suddenly, and a woman fairer than Aoife or Maev, seated in a rich chariot drawn by dwarfish horses, drove up to the bed. She addressed him in musical tones, requesting him to take his seat beside her, and come with her to her hill palace. Fion was enchanted with her beauty, but had presence of mind to put his thumb between his teeth, and an old withered creature was before him, seated on a car of rotten sticks. He turned to the wall and remained immoveable. After some seconds the light changed to gloom, and at the moment, he put his enchanted bugle the Dord Fionn between his lips, and blew some notes on it expressive of imminent danger and caution. It was heard by Fergus, Caeilte, Diarmuid, Oisin, Luacha, Goll, and Conan; and much as each knight was under the thrall of female loveliness, each turned his face to the wall at the Sighe's appearance, even as did his chief.

At last all had been visited but Conan the incontinent, the abusive, the cunning, and the only one of the Fians unpossessed of a noble soul. At the first invitation of the fay he sprang into the chariot, and found himself tumbling headlong into a deep well in which he could hear the roar of uprushing waters, and feel the hot steam scalding him to the bone. He caught at a beam that lay across, uttered a roar that might be heard from Ceash (in Sligo) to Inis na Gloria, and was soon surrounded by his brother Fians. By the dull firelight they found him astride on a flesh-fork that lay across the caldron in which their supper had been cooked. After administering some comfort of that quality once so liberally bestowed on Job, they left him to his repose, first exhorting him to resist temptation.

He had not time to fall asleep when the same bright vision again filled the room. This time he delayed ten seconds before he sprung into the car; when he did so he found himself in the midst of a forest, and a dreadful beast, resembling a wild cat, gigantic, such as he had heard of, but never seen, springing on him from behind a tree, pinned him to the earth, and got his head in a moment into its horrid mouth. While power was left him to roar he roared, and the room was soon filled by the knights. They found him on his back writhing and crying out, and a large cat sitting at his head, and licking his greasy chin and *crommeal*[1] (moustache). "Misfortune be on you for a troublesome Conan," said Caeilte; "if you disturb us again you shall receive the discipline of the sword-belts."

Alas! when all was quiet for a while, such shouts shook the house as if the *Donn Cuailgne* and the *Donn Finnbeanach*[2] were employed at single combat. When the champions entered they could see no outward cause of torment; but the unfortunate victim was lying on his back, his hair fastened to the floor, and he twisting about in agony. "What is the matter now, you unblest Son of Mischief?" cried Fion. "Oh, have pity on me!" he cried. "I am suffering the pangs inflicted on woman-

---

[1] The ancient Irish gentry let their hair grow as long as it would, but carefully shaved the face and neck, with the exception of the upper lip.
[2] The two rival bulls in the *Tain Bo Cuailgne*, the Cattle Raid of Cooley (in Louth), the queen of Celtic epics.

kind. Chew your thumb, O son of Cumhail, and give me relief." He did so, and beheld through walls and doors the dwarf in a far-off cell, rocking himself and singing a cronan. Doors and gates gave way before the feet of the Fianna, and they were all soon surrounding the sorcerer with their javelins at his throat. " Release our companion, O Danaan of evil, or taste the bitterness of dissolution." He drew a vial from his breast-clothing, and handed it to Fion, who placed it in Oisin's hand, motioning him to go to the relief of Conan. The rest remained to watch the Druid, till they heard from the distant room a burst of laughter. Hastening back they found Conan sitting painless, but silent and sad—the upper part of his head resembling the moon at full, while a long veil of his black hair hung sorrowfully from its outer rim.

A laugh rung out from the warriors as they entered, but it was soon checked by the chief; and for fear of further evils they immediately quitted the ill-omened abode of the sorcerer; and to this day it is said to a traveller or seeker of adventures, " May you come off with better fortune than Conan did at Ceash ! "

Students of Homer and Ovid are not ignorant of the transformations their unedifying divinities spontaneously underwent, and for what purposes. Events of a similar but much less revolting character are gleaned among the dim traditions of our Celtic mythology. In a former legend is recorded how Tuirrean, Fion's aunt, having been changed into a female stag-hound by the Lianan Sighe of her husband, her nephew's celebrated hounds, Brann and Sceoluing, were born while she was enduring the transformation. In the tale which follows is recorded the double existence of Oisin and his mother as deer and human beings.

THE YOUTH OF OISIN.

As the Fianna were one day returning from the chase, a beautiful fawn was started, which fled towards their own dun. At last all had fallen back, both men and dogs, except Fion and his two favourite hounds. Sweeping along a valley-side the animal suddenly ceased her flight, and lay down on the smooth grass. Fion was amazed at this, but much more when he saw the hounds frolic round her, and lick her face and neck and limbs. To kill so beautiful and gentle a beast under the circumstances was out of the question. She followed him home, playing with the hounds, and was housed in Almuin that night.

When Fion was left alone late on that evening, a woman of fair features and rich dress presented herself before him, and declared herself the hunted fawn of that day. "For refusing the love of the Danaan Druid, Fear Doirche," said she, "I have for three years endured the nature and the dangers of a wild deer's life in a far district of Erinn, which dread 'Geasach' prevents me from naming. A pitying slave of the Druid at last revealed to me, that if I were once within any fortress owned by the Fians of Erinn, his power over me would be at an end. I flew with untiring limbs for a day, until I came into the territory of the chief of Almuin, and ceased not my flight till Brann and Sceoluing of human intellect were the only pursuers on my track. With them my life was safe; they knew me to be of a nature like to their own."

Some months passed away, during which Fion went forth neither to the fight nor to the chase, so lost was he to all his former amusements and pursuits, through his deep love for the rescued princess. But at last the *Loch-Leannach* (the Scandinavians) were in the bay of the Hill of Oaks (Howth). Seven days were the Fians absent, and on the eighth the chief was crossing the plain of Almuin with rapid strides, and wondering that his sweet flower was not looking towards him from the top of the mound. The dwellers of the fort rushed out in joy to greet their chief; but sadness sat on their faces. "Where is the flower of Almuin, the beauteous, the tender Saav?"

"Blame not her nor us, O father of your people! While the white strangers were falling beneath your axe of war, your likeness and the likenesses of Brann and Sceoluing appeared before the dun, and we thought we heard the sweet-sounding Dord Fionn blow from your lips the music that makes wounded men and women in travail forget their pains. Saav the good, the beautiful, came forth; she flew down the pass; she issued through the gates; she would not listen to entreaty or command. 'I must go and meet my protector, my love, the father of my unborn infant,' she cried, and in a few moments she was rushing into the arms of the phantom. Alas! we saw her start back with a scream, and the form strike her with a hazel wand. A gentle, slender doe was on the plain, where she stood a moment since, and with wild yelpings the two hounds chased her from the dun. Thrice, four times, she sprang towards the moat, but every time she was seized by the throat and pulled away. By your hand, O Fion, we were not idle. What we have told passed while ten could scarcely be counted twice, and by that time we were on the plain with glaive, lance, and javelin. *Mo chuma!* (my sorrow) neither was woman, nor hind, nor sorcerer, nor dog to be seen, but we still could hear the beating of rapid feet on the hard plain, and the howling of dogs. If you were to ask every four of us in which quarter the noise was heard, each would name a different one."

Fion looked upwards in anguish, and repeatedly struck the mail that guarded his breast with his clenched hands. Word he spoke none, but retired to his private apartment, and did not show himself to his people for the rest of that day, nor till the sun rose over the plain of the Liffey next morning. For seven years from that time, whenever he was not called with his Fianna to make head against the white strangers, he continued to explore every remote corner of the land for the beloved Saav; and, except in the excitement of the chase or battle, an unchanging sadness had possession of him. Nor for seven years more did he forget the matchless princess who had shed such happiness, fleet as it was, on his life. He never during that time took to the chase more than his five favourite hounds—Brann, Sceoluing, Lomaire, Brod, and Lomluath—lest he should endanger the life of Saav if his good destiny led him upon her track.

At the end of the second period, as he and some of his knights were hunting on the side of Bengulban, in Sligo, they heard a terrible clamour among the dogs, who had got before them into a defile. On coming up they found the five hounds of Fion in a sort of circle, opposing the furious efforts of their companions to seize on a stripling of noble features, but entirely naked, except for the long hair which covered him from head to foot. He stood within the circle with no sign of fear on his countenance, and, forgetful of his own peril, did nothing but gaze on the stately forms of the curai as they surrounded the dogs. As soon as the fight was stopped, Brann and Sceoluing came to the wild youth, and whined and fawned on him, and licked him, and seemed as if for the moment they had forgotten their master. Fion and the others approached, and laid their hands on his head and caressed him, and his wild nature began from that hour to be changed. They brought him to their hunting sheds, and he ate and drank with them, and soon became as one of themselves. Fion, considering his features, and seeing in them some reflexion of the sweet countenance of Saav, and comparing his apparent age with her disappearance, hoped that he was her child, and kept him continually at his side. The youth fully returned his affection, and Brann and Sceoluing seemed never tired of bounding round him and receiving his caresses. His long hair soon disappeared with the use of clothes, and as soon as he acquired the gift of speech he gave this account of what he remembered :—

He and a hind whom he tenderly loved, and who sheltered him and tended him, inhabited a wide park, in which were hills, deep valleys, streams, rocks, and dark woods. He lived on fruits and roots in summer, and in winter he found provisions left in a sheltered cavern. A dark-visaged man came at times, and spoke sometimes in soft and tender, sometimes in loud and threatening tones, to the hind, but she ever shrunk away, and looked at him with fear expressed in face, and limb, and attitude. He always departed in great anger. All this time there was no way of escaping from this park; where high steep cliffs were wanting, there were straight descents of such depth as could not be passed with life. The last time he beheld his mother, the Fear Doirche had been speaking in soft and in harsh tones alternately for a long time; but still the hind kept aloof from him trembling. At last he struck her with a hazel wand, and she was obliged to follow him, still looking back at her son and bleating piteously. He made violent efforts to follow her. He cried out in rage and sorrow, but had not power to move. He fell on the ground insensible, just as he was listening to what he supposed the expiring cries of the deer, and when he awoke he found himself on the side of the hill where some days after the dogs discovered him. He had searched days and days for the inclosure where he had so happily lived, but could discover no appearance of cliffs springing up or descending, such as had long been so familiar to his eyes.

This youth received the name of *Oisin*, and in time he became the sweet singer of the Fianna of Erinn.

In the Book of Leinster are preserved some poetic pieces attributed to Oisin, the son of Fion. Oisin and Oisin's poetry may have belonged to the real world, but if so, succeeding poets so carefully surrounded his remains with their own compositions imposed on the world as his, that they became lost to sight and hearing, and are now either extinct or dispersed in very small portions through the inferior productions of his imitators. Subjoined is a literal translation of a poetical answer given by Fion to Conane of the hill ridge, on his asking him what kind of music he preferred:—

THE FAVOURITE MUSIC OF FION MAC CUMHAIL.

"When my seven battalions gather on the plain,
And hold aloft the standards of war,
And the dry cold wind whistles through the silk,—
That to me is sweetest music!

"When the drinking-hall is furnished in Almuin,
And the pages hand the carved cups to the chiefs,
And the musicians touch the wires with their fingers,
And the drained cups ring on the hard polished table,—
Sweet to my ears is that music!

"Sweet is the scream of the sea-gull and heron,
And the waves resounding on the Fair Strand (Ventry);
Sweet is the song of the three sons of Meardha,
Mac Luacha's whistle, the Dord[1] of Fear-Scara,
The cuckoo's note in early summer,
And the echo of loud laughter in the wood."

The next tale may be considered the latest that had reference to the Fianna.

THE OLD AGE OF OISIN.

After the fatal battle of Gavra the only surviving warrior, Oisin, son of Fion, was borne away on the Atlantic waves by the Lady Niav of resplendent beauty, and for a hundred and fifty years he enjoyed her sweet society in the Land of Youth below the waters. Getting at last tired of this monotony of happiness, he expressed a wish to revisit the land where his youth and manhood had been spent, and the loving Niav was obliged to consent. She wept bitterly on seeing him mount the white steed, and warned him that if his feet touched earth, he would never see her nor Tir-na-n-Oge again, and that his strength would be no more than that of a newly-born child.

Alas! Fion and his heroes were scarcely remembered on the plains and by the streams of Erinn. The fortress of Almuin was a mound and moat overgrown with docks and thistles, and moss had covered the huge casting-stones of the Fianna. Where strong mounds and ditches once secured armed warriors from their foes, he found unchecked entrance, and prayers and hymns recited and sung in stone buildings surmounted by cross and spire. He saw fewer spears and many more sickles than in the days of Fion, and near the Pass of Wattles (Dublin) he found Patrick the missionary raising a lowly

[1] A war-bugle.

house of worship. As he sorrowfully rode up the Glen of Thrushes (*Glann-a-Smoll*), a crowd of men striving to raise a huge stone on a low waggon, craved his aid. Stooping, he heaved the mass on to the car, but in doing so the girth snapped, the saddle turned round, away flew the white steed, and the last of the heroes lay on the hill-side, a grizzly-haired, feeble man.

He was conveyed to Bal a' Cliath, and St. Patrick gave him a kind reception, and kept him in his house. Many an attempt did he make to convert him to Christianity, but with little success; and the conferences generally ended with Oisin's laments for the lost heroes. The saint, pitying the desolation of the brave old man, would then introduce some remark on past events, which would be sure to draw from the bard a rhymed narrative of a Fenian battle, or hunting, or invasion by the king of the world—at least of Greece—or an enchantment worked on Fion or Fergus by some Danaan Druid, such as the ones just told. The winding up would be a fresh lament over his own desolate state, and the faded glories of the once renowned Fianna.

Poor Oisin did not find the frugal larder of the saint at all to his mind—he that had been used to the profuse feasts of former hunting days, when they cut up the deer, and baked it between the heated stones in the large oven on the wild moor or mountain side. When the housekeeper twitted him with his mighty appetite, he said that when he was young the leg of a lark was as large as the present shoulder of mutton, that the berry of the wild ash was as large as a sheep, and an ivy leaf as broad as a knight's shield. He was not believed, and feeling sore in consequence, he induced a stout fellow to drive him outside the town next day in a war-chariot. They held on till they came to a mighty *dallan* (pillar-stone) on the plain of Kildare, and there the blind poet directed his companion to alight, and dig out the earth at the south side of the pillar. At a certain depth he found a rusted spear of great size, the Dord Fionn, or great war horn of Fion, and a lump of bog butter. "Sound the horn," said Oisin, "and tell me the result." The guide blew a blast, but so terrible and unearthly was the tone, that he flung down the bugle in mortal terror. A sound as of distant thunder replied, and he cried, "Oh, Oisin, a flock of furious, gigantic birds are running this way, with wings outspread, and legs like those of a battle-steed: the hound is shivering in his chain." "Give him a piece of the butter, and untie his leash." "Ah! he is now yelling and charging the fowl. He has seized one, and the rest are dispersing to the four winds. He has pulled it down and bit its throat across. Oh! he is now flying back on us with madness in his eyes, and red jaws open as a cave's mouth." "Hold the spear levelled, and let it enter his breast." And so it befel: the dog was transfixed; and the guide separating the leg and thigh of the slain fowl they returned to Ath Cliath. In Glann-a-Smoll they gathered a berry of the quicken or rowan tree, and at Izod's Tower, an ivy leaf. The lark's thigh, the berry, and the leaf were larger than those vaunted by Oisin, and thenceforward he was treated with as much consideration by St. Patrick's household as by the saint himself.

The subjoined legend was heard from the lips of an intelligent woman, who, despite the want of books in her neighbourhood, had amassed a considerable stock of information on the legendary history of Ireland, on sacred history, and even on the subject of heathen mythology. She had a retentive memory for poetry, and could recite many passages from the Iliad and Paradise Lost, and the greater part of the Battle of Aughrim. She was a woman of gentle manners, and rather looked up to by her neighbours. Much of her literary stores were obtained from one who was a wandering pedlar, a poet, and a usurer. He was gifted with a surprising memory, and would recite passages from Milton and other masters in the art for hours on winter nights at his established resting-places through the country.

Before he would begin his passages from Irish History, or Milton, or the Iliad, the children should be sent to bed; and if any ignorant yet inquisitive listener interrupted him by what he considered an untimely question, he would suspend his recitation for half an hour, or, in some cases, the entire evening. Notwithstanding his literary attainments, he was sadly deficient in what were considered good manners among the small farmers, tradesmen, and comfortable peasants. But Dhonocha Rua, his poetry, his pamphlet, for which he was tried for his life at the Summer Assizes in Wexford, in 1775, and acquitted chiefly through the exertions of George Ogle, his sayings, his eccentric manners, and his lawsuits, would make an article in themselves. We must return to Mrs. K. and her.

LEGEND OF LOCH NA PIASTA.[1]

A long time ago, the pool near the bridge of Thuar was infested by a terrible beast in the shape of a dragon. He laid waste all the Duffrey from Kilmeashil out to Moghurry, and the king of this part of the country didn't know what to do. His very breath was so strong that he could suck a horse into his throat, if he smelled him within three miles of his pool.

At last messengers were sent to the court of the head king of Ireland, who lived somewhere in Munster, to see if he would sent some great warrior to circumvent this devil of a serpent, that would soon not leave a single family alive on this side the Slaney.

Off went the messengers, and nothing need be told of their travels till they came to the court. They up and told their story, but the king was unwilling to fix on any one, it was so entirely dangerous. However, the hot blood was never wanting among the Irish, and so three brave fellows—an O'Brien, an O'Farrel, and an O'Kennedy—volunteered.

Well, one of these, I won't say which, was so impatient to set out, nothing could be like it; and "if the

[1] Pool of the *Worm* (Serpent).

first lot didn't fall on him, he'd roar his arm off." But what will you have of it? The day before they were to leave, the buck got an impression on his chest, or the palate of his mouth was down—some *meeah* was over him, at any rate : he said he wasn't fit to go, and sure enough it's the truth he was telling. There was a brother of his in the house—a big slob of a boy, that never got anything better to do than turn out the cows or thrash fodder for the cattle. Well becomes my brave lad, he goes to the king, and says he, " My family will be disgraced for ever if your majesty doesn't let me go instead of my brother." The king looked at him as if he had horns on him, but he was a fine strong young fellow, and had a good innocent look, and something very resolute in his eyes. " Well, go in God's name," says the king; " David killed Goliath with a small stone."

Off they set, by valleys and mountains, till they came to Bullawn-a-Rinka, there on the top of Coolgarrow-hill. They put up their spy-glasses, and saw the beast stretched out down below, very stupid after a fog-meal he got on a small party of strange soldiers.

"Now, if you'll consent," says the big boy, "I'll try the battle first, and if I fall it will be no great loss." But they would not agree to his offer; so they cast lots, and sure enough he got the chance. " Now," says he again, " bear a hand while the thief is asleep ; " and so they cut down trees, and made the full of a big sack of charcoal.

He got into it with a sharp skian, and made them fill all about him with the black logs. Before they closed it he says to his comrades, " Get to the top of the nearest part of Mount Leinster there beyond, and if you see a smoke near the pool after three hours, kindle a fire, and that will be a sign to all the country that the piastha is slain. You, messengers, get across to Ferns as fast as you can lay leg to ground, and tell your king what's going on."

Just as he said, just so they did, and the two knights were hardly up on the mountain when they saw the monster waking up and stretching himself. He began to snuff about, and when he turned his nose towards Coolgarrow, he began to suck like vengeance. The sack came through the air like a bow-arra, and struck the inside of his jaw with such force that it almost knocked him down. He didn't like the taste of the coals, so he swallowed the sack, body and bones; and when the boy found himself in his belly, he got out his skian and gashed away under him, and the piastha finding something going wrong in his inside, rolled away to the pool. The pain was growing worse and worse, and just as he was tumbling heels over head into the water, his belly was cut through, and out tumbled the Munster man safe and sound on the sod.

He lost no time till he made a fire; and, by my word, there was another fire soon on Mount Leinster, and another on Black Stairs and every hill round, and such joy and delight as there was *we'll* never see any way.

But the brave boy was devout, too. He determined he'd build a church out of gratitude, and he prayed that he might be shown a proper place to make the foundation. So he had a dream, and the next morning he saw a duck and mallard flying along. He followed them across Thuar Bridge, and over the hill to Templeshambo. There they lighted, the drake on the near side of the stream, and the duck on the far one. So he built a monastery on one side and a nunnery on the other, and even when there wasn't a stick nor a stone of either of them left, there was not a woman buried on one side, nor a man on the other, till the devil bewitched the people of Ballinlugg to bury Blue Cap on the men's side, within a foot of the body of brave ould Daniel Jourdan, that fought with Sarsfield at Aughrim, and you all know how it fared with her.

There is scarcely a lake in Ireland without its legend of a worm or piastha, destroyed by Fion Mac Cumhail, or one of the old saints. As the early missionaries were unable to induce their converts to give up the recitation of these pagan fables, they turned them to account by investing them with a new character. The worm or serpent was the devil, and his conqueror was St.

Michael. Kilmeashil churchyard lies a little better than a mile away from Lough-na-Piastha: the name is a corruption of *Cil-Mihil*, "Church of St. Michael." The later story-tellers, however, found it more to their purpose to leave out the spiritual element, and so the legend by degrees resumed its ancient character, substituting Christian knights for three of the Ossianic heroes.

About the year 1808 a report ran through the Duffrey that some spawn of the old serpent had made its appearance in the pool, and was seen tearing across the fields that divide it from Kennystown bog, and plunging into one of the deepest bog-holes. Some hundreds of people collected after Mass one Sunday, and, armed with pitchforks, fishing spears, and spades, perambulated the bog the whole afternoon, with intent to slay the young worm. They were obliged to separate towards nightfall without a glimpse of him—head, body, or tail.

Our authority for the following legend was Owen Jourdan, already mentioned. Poor Jourdan was a genuine story-telling genius. He was not the mere talented Scealuidhe; he not only had a sense of what pleased and interested, but he could invent, if needful —*i.e.* he could form a good narrative out of two or three independent ones. With all his native powers of deceiving his auditors while relating extraordinary things, as if they had happened to himself, he was suspected of believing in the existence of fairies, and their dwelling in peculiar localities, such as the Rath of Cromogue. As for raths in general, he would as soon think of planting a ridge of potatoes in the ancient cemeteries of Kilmeashill or Templeshambo as of ploughing up the green area of one of these circular remains. We have endeavoured to retain his style of narrative; but alas! it is more than thirty years since we sat near his throne, viz., the big kitchen griddle in Tombrick.

THE KING WITH THE HORSE'S EARS.

The story I'm going to tell yous is not to be met every day. I heard little Tom Kennedy, the great schoolmaster of Rossard, say that he read it in the history of Ireland, and that it happened before the people wor Christians. It is about a king that never let himself be docked only once a year. He lived in some ould city on the borders of Carlow and Kilkenny, and his name was a queer one —Lora Lonshach it was. So, as I said, he got his hair cut once a year; and tale or tidings was never after hard of the barber that done it. About seven unlucky fellows got the honour, and after that, dickens a barber would come for love or money within a hen's race of the castle. So the king made an Act of Parlement, that all the shavers through the country was to cast lots; and if any one that got the short straw daared say boo, down went his house.[1]

So the first lot came to the son of a poor widow woman, and the bellman proclaimed it through the town; and when the poor mother heard it she had like to fall out of her stanin'; but as that wouldn't save the poor fellow's life, she thought betther of it, and run up the street like wildfire, till she came to the palace gates. She broke through the guards (I don't think the old kings in Ireland took any trouble about mindin' the gates; for if they did, how could such crowds be always at the fastes withinside?)—She broke in, as I said, and came into the big stone hall, where the king was takin' his tay—if it's tay they used in them days.

"What brings this mad woman here?" says he, flying into a passion. "Go," says he to the butler, "and put the guards into the dungeon, for lettin' me be disturbed at my break'ast, and bid the drummer give 'em thirty lashes apiece wud the cat-o'-noine-tails. What brings you here, you unfortunate ould sinner?" says he to the poor woman, that was sitten' an her heels, and pulliluin' fit to blow the roof off o' the house.

"Oh, plase your noble majesty," says she, "don't take

[1] Idiomatic for "being put to death."

Thigueen from me. If you do, who'll I have to wake and bury me dacent?" "An' who is Thigueen?" says he; "an' what have I to say to him?" "Oh, an' isn't he the unfortunate disciple that's to clip your majesty to-morrow, an' sure after that I'll never see him again." "Call the butler here," says the king to the little page. "Plaze your majesty, he's gone to see the floggin'." "It doesn't plaze my majesty, I tell you, for him to take the liberty. Call the footman." "Sir, he's gone to mind the butler." "Well, then, tundher and turf! call the coachman." "Sir, he said he'd go have an eye on the other two, for fraid they'd go look at any one dhrinkin'." "Well, then, call in the guards." "Oh, sure, they're all gettin' the floggin'." "Cead millia mollaghart—Oh, tattheration to yez all; isn't this the purty way I'm circumvented! Begone, you oul' thief," says he to the poor woman, "since I can't give you the chastisement you desarve. You'll get your *paustha* (boy) back safe an' sound; but if ever I lay eyes on you again, I'll have you hung as high as Balffe or Gildheroy."[1] "Oh, may heavens be your bed! May all the sowls that ever left you——" "Out o' my sight, you torment! My break'ast is spiled, an' I'll be all through other the whole day."

You may be sure the guards kep' an eye about 'em next day, till the king was done his break'ast; and then the poor barber came in, like a dog with a kittle under his tail. He stood, bowin', bowin', and all the blood in his body down in his brogues. So the king looked at him, an' says he, "My good fellow, you'll be at liberty to go where you please after cutting my hair; but you must first take your Bible oath——" Ah, that's true, they didn't know anything about the Bible; the oath he made him swear was, *Dar lamh an Righ* (by the king's hand), that he'd never tell anything that had ears and tongue what he'd see that day.

So he sat down on his throne, took off his green

[1] The biography of these unlucky heroes *was* to be found in the once familiar school-book—"The Adventures of the Irish Rogues and Rapparees." It has been a desideratum in our little collection these thirty years. We cannot bear the sight of the modern edition.

birredh, with his eyes fixed on the barber; and when the cap was off, up flew two brown horse's ears (but they were as long as if they belonged to an ass), and bid Thigue fall on with his scissors.

The poor lad never could rightly tell how he got through the job. He had like once to cut the edge of one ear; but such a roar as the king let at him, while he put down one ear and cocked up the other, almost terrified him to death. He'd give the world to be away some place where he could faint, and be done with the business, head and pluck.

When he was over the job, the page handed him five guineas—if it's guineas they had; and says the king, "Now, my lad, if I ever hear the wind o' the word of this after you, if I don't hang you, or thransport you to Bottomy Bay, I'll do worse; I'll get you married to a tay-dhrinking *bawrshuch* (scold) of a woman, that'll make you wish you never was born before you're three months man and wife. I will do that, by this scepthre, an' there's both wood and stick in it [1]—so mind yourself."

The poor mother was there, looking over the halfdoor, seeing if her son 'ud ever come back to her; an' at last, bedad, there he was, comin' down the street, pullin' one leg after the other; and when he came in, he tumbled head and heels into his bed, without so much as blessing himself. Ovoch, I'm always forgetting it's a hathen story I'm telling. The poor mother begged and beseecht him to tell her what ailed him, but dickens a word he let on about it. At last, after two days and nights, the doctor came; and as sure as he did, he bid Thigue put out his tongue, and let him feel his pulse. "Docthor," says the poor fellow, "there's no use in sthrivin' to blindfold the divel in the dark: I have a saycret. If I can't tell it, I'll die; and if I *do* tell it, I'll not be allowed to live." "*Sha gu dheine*," says the doctor, "is that the way the wind blows?" When he heard that the people the secret was not to be told to were to have tongues and ears on 'em, says he to Thigue, "Go into the wood there below; make a split in the

[1] The editor has not ventured to print this bizarre pleonasm without legitimate authority.

bark of one of the trees, tell your secret into the cut, and try how you'll feel after it."

The doctor was hardly out of the house when Thigue was up, and creeping off to the wood. He was afraid to stop, for fear he'd be seen, till he got into the heart of it, where two paths crossed one another. There was a nice sally tree at the spot, and so Thigue went no farther; but cut the bark in a down gash, and stooped down, and whispered into it, "*Da Chluais Chapail ar Labhradh Loingseach.*" And the maning of them words is, "The two ears of a horse has Lora Lonshach."

Well, the poor fellow was hardly done whispering, when he felt as if a mountain was lifted off his back. He'd be out of the wood home again in three jumps, only for the wakeness of hunger that was on him, and that he never felt while the secret was troubling him. A neighbour, that was strainin' her dinner on the flags outside of her door, just as he got into the town, seein' him go by so miserable-lookin', made him come in, and never did he enjoy such a dinner of good potatoes and milk before or since.

Well, with the joy, and the five guineas, and that, himself and his mother lived like fightin' cocks for a long time; but the day twelvemonth was drawing near, when he'd have to cut the king's long hair again, and his mornings began to grow very dismal on him. But, before the day come round, there was great coming and going; for the other four kings of Ireland were invited, along with all the lords and ladies that choose to travel so far, to listen to a great match of harp-playing between Craftine, the king's harper, and any one that had the consate to play again him.

Well and good, a week before the day appointed, the harper found some cracks or worm-holes, or some *meea* or other in his instrument, and so he went into the wood to look for the makings of a new one. Where should bad luck send him but to the very sally that Thigue told his secret to! He cut it down, and fashioned it into the finest harp that ever you see (an' the dickens a harp ever I saw but on a halfpenny); and when he tried it, he was enchanted himself, such beautiful music as it played!

So at last the great day came, and the streets wor filled with coaches and horses, and the big hall in the palace was crammed. The king was on his high throne, and the four other kings were before him, and behind him, and at one side of him, and at the other; and the great lords and ladies were round the open place in the centre where all the harpers were sitting; and all such people as you and me surrounded the quality, till you couldn't put the blade of a knife between the walls and themselves.

So the king gave the word of command, and up got Craftine, and the music he made was so mournful that those who couldn't cover their faces put a cross look on themselves to hide their grief. This didn't please the king; so he waved his hand, and Craftine struck up a jig, and so bothered were they all, gentle and simple, that they had no room for dancing, that they shouted out for merriment, and any one that had a hat or a cap flung it up to the rafters. By and by he got afeared that they would all rush in on himself and the other harpers for dancing room, and he changed the air to "Brian Boru's March." Well, they were not so uproarious while it was playing; but the blood was galloping through their veins like mad. Every one that had room drew his sword, and waved it over his head (and such a clatter as these swords made striking one another!), and every one cried out the war-cry of his own chief or king. This wouldn't do at all for a continuance; so he changed his hand, and made such music as angels do when they are welcoming good souls to heaven. Every one shut their eyes and leaned back, and hoped that the beautiful tune would never come to an end.

But it was forced to come to an end, and the harper let his arms fall on his knees, and every one sighed and groaned for being brought back to the world again. You may depend that Craftine was praised, and gold and silver was thrown in showers to him. Then the harpers of Leinster, Munster, Connaught, and Ulster tried their hands, and, sure enough, fine music flew out from under these hands; but all did not come within miles of Craftine's. So when they stopped, says the king to his harper,

"Give us one tune more to finish decently, and put all that we invited in good humour for their dinner. I'm afraid if you go on in this way the King of Greece or the Emperor of Morōco will be sending for you one of these days." "By your hand, my king," says Craftine, "I'm afeard of the same harp. It wasn't my fingers at all that struck out that music; it was the music that stirred my fingers. There's some pishrogue on the instrument, and I'm in dread it will play us some trick." "Oh, trick be hanged!" says the king; "play away." "Well," says the other, "I must obey your majesty—why shouldn't I? Here goes!"

Well, his fingers hardly touched the strings, when they felt like sand-paper that was powdered with nettle-tops, and out they roared as if thunder was breaking over the roof, and a thousand men were smashing stones. Every one was going to stop his ears, but a loud voice began to shout out from the strings that were keeping hold of Craftine's fingers, "*Da Chluais Chapail ar Labhradh Loingseach!*"

Well, to be sure! how the people were frightened, and how they looked at the unfortunate sinner of a king, that didn't know whether he was standing on his feet or his head, and would give half Ireland to be ten miles under ground that moment. He put up his poor hands to his head, not knowing what he was doing, and, bedad, in his fumbling he loosed the band of his birredh, and up flew the two long hairy ears. Oh, what a roar came from the crowd! Lora wasn't able to stand it; he fell in a stugue down from his throne, and in a few minutes he had the hall to himself, barring his harper and some of his old servants.

They say that when he came to himself, he was very sorry for all the poor barbers that he put out of the way, and that he pensioned their wives and mothers; and when there was no secret made of it, Thigueen made no more work about docking him than he would about you or me. Only for all the blood he got shed he'd never be made the holy show he was in the sight of people from all parts within the four seas of Ireland.

But for fear of being detected, we should willingly claim this as an original Celtic legend. But alas! the learned in classic mythology would soon humble our national vanity by quoting that troublesome old Midas of Asia Minor, renowned for the fatal pair of ass's ears bestowed on him by Apollo, the secret told to the reeds, the minstrel fashioning a Pandean pipe out of these reeds, and the treacherous miniature organ squeaking out, "King Midas has the ears of an ass!"

THE STORY OF THE SCULLOGE'S SON FROM MUSKERRY.[1]

A long time ago, before the Danes came into Ireland, or made beer of the heath flowers, a rich man, though he was but a sculloge, lived in Muskerry, in the south, and he died there too, rolling in riches, for he was a saving man. It is not often that a very thrifty and hard-working man has a son of the same character to step into his shoes, and the Muskerry sculloge was no worse off than many of his neighbours. When the young sculloge came to own the chests and the stockings full of gold, said he to himself, "How shall I ever be able to spend all this money?" Little he thought of adding anything to it. So he began to go to fairs and markets, not to make anything by buying and selling, but to meet young buckeens like himself, and drink with them, and gamble, and talk about hunters and hounds.

So he drank, and he gambled, and he rode races, and he followed the hounds, till there were very few of the guineas left in the chests or the stockings; and then he began to grope among the thatch, and in corners and old cupboards, and he found some more, and with this he went on a little farther. Then he borrowed some money on his farm, and when that was gone, he bethought him of a mill that used to earn a great deal of money, and that stood by the river at the very bounds

[1] *Sceal Vhic Scoloige O'Muscridhe.* Scolog means either a small farmer, or a generous, hospitable person.

of his land. He was never minded to keep it at work while the money lasted. When he came near it he found the dam broken, and scarcely a thimbleful of water in the mill-race, and the wheel rotten, and the thatch of the house and the wood-work all gone, and the upper millstone lying flat on the lower one, and a coat of dust and mould over everything. Well, he went about in a very disconsolate way, and at last sat down for grief and weariness on a seat fastened to the wall, where he often saw his father sitting when he was alive. While he was ready to cry in his desolation, he recollected seeing his father once working at a stone that was in the wall just over the seat, and wondering what he wanted with it. He put his fingers at each side, and by stirring it backwards and forwards he got it out, and there behind in a nook he found a bag holding fifty guineas. "Oh ho!" said he, "maybe these will win back all I lost." So instead of repairing his mill, and beginning the world in a right way, he gambled, and lost, and then drank to get rid of his sorrow. "Well," said he, "I'll reform. I'll borrow a horse, and follow the hunt to-morrow, and the day after will be a new day."

Well, he rode after the hounds, and the stag led him a fine piece away; and late in the evening, as he was returning home through a lonely glen, what should he see there but a foolish-looking old man, sitting at a table, with a backgammon-board, and dice, and box, and the *taplaigh* (bag for holding all) lying by him on the grass. There he was, shouting, and crying, and cursing, just as if it was a drinking-house, and a dozen of men gambling. Sculloge stopped his horse when he was near the table, and found out by the talk of the man that his right hand was playing against his left, and he was favouring one of them. One game was over, and then he began to lay out the terms of the next. "Now, my darling little left," said he, "if you lose you must build a large mill there below for the right; and you, you bosthoon!" said he to the right, "if you lose, but I know you won't, you thief, you must make a castle, and a beautiful garden, and pleasure-grounds spring up on that hill for the entertainment of your brother. I know I'll lose, but still I'll bet for the left: what will you venture?" said he to the young Sculloge. "Faith," said the other, "I have only a tester (sixpence) in the world, so, if you choose, I'll lay that on the right." "Done!" said he, "and if you win I'll give you a hundred pounds. I have no luck, to be sure, but I'll stick to my dear little left hand for all that. Here goes!"

Then he went throwing right and left, cheering whenever the left hand gave a good throw, and roaring and cursing at the other when two sixes or two fives turned up. All his fury was useless; the right won; and after the old fool had uttered a groan that was strong enough to move a rock, he put his left hand in on his naked breast under his coat, muttered some words that the Sculloge did not understand, and at the moment a great crash was heard down the river, as if some rocks were bursting. They looked down, and there was plain in sight a mill, with the water tumbling over the wheels, and the usual sounds coming from within. "There is your wager," said he to the right hand; "much good do you with it. Here, honest man, is your hundred guineas. D—— run to Lusk[1] with you and them."

Strange to say, Sculloge did not find himself so eager for the bottle, nor the cards and dice next day. The hundred pounds did not turn out to be withered leaves, and he began to pay the poor people about him the debts he owed, and to make his house and place look snug as it used to do. However, he did not lose his love of hunting; and on that very day week he was coming home through the same valley in the evening, and there, sure enough, was the foolish old man again, sitting at his table, but saying nothing.

[1] The original MS. being here injured, and the best lenses found ineffective, the translator of the story was at a sore nonplus, being ignorant of the locality to which Cork and Kerry people are in the habit of consigning their ill-wishers. People of Wexford, certainly, and those of Wicklow and Carlow, probably, have established the town mentioned as their social Norfolk Island; so he has ventured on the substitution. He has questioned sundry archæologists on the reason of this undesirable distinction being conferred on the little Fingallian burgh, but to no sure result, the causes assigned delightfully contradicting each other.

"If I knew your name," said Sculloge, "I would wish you the compliments of the evening, for I think it is lucky to meet you." "I don't care for your compliments," said the other, "but I am not ashamed of my name. I am the *Sighe-Draoi* (Fairy Druid), Lassa Buaicht, and my stars decreed at my birth that I should be cursed from my boyhood with a rage for gambling, though I should never win a single game. I am killed all out, betting on my poor left hand all day, and losing. So if you wish to show your gratitude get down and join me. If *I* win, which I won't, you are to do whatever I tell you. You may say now what is to be yours if *you* win, and that you are sure to do."

So Sculloge said that all he required was to have his old mill restored, and they began the game. The Sheoge Druid lost as usual, and after rapping out some outlandish oaths, he bade the other take a look at his mill at an early hour next morning.

It was the first thing that Sculloge did when he went out at an early hour, and surprised and delighted he was to find as complete a meal and flour mill in ready order for work as could be found in all Muskerry. It was not long till the wheel was turning, and the stones grinding, and Sculloge was as happy as the day was long, attending to his mill and his farm, only he felt lonely in the long evenings. The cards and the dice, and the whiskey-bottle were gone, and their place was not yet filled up by the comely face and the loving heart of the Bhan a teagh.

So one evening about sunset he strolled up into the lonely valley, and was not disappointed in meeting the Sheoge Druid. They did not lose much time till they were hard and fast at the dice, the Druid to supply a beautiful and good wife if he lost the game; if not, Sculloge to obey whatever command he gave him. As it happened the other evenings it happened now. Sculloge won, and went to bed, wishing for the morning.

He slept little till near break of day, and then he dozed. He was awaked by his old housekeeper, who came running into the room in a fright, crying, "Master, master, get up! There's a stranger in the parlour, and the peer of her I never saw. She is dressed like a king's daughter, and as beautiful as—as I don't know what, and no one saw her coming in." Sculloge was not long dressing himself, and it wasn't his work-day clothes he put on.

He almost went on his knees to the lovely lady, whom he found in the parlour. Well, he was not a bad-looking young fellow; and since he was cured of gambling and drinking his appearance was improved, as well as his character. He was a gentleman in feeling, and he only wanted gentle society to be a gentleman in manner. The lady was a little frightened at first, but when she saw how much in awe he was of her she took courage. "I was obliged to come here," said she, "whether I would or no; but I would die rather than marry a man of bad character. You will not, I am sure, force me to anything against my will." "Dear lady," said he, "I would cut off my right hand sooner than affront you in any way."

So they spent the day together, liking one another better every moment; and to make a long story short, the priest soon made them man and wife. Poor Sculloge thought the hours he spent at his farm and his mill uncommonly long, and in the evenings he would watch the sun, fearing it would never think of setting. She learned how to be a farmer's wife just as if she had forgot she was a king's daughter; but her husband did not forget. He could not bear to see her wet the tip of her fingers; and the only disputes they had arose from his wishing to keep her in state doing nothing, and from her wishing to be useful.

He soon began to fret for fear that he could not buy fine clothes for her, when those she brought on her were worn. She told him over and over, she preferred plain ones; but that did not satisfy him. "I'll tell you what, my darling Saav,"[1] said he one evening. "I will go to the lonely glen, and have another game of backgammon with the Sighe Draoi, Lassa Buaicht. I can mention a

[1] *Sabh* or *Sadbh* is one of the many Irish words perplexing for the variety of their significations. Some only of the meanings of this name follow. An airy shape, a fantasy, a salve, the sun, a good habitation. It is Englished by Sabia or Sabina.

thousand guineas if I like, and I am sure to win them. Won't I build a nice house for you then, and have you dressed like a king's daughter, as you are!" "No, dear husband," said she; "if you do not wish to lose me or perhaps your own life, never play a game with that treacherous, evil old man. I am under 'geasa' to reveal nothing of his former doings, but trust in me, and follow my advice."

Of course he could only yield, but still the plan did not quit his mind. Every day he felt more and more the change in his wife's mode of living, and at last he stole off one evening to the lonely glen.

There, as sure as the sun, was the foolish-looking old Druid, sitting silent and grim with his hands on the table. He looked pleased when he saw his visitor draw near, and cried out, "How much shall it be? What is it for this evening?—two more mills on your river, a thousand guineas, or another wife? It's all the same, I'm sure to lose. You may make it ten thousand if you like. I don't value a thousand, more or less, the worth of a thraneen. Sit down and name the stake. If I win, which confound the Sighe *Aithne* (knowledge) I won't, you will have to execute any order I give you."

Down they set to the strife. Sculloge named ten thousand guineas to have done with gambling, and went on rather careless about his throwing. Ah! didn't his heart beat, and blood rush to his face, and a flash dart across his eyes when he found himself defeated! He nearly fell from his seat, but made a strong effort to keep his courage together, and looked up in the old man's face to see what he might expect. Instead of the puzzled, foolish features, a dark threatening face frowned on him, and these words came from the thin harsh lips :—" I lay geasa on you, O Sculloge of folly, never to eat two meals off one table, and never to sleep two nights in one rath, or bruigheen, or caisiol, or shealing, and never to lie in the same bed with your wife till you bring me the *Fios Fath an aon Sceil* (perfect narrative of the unique story) and the *Cloidheamh*[1] *Solais* (Sword of Light) kept by

---

[1] Pronounced *Chloive*; *Fath* nearly as faw. *Claymore* is made up of *Cloidheamh* and *mhor*, large. *Glaive* is evidently a cognate word.

the *Fiach O'Duda* (Raven, grandson of Soot) in the *Donn Teagh* (Brown House)."

He returned home more dead than alive, and Saav, the moment she caught sight of him, knew what had happened. So without speaking a word she ran and threw her arms round his neck, and comforted him. "Have courage, dear husband! Lassa Buaicht is strong and crafty, but we will match him." So she explained what he was to do, made him lie down, sung him asleep with a druidic charm, and at dawn she had him ready for his journey.

The first happy morning of her arrival, the Sculloge had found a bright bay horse in his stable, and whenever his wife went abroad, she rode on this steed. Indeed, he would let no one else get on his back. Now he stood quiet enough while husband and wife were enfolded in each other's arms and weeping. She was the first to take courage. She made him put foot in stirrup, smiled, cheered him, and promised him success, so that he remembered her charges, and carefully followed them.

At last he started, and away at a gentle pace went the noble steed. Looking back after three or four seconds he saw his house a full mile away, and though he scarcely felt the motion, he knew they were going like the wind by the flight of hedges and trees behind them.

And so they came to the strand, and still there was no stoppage. The horse took the waves as he would the undulations of a meadow. The waters went backwards in their course like arrows shot from strong bows. In shorter time than you could count ten, the land behind was below the waters, and the waves farthest seen in front came to them, and swept behind them like thought or a shooting star.

At last when the sun was low, land rose up under the strong blaze, and was soon under the feet of the steed, and in a few seconds more they were before the drawbridge of a strong stone fort. Loud neighed the horse, and swift the drawbridge was let down upon the moat, and they were within the great fortress.

There the Sculloge alighted, and the horse was patted

and caressed by attendants, who seemed to know him right well, and he repaid their welcome by gentle whinnyings. Other attendants surrounded the Sculloge, and brought him into the hall. The noble-looking man and woman that sat at the upper end, he knew to be the father and mother of his Saav. They bade him welcome, and ordered a goblet of sweet mead to be handed to him. He drank, and then dropped into the empty vessel a ring which his wife had put on his finger before he left home. The attendant carried the goblet to the king and queen, and as soon as their eyes fell on the ring they came down from their high seats, and welcomed and embraced the visitor. They eagerly inquired about the health of their child, and when they were satisfied on that point, the queen said, "We need not ask if she lived happily with you. If she had any reason to complain, you would not have got the ring to show us. Now, after you have taken rest and refreshment, we will tell you how to obtain the Fios Fath an aon Sceil and the Cloidheamh Solais."

The poor Sculloge did not feel what it was to pass over some thousand miles of water while he was on the steed's back, but now he felt as tired as if he had travelled twenty days without stop or stay. But a sleeping posset and a long night's rest made him a new man; and next morning after a good lunch[1] on venison steaks, a hearthcake, and a goblet of choice mead, he was ready to listen to his father-in-law's directions.

"My dear son," said the king, "the Fiach O'Duda, Lassa Buaicht, and I are brothers. Lassa, though the youngest, and very powerful in many ways, has always envied his eldest brother Fiach the Sword of Light. *I* only have the means of coming at it, but he knew I would not willingly interfere to annoy the poor man, who, after all, is my eldest brother, and has been sadly

[1] It is maintained that the ancient Celts, as well as the Romans and other peoples of old times, ate only once a day, viz. after sunset. That was undoubtedly the principal meal, but the most determined Dryasdust in Ireland, or Scotland, or Wales, shall not persuade us that they did not partake of lunch or collation, say from 8 to 11 A.M. to enable them to endure life till Beal chose to sink into his western bed.

OSSIANIC AND OTHER EARLY LEGENDS 233

tormented during his past life, and has never done me the slightest harm. So he laid out this plan of stealing my daughter from me. I can't explain to you who know nothing of Droideachta, how he enjoys this and other powers. He got you into his meshes, blessed you with Saav's society, and then put this geasa on you, judging that I would help him to do this injury to my brother, rather than make my daughter's life miserable. Fiach lives in a castle surrounded by three high walls. It is on a wide heath to the south. Everything inside and outside is as brown as a berry. The black steed which I am going to lend you will easily clear the gate of the outer wall, and then you make your demand. As soon as the Fiach comes into this outer inclosure you have no time to lose; and if you get outside again without leaving a part of yourself or of your horse behind, you may consider yourself fortunate."

He mounted his black steed, rode southwards, came in sight of the Brown Castle, cleared the gate of the outer wall, and shouted, "I summon you, great Fiach O'Duda, on the part of your brother, the Sighe Draoi, Lassa Buaicht, to reveal to me the Fios Fath an aon Sceil, and also surrender into my keeping the matchless Cloidheamh Solais." He had hardly done speaking when the two inner gates flew open, and out stalked a tall man with a dark skin, and beard, hair, birredh, mantle, and hose as black as the blackest raven's wing. When he got inside the inclosure he shouted, "Here is my answer," at the same time making a sweep of his long sword at the Sculloge. But he had given the spur to his steed at the earliest moment, and now safely cleared the wall, leaving the rear half of the noble beast behind.

He returned to the castle dismally enough, but the king and queen gave him praise for his activity and presence of mind. "That, my dear son," said the king, "is all we can do to-day: to-morrow will bring its own labours." So the sun went to rest, and the Sculloge and his relations made three parts of the night. In the first they ate and drank. Their food was the cooked flesh of the deer and the wild boar, and hearthcakes, and water-cress; and their drink—Spanish wine, Greek honey, and Danish beer. The second part of the dark time was given to conversation, and the bard, and the story-teller. The third part was spent in sleep.

Next day Sculloge rode forth on a white steed, and when he approached the fort, he saw the outer wall lying in rubbish. He cleared the second gate, summoned the Fiach, saw him enter the inclosure, and if his face was terrible yesterday it was five times more terrible to-day. This time he escaped with the loss of the hind legs of his steed only, and he was joyfully welcomed back by the king and the queen. They divided the night into three parts [1] as they did the last, and the next day he approached the *Donn Teagh* on the *Eich Doun*, the brown horse that brought him over the sea.

The second wall was now in *brishe* as well as the first, and at one bound of the brown steed he was within the courtyard. He had no need to call on Fiach, for he was standing before his door, sword in hand, and the moment the horse's hoofs touched the ground he sprang forward to destroy steed and rider. But the druidic beast was in the twinkling of an eye again on the other side, and a roar escaped the throat of Fiach that made the very marrow in Sculloge's bones shiver. However, the horse paced on at his ease without a hair on his body being turned, and Sculloge recovered his natural courage before you could count three.

Great joy again at the castle, and the day was spent, and the night divided into three parts as the day before, and the day before that again. Next morning the king sent out no horse, but put a *Clarsech* (small harp) into his son-in-law's hand, and a satchel by his side filled with withered leaves and heath-flowers, tufts of hair, pebbles, and thin slates, passed his hands down Sculloge's arms from shoulder to wrist, and gave him directions what to do.

When he came within sight of the castle, he began to

[1] A circumstance frequently repeated in Celtic tales. Such repetitions were never omitted by the story-tellers. They were used as resting-places, and aids to arrangement or recollection of what was to follow.

touch the harp-strings, and such sounds came from them that he thought he was walking on a cloud, and enjoying the delights of Tir na-n-Oge. The trees waved their branches, the grass bent to him, and the wild game followed him with heads raised and feet scarce touching the ground. All the walls were in confused heaps, and as he approached them, servants and followers were collected from wherever they were employed, and standing in a circular sweep facing him. No noise arose from the crowd ; their delight was too great. As he came close he ceased for a moment, and flung the contents of his satchel among them. All eagerly seized on scraps of leaves, or hair, or heath-flowers, or slates, or pebbles, for in their eyes they were gold, and diamond ornaments, and pearls, and rich silks. He struck the strings again, and entered the castle, accompanied by the enchanted sounds from the harp-strings. He passed from the hall through a passage, then up some steps, and he was in the small bedchamber of Fiach O'Duda. He had heard the sounds, but the effect they had was to throw him into a deep sleep, in which the music was still present to his brain, and kept him in a sleepy rapture.

This room was as light as the day, though window it had none. By the wall hung a sword in a dark sheath. Bright light flashed round the room from the diamond-crested hilt and about three inches of the blade not let down into the scabbard. Taking it down, he approached the sleeping Druid chief and struck him on the side with the flat of the blade. "Arise," said he, "great Fiach O'Duda ! reveal to the Sighe Draoi, Lassa Buaicht, through me, the Faos Fath an aon Sceil. I will not ask for the Cloidheamh Solais ; I have it in my keeping." The Druid's looks were full of surprise at first, and then of fright, but in a short time he became calm, and proceeded to relate the

FIOS FATH AN AON SCEIL.

"I am," said he, "the eldest of three brothers, the Sighe Draoi, Lassa Buaicht, being the youngest. By birthright I inherited the great family treasure of the Cloidheamh

Solais, and my youngest brother envied me from the beginning, and made many an attempt to take it from me. But I was a Draoi as well as he, and always was able to disappoint him. At last, wishing to get out of the reach of his villainous tricks, and see the world, I went on a voyage to Greece, and when I returned I was a married man. The King of Greece had grown to like me so much, that he gave me his daughter. The king and his daughter were deep in Draoideachta, and he had in his possession a *slat* (enchanted rod) which could change any living being into whatever form he wished. I never dreamed, as my wife and I talked so lovingly, and were so happy, sitting on the deck of our vessel as we returned over the calm central sea, that she had stolen that rod from her father's chamber before we set out on our return.

"About a week after I came home, as I was hunting, the hounds gave chase to a wild-looking but very handsome man, all covered with long hair, and when I got up to them they had seized him, and were on the point of tearing him asunder. He stretched out his hands to me, while the tears ran down his cheeks, and I drove off the dogs and brought him home to my castle. I got his hair cut off, and had him clothed, and I amused myself in teaching him to speak. Little did I think he was a disguised follower of my brother, who had sent him into my family by this stratagem, to corrupt my wife, and to get possession of the sword of light for him.

"One day as I was returning from hunting through a grove near this castle, I heard voices in a thicket. They were familiar to me, and when I had arrived at a convenient place, what did I espy but my wife seated under a tree, and the villainous wild man, with not a trace of wildness about him or in his speech, stretched on the grass, his head upon her knees, and he looking up lovingly into her face, and entreating her to secure the Cloidheamh Solais for him. I had no further patience, but rushed on ready to strike him through with my hunting spear, but the moment my wife caught sight of me, she flung the magic rod at me, and I found myself, in the twinkling of an eye, changed to a horse. I did not lose my memory, but rushed on the villain to trample out his life. However, he had got up into the tree before I could reach him. I had neither the power nor the will to trample or strike my wife. So the guilty pair escaped for the time.

"She managed to have me caught very soon, and hard worked, but that was going too far with the joke. I kicked and bit every one she sent to yoke or bridle me, and no one would venture to come near me. This did not meet her views. So she came where I was one day, struck me with the *slat* once more, and I was a wolf on the moment. Great as her power was, she could not kill me, but she contrived to get her father, who was just then with her on a visit, to hunt me with a great pack of wolf-dogs. I led them a good chase, but was taken at last.

"Just as they were on the point of devouring me, the King of Greece himself came up, and so I howled out dismally to him, imitating the human voice as well as I could. I held up my fore-paws, and he saw the big tears rolling down from my eyes. He knew there was something mysterious about me, and rescued me from the dogs at once. I walked home by his side, and he kept me about him, and grew quite attached to me. All this terribly annoyed my wife, but she was prevented by a higher power from killing me with her own hands, and I kept too close to her father to be in danger from any one else. All this time she and the false wild man searched for the sword of light, but could not find it. It was kept in a thin recess in a wall, under a spell, and no one but I could discover the method of coming at it. She did all she could to persuade the king to send me away, but he would not gratify her. At last one day she brought a druidic sleep on our child in the cradle, so that he seemed without life, and she sprinkled him with blood, and threw some also on me. For I used to stay in the room with the infant whenever I could. She then began to shriek and cry till her father and the servants ran in to see what the matter was. 'Oh, father, father!' said she, pointing to the cradle, and then to me, 'see what your favourite has done!'

All were rushing to kill me at once, but he ordered them to stop. He took the *slat* in his hand, and drew it down the child's body from its breast to its toes, and again from its breast to its finger ends, muttering some words, and it sat up, and began to stretch out its arms to him. He examined the places where the blood spots were, and found no wound. Then he called me to him, and said to those around him, ' Here is some treachery and mystery which I must clear up. *Mac Tire*,' he continued, addressing me, and striking me with the rod, ' I command you by my druidic power to take on your natural form, if you be not a true *madralamh*.' In a moment I was restored to my own face and figure before them, and saw my wife and her favourite hastening from the room as fast as their legs could carry them. The king saw this as well as I, and ordered both to remain, and the doors to be closed. I directed one of the servants to fetch cords, and have the two bound hand and foot. 'No need,' said the king, ' as far as my daughter is concerned.' He waved his hand towards her, and muttered a charm, and she sank on a chair without power to move. I then explained all that had happened from the day when I detected them in the wood, and declared my belief that the pretended wild man was not present in his natural appearance. ' We shall soon know the truth,' said the king. He struck the villain across the face, and instead of the handsome *gaisceach* (brave young fellow) we knew, he stood before all an ugly featured humpback, who was known to every one as the confidential follower of my brother Lassa Buaicht. The wretched woman on the chair, though not able to move, uttered a piercing cry, and her face was covered with a stream of tears. The servants did not wait for further orders. They tied the humpback hand and foot, made a roaring fire in the bawn, and pitched him into the middle of it. The King of Greece asked me what punishment I wished to inflict on my false wife, but I said he might do as he pleased, but that I wished her life to be spared. When he left me to return to his own country, he took her with him, and since I have heard no news of either. And now you know why I have kept myself so well guarded from the designs of my wicked brother, and you have heard the Fios Fath an aon Sceil, and got the chloive solais. In return, tell me why a stout, noble-looking young gaisceach like you should come and throw down my walls and take my bright treasure, and why my good brother should aid you. You could not have done it without his help."

So Sculloge related his history, and assured him that he should not be long deprived of the chloive solais, and would have no occasion for any more walls to fence himself from his evil-minded brother. He was soon back to the king and queen, and soon over the wide ocean on his bay steed, and on the evening of the same day was sitting in the *Glean Raineach* (ferny glen) at the table with the Sighe Draoi, Lassa Buaicht, and the sword of light in its dark sheath, and its hilt covered by his sleeve, grasped tightly in his strong right hand. The Druid gave him a hearty welcome, and mentioned how rejoiced he was to see him safe back, never removing his eyes from the weapon.

"My brave gaisceach," said he, "I need not trouble you about the fios fath. I know it already. Hand me the chloive solais, and my hand shall not be slack in showering guineas on you." "Oh, just as you like. You don't care how I give you the sword?" "Ah, what matter how you give it!" "Thus then it shall be, treacherous wretch," said Sculloge. The valley was lighted up in a moment as if in noon-day, and the head of the Druid was in the next moment lying at his feet.

Very soon his beautiful, gentle, and loving wife was laughing and crying in his arms, for she was not far off awaiting the issue, and the sudden blaze brought the happy news to her, and the bright bay steed was soon bearing them over the waves again to her native land. Fiach O'Duda was once more happy in the possession of his chloive solais, and there was no more happy palace than that in which the Sculloge and his princess, and her father and mother, spent their days. The Lords of Muskerry trace their genealogy from the son of the gaisceach of our story.

The following is a fair specimen of the Celtic variety of fiction in which suitors for the hand of some lady of matchless beauty enter on dangerous and generally unsuccessful quests. The mortal hero in all cases needs the aid of benevolent fairy, elf, or genius, to bring the adventure to a successful issue. Parts of the story will be found rather obscure by those who look for a close connexion of cause and effect in works of imagination. But change, and loss, and corruption may be looked for in compositions more than a thousand years old, left for a large part of that time to the chance guardianship of such of the community as had a taste for legendary traditions.

AN BRAON SUAN OR.[1]

The lovely Fiongalla (fair cheek) was daughter to Glas, chief of a district in the south-west of Desmond.[2] She would have been his great happiness, but for a fate that had brooded over his house for nearly two centuries. No woman of the family could be married till her suitor had brought from the *Donn Thir* (brown or dark land) the Craov Cuilleann (holly-bough), the Luis Bui (marigold), and the crimson berries of the Uhar (yew). These were to be found in the dim and distant Donn Thir, in the Western Sea, near the Stone Circle of Power; and for some generations no knight had been so fortunate as to secure them. A corrochan (leather-covered bark) lay in a wooded nook near *Bean Tra* (Fair Strand, Bantry), and had lain there time out of mind. The daring adventurer entered it, and readily made the open sea. A day and a night were allowed for the voyage going and coming; but hitherto the fated bark had been in every instance seen entering its little cove within the time, unfreighted by the hero or the magic prizes.

---

[1] The golden pin of sleep.
[2] Desmond—*Deas*, south; *Muimhe*, Munster; *Tuaig Muimhe*, Thomond, North Munster.

OSSIANIC AND OTHER EARLY LEGENDS

In the family lived the sage woman Amarach (lucky, fortunate), whom no one living remembered ever to have seen look a day younger, and of whom their fathers and mothers had made the same report, handing down the assertions of their ancestors for two generations to the same effect.

More than one suitor had essayed the adventure, hoping for the hand of fair Fiongalla. All had perished in the rough western waves, when at last the court was visited by the young *Feargal* (nobleman), son of Ciocal. In his father's hospitable hall in Thomond he had heard of the matchless beauty and good qualities of Fiongalla, from the lips of more than one wandering bard; and despite all opposition from his parents and the Duiné Uasals of his tribe, he travelled to the Court of Glas, saw the damsel, found his resolution confirmed, and demanded of the lady and her father permission to try the adventure.

The love felt by Feargal was fully returned by Fiongalla, yet she used her influence to dissuade him from the attempt. "How could he hope for success, when so many bold and skilful young knights had failed and perished for the past two centuries?" But the young hero on his journey had a vision of the tutelar Sighe of his family, the benevolent and powerful *Finncaev* (fair love), who had promised him her assistance at his utmost need. Confident in her protection, and inspired by strong love, he told her that the only words from her mouth that could turn him from his purpose were, "I love you not." These words she could not force herself to utter, and forth fared the knight to find the magic coracle, while the shadow of night still lay on sea and land.

Amarach had joined her entreaties to those of father and daughter. But Amarach was the evil being that had, two centuries before, imposed this cruel fortune on the family. She knew by her art that the youth was protected by the powerful Sighe Finncaev, and she feared that her influence and her spells would become things of nought.

Passing from the heights on which the dun of the

chief stood, he had to traverse a rough glen strewed with rocks and brushwood, and his path led by a circle of tall stones marking the burial-place of some chief of former days, and still the favoured resort of those who practised druidic rites. He felt a sudden awe creep over him as he was hurrying by the ring of power, and which was increased by the appearance of a tall figure. His courage was restored when he discovered it to be the friendly Sighe, who gave him a few brief directions. "You have rashly engaged in a most perilous enterprise, but follow my instructions punctually, and I trust to bring you out of it with safety and honour. When you reach the corrach and enter it, wish yourself outside the bay, and there remain till the darkness of evening comes on. If you return and touch the land before you see on the shore my three servants, you are lost. Those servants I will now present to your sight." She struck one of the stones with her druidic wand, and at the touch it fell to pieces. "*Cush fe Crish* (Tied Foot), come out," and a stout figure with his right foot in his hand stood before them. She struck another stone and cried, "*Fir na Saghaidh* (Man of the Arrows), come out." The stone parted, and yielded an archer with a well-furnished quiver. She struck the third, "*Fir na Mulla Headha*, come forth," and a figure with an enormous mouth and swollen cheeks sprung from the fragments of his stone.

All bowed before the youth, and asked to know his will. He turned to Finncaev, but she had vanished; and he addressed the powerful beings before him in some perplexity. "I am ignorant of your means of helping me. I only know that I require you to be on the shore by sunset of the coming day with the holly bough, the marigold, and the red berries of the yew from the ring of power in the obscure land in the great sea! "Hard," said Cush, "will be the task, O noble knight, to foil the powerful Amarach. If when you approach the land at sunset she get into the boat, or you touch the land till you see us, you are lost; so will be our services. Come, brothers, I am obliged to keep one foot tied for fear of out-distancing my object. You, O

Fir na Saghaidh, are unerring in aim; you, O Fir na Mulla Headha, can see through the earth and to its farthest rim, and can blow tempests from your mouth. To your tasks! I hasten before you to the extreme verge of Hy Conaill (Donegal). There at the base of the mighty rocks lies the boat to convey me to the dim land and the circle of power. The voyage which you, Sir Knight, would not accomplish within a year I will execute in half a day. Brothers, await my return on the summit of Rinkan Barra on the brink of the North Sea."

Tied Foot was on the coast of Hy Conaill at an early hour, and discovered the fated boat which Amarach was obliged to keep in the dark cove for the service of adventurers. She was sitting within it in the appearance of a fair young woman, and received Cush fe Crish on his first call. A mether stood in the bow, filled with brown mead, and the sight enchanted the wearied and thirsty traveller. The maiden courteously offered the vessel, which he gratefully took, and drained to the bottom. "Lovely maid," said he, "you were beautiful when I entered your boat; you are now the most beautiful within the coasts of Erinn. I want your boat for a passage to the dim land to fetch the three magic gifts for Feargal, son of Ciocal. I shall be there and back by the first hour after mid-day; but there's no hurry. I must sit here and converse with you, enslaver of my heart, for a small hour." As he was endeavouring to take her hand, his foot escaped from his grasp, and he fell, overpowered with the magic drink, and lay motionless at the bottom of the boat. The treacherous woman then took from her hair the *braon suan or*, the magic sleeping pin, and stuck it through his long glibbs; and while it lay in his hair no power could wake him.

His two companions arrived on the rocks an hour later, and were dismayed at sight of him, far below them, in dead sleep. In his hair they espied the magic pin, and in a moment they recognised it, and guessed at what had occured. The archer had his bow bent in a trice, and the next the braon was dashed from the hair of

Cush, and lay powerless at his feet. He awoke, took his foot again in his hand, looked at the pin, then up at the cliff, waved his free arm in gratitude, seized on the oar, and the skiff went skimmimg over the great sea fleeter than the swiftest arrow. Fir na Mulla Headha put his hand to his eyebrow, and spoke to his comrade :—" Through the thick air and the mist I still see the shooting bark; the dim veils are clearing a little round Cush, and he seems almost at the world's end; a low, thick fog lies beyond; the boat speeds to it, and it becomes a land of rocks, and woods, and valleys, as grey as clouds. He enters a bay, secures his boat, advances inland. A grove is before him, and under the shade of trees as old as the world stands a ring of mighty stones. Within is a cromleacht, and overshadowing it the holly-bough and berry-bearing yew; at its foot springs the marigold. He leaves the dim land behind him. I see the boat more plainly, but the land has become a cloud. The boat is larger, but the cloud bank has vanished. Here he comes swifter than the arrow from your own bow-string."

Great was the joy of the druidical servants as they met; but after a moment Cush fe Crish cried out, " Our work is only half accomplished. The powerful Amarach is speeding south, and if she reaches Bean Tra she will induce Feargal to touch the land, and then our labour is void. You, O *Boghadoir* (archer), have done your duty —follow at your leisure. Get on my back, O Mulla Headha. I value not your weight a dry leaf. Now for the southern bay. On they swept, leaving the breeze behind them, and at last spied the sage Amarach as she skimmed by the side of Ben Gulban, and passed the mound of the sword hilt, where Diarmuid the peerless perished by the tusk of the fell wild boar. She found herself pursued, and increased her speed; but Cush fe Crish found new vigour in his limbs at sight of her, and still was gaining as they brushed the hills of Iar-Conacht.[1]

[1] *Siar* or *Iar*, West ; *Soir*, *Oirthir*, East ; *Thuaig*, North ; *Deas*, South.

As they approached *Knoc an Air* (hill of slaughter),[1] Tied Foot, who had not yet put forth his utmost speed, swept past, and his rider, making him stop and turn about, blew from his mouth such a mighty tempest as rooted up the oaks in its path. Catching up the sorceress, she was blown through the air to a great distance, and a second blast put all further struggles on her part at an end.

Feargal had waited wearily in the fated boat the long hours of the day. Toward the gathering of the dark he heard the distant tempest, which astonished him, for, wild and horrifying as it was, it lasted only for a few seconds. Approaching the shore, he perceived as it were a flash of lightning darting from the bosom of the hills, and ceasing at the near strand. He then distinguished, in a soft, dimly-bright vapour that hovered on the shore, the servants and their powerful mistress. He sprung to land, and Finncaev, advancing and smiling on him, placed the magic gifts in his hand. While he was pouring out his thanks, she turned to her ministers, and laid her hands caressingly on their shoulders. Smiles of pleasure came over their weird features, and while Feargal was looking on in awe, the figures and the soft vapour vanished

But shouts of joy were heard on every side, and crowds bearing torches were hurrying through various defiles to the shore. The figure of Feargal had been descried, and he was now conducted in triumph to the dun, and the trophies were hung in the great hall. Amarach had not been seen since the previous night, and the meeting of the lovers and their speedy marriage was undisturbed by fears of the sorceress, or of her hellish spells.

THE CHILDREN OF LIR.

Lir, though the father of a demi-god, was not able to secure domestic comfort. Having lost his beloved wife he sought relief in travel; and being on a visit with

[1] In Kerry, where princes and chiefs of Greece, pursuing the hapless Princess Niav Nua Chrotha, slaughtered many of the Fianna, but were in the end completely annihilated.

Bogha Derg, King of Conacht, he was induced to enter on the married state again, taking the beauteous and virtuous Princess *Aebh* (Eve) as his new partner. She bore him twins, *Fionula* (Fair-shoulder) and *Aodh* (Hugh), and at a second birth, Fiachra and Conn. This was followed by her death; and after some time the bereaved widower again sought the court of his father-in-law. He was there tempted to commit matrimony again, hoping that the sister of his lamented wife, the Princess Aoifé, would do the duty of an aunt, at least, to his orphans. For a year there was nothing to be complained of, but then she began to be jealous of the tenderness and attention ever exhibited by Lir to the Princess Fionula and her brothers. From mere despite she took to her bed, and there remained a year. At last a skilful but wicked Druid visited her, extracted her heart's secret, and tendered his advice. Rising from her bed, she arrayed herself in her best, and taking the children with her, got up into her chariot, and set out for her father's court, near Loch Derg, on the Shannon. On the route she urged her charioteer to destroy the children; but he was deaf to her entreaties, and she was obliged to enact the part of executioner herself. Fionula, with a girl's acuteness, sorely distrusted her stepmother; and when they arrived at the edge of a lake, and she and her brothers were commanded to get down and bathe, she refused in the most decided manner for them and herself. However, Aoifé, with assistance from her retinue, forced them into the water, and then and there, by a stroke on the head of each with a wand, the wicked Druid's gift, she changed them into four beautiful swans.

On arriving at her father's palace, he made inquiry about his grandchildren, and suspecting that her representation of their being in health at home was not true, he cast her into a druidic sleep, and made her reveal her wickedness. Restoring her to her ordinary state, he bitterly reproached her in the presence of the court, changed her into a grey vulture by a stroke of his wand of power, and doomed her to live in the cold, and windy, and sleety air, while time was to endure.

All repaired to the lake where the enchantment was effected, and were kept in a state of delight listening to the magic songs of the birds. The chariots stood by the shore, and the steeds consumed their provender, and the knights and ladies still listened entranced, night and day, until by the power of Aoifé's words, they were obliged to rise in the air, and direct their flight to Loch Derg. There through the mildness of summer, and the harsh winds and ice of winter, they abode three hundred years ;—Fionula pressing her dejected and shivering brothers to her side, covering them with her wings, and cheering them with her grandfather's prophecy—that when men with shaved heads came over the sea, set up their tables in the east ends of their houses, and rung their bells, the first sound would again restore their human form.

Three hundred years being gone, they once more were obliged to take their flight to the sea of Moyle, between Erinn and Alba, and there, for three hundred years more, endured unspeakable sufferings. In their flight they passed over the pleasant rath where their childhood had been spent, and now it was but a grass-covered mound, with a slimy ditch at its base. The last three hundred years of their sad pilgrimage were passed on the wild waves of the great western sea near *Irrus Domnann* (Erris). The bell that rung in the first Mass celebrated on *Inis na Gluaire* (Isle of Glory), restored them to their human shapes ; but they were now emaciated and decrepit, and only waited for baptism, to flee away to rest eternal.[1]

Our ancient annalists took it upon them to assign the year on which sprung forth certain rivers and lakes, and

[1] The "children of Tuirrean," the "children of Lir," and the "children of Uisneach," form the "Three Sorrows of Story" so lovingly quoted by admirers of Celtic literature. It is a grief to us to have spoiled one of them by inevitable contraction, and to be obliged, by want of space, to omit the other. There being nothing of a magical character about the last-named one, it has no place in this article ; but a charming version furnished by Samuel Ferguson may be found in the Hibernian Nights' Entertainments in an early volume of the *University Magazine*.

consequently it was not at all strange that their associates who took charge of the imaginative affairs of the island, should improve the hint; and, neglecting the trifling circumstances of dates, and names of contemporary monarchs, proceed to tell their willing listeners to what faults or negligences it was owing that the once fertile vale, dotted with the habitations of happy mortals, was flooded over, and how keen-sighted guides can to this day behold through the deep waters the pinnacles of churches, and occasionally the conical cap of a round tower. There being no need, in this instance, to rank our fine sheets of water by the more or less beauty of the surrounding scenery, we take them at random, and commence with

LOUGH NEAGH.

This beautiful sheet of water issued from a spring well which only waited an opportunity of being left uncovered, to send forth a mighty flood. The inhabitants of the neighbourhood, aware of the danger, kept it securely covered, till at last one luckless gossip walked off with her pitcher, forgetting to replace the smooth round flag, and in consequence the water burst forth in such a volume that the poor woman was drowned before she reached home. Incredulous readers objecting to this mode of lake-making, have only a choice between it and another theory somewhat less probable. Fion Mac Cuil having routed a Scotch giant with red hair, was pursuing him eastwards, but the canny Scotch monster was rather more fleet of foot than his Irish rival, and was outrunning him. Fion, fearing that he might reach the sea and swim across to Britain before he could overtake him, stooped; and thrusting his gigantic hands into the earth, tore up the rocks and clay, and heaved them after the Albanach. As Fion miscalculated height and distance, the mighty mass which had filled the whole bed of the present lake, launched from his hands, flew past the giant at a considerable height above his head, and did not lose its impetus till it came over the mid sea. There dropping, according to the laws of gravitation, it formed an island, afterwards called Man, from its Danaan patron, Mananan, son of Lir.

KILLARNEY.

Killarney's fair lake was formed under the following romantic circumstances—the historian omitting to state whether the inhabitants that dwelt beneath the level of its present waves were good or bad, or distinguished by an uncomfortable mixture of both qualities. A knight from foreign parts wooed the fair daughter of a man of the valley, rich in corn-fields and cattle, and earnestly urged her to depart with him to his rath in the north. He made no particular mention of the marriage ceremony, so she, while taking no pains to conceal her love, gave him decidedly to understand that, unless as his married wife, she would never quit her native vale in his company. He had a short struggle between his innate pride of chieftaincy and the deep love he bore to the pure-minded maid. At last he came to her house as evening was closing in, and gladdened the hearts of her parents by earnestly requesting the hand of their fair daughter. On inquiring where she was at the moment, he learned that she had gone to the fairy well for water, as was the custom of the young women of the valley. Thither he hastened without delay, and found two of her handmaids just leaving the fountain with their vessels balanced on their heads, and their forms gracefully swaying under them as they proceeded home. Before she could express displeasure or surprise, he told in abrupt and eager tones where he had been, and what he had done, and in a moment she could think of nothing but her new-found happiness. Her half-filled pitcher was forgotten, and in the cool evening they walked about on the russet turf, between the rocks and bushes; and in talking over their bliss, the time went by unmarked. At last a sudden recollection of her neglect, and of the fatal nature of the gifted spring, rushed on her mind. She shrieked aloud, and, quitting her lover's arm, she rushed down the side of the hill. But on looking towards the spring, she found a sheet of water surrounding the little eminence, and a bubbling flood bursting upwards where the still fluid was peacefully lying within its circular wall only a quarter of an hour before. She would have awaited death where she stood, so much was she overpowered with remorse for her fault, but such was not the purpose of her knight. Lifting her on his shoulders, he dashed through the channel nearest the neighbouring slope, and bore her still alive to her home. The dismayed dwellers in the valley had time to gain the heights before their dwellings were covered with the water; but the young maiden was denounced. The legend leaves us in ignorance of the after-fortunes of the lovers.

A once king of Cork and all his household are still living in comfortable seclusion at the bottom of the Lough of Cork, which burst out, as in the other instances, on account of the negligence of a domestic.

LEGEND OF THE LAKE OF INCHIQUIN.

Below the present surface of this lake was once a level plain, over one part of which towered a castle, or dun at least. A cavern under this castle led to some unexplored region, and a beautiful spring-well lay not far from its mouth. The lord of the dun was informed that three beautiful women were seen at times to come forth from the cavern's mouth, on calm moonlight nights, and bathe in the well; and the tale was not told to inattentive ears. He concealed himself just within the entrance of the passage, and saw the three beauties pass forth into the moonlight. He waited impatiently till they were returning, and he allowed two of them to glide by his hiding-place. As the third, who was the youngest and most beautiful, went by, he grasped her, and bore her into the open air. The others fled into the cavern, and the imprisoned nymph pleaded hard for her liberty. But he was handsome and gentle, and resolute at the same time, and at last she agreed to reign as mistress of his heart and his domains. They lived in happiness for many years, and two children were born to them. She had made it a condition that he should never invite company to the castle, and for many years he felt no desire to break his engagement.

Having in his stables a fine race-horse, a desire of going to the races of Kood at length seized on him, and he asked permission to attend that assembly. She gave consent, but warned him against bringing home any friends or acquaintance he might meet there. He returned home alone in the evening, rejoicing in a prize won by his steed, and induced his *Sighe* lady to agree to his repeating the excursion next day. Her consent was granted, accompanied with a solemn caution. The second evening also he kept to his word. But woe the while! on the third day some thoughtless and other envious acquaintances beset him, intoxicated him, learned his secret, and were invited to accompany him to his castle, and be introduced to his lady that evening. The beautiful Sighe had been watching for his return, and when she saw him cross the plain, surrounded by a disorderly crowd, he and they indulging in boisterous mirth, her love and esteem for him melted into thin air. The noise of the unthinking group ceased as they beheld a woman of superhuman beauty advancing towards them from the castle door, leading a child by each hand. The chief's heart began to throb wildly, and immediately after he uttered a wild cry of anguish, and rushed on as he saw her and his children disappear in the enchanted spring. The wonder and surprise of his companions were soon changed into personal fears, for water began to burst forth in a large body from the well and fill the plain. Out it kept rushing till it acquired the level it occupies at this day—a signal warning against all unsuitable associates, and breaches of solemn engagements.

HOW THE SHANNON ACQUIRED ITS NAME.

A long time ago there was a well in Ossory, shaded by a rowan-tree. When the berries became ripe they would drop into the water, and be eaten by the salmon that had their residence in the well. Red spots would then appear on the fish, and they received the name of "Salmon of Knowledge." It was not so easy to take these salmon, for there were shelving banks, and they could also retreat into the cavern from which issued the waters that supplied the well. However, one was occasionally caught, and the captor, so soon as he had made his repast on it, found himself gifted with extraordinary knowledge, even as Fion, son of Cumhail, when he had tasted of the broiled salmon of the Boyne. It was understood that no woman could taste of this delicacy and live. Yet Sionan, a lady cursed with an extraordinary desire of knowledge, braved the danger, suspecting the report to be spread abroad and maintained by the male sex from merely selfish motives. So, in order to lose no time, she had a fire ready by the side of the well, and the unfortunate fish was scarcely flung out on the herbage when he was disembowelled and frying on the coals. Who can describe the rapture she felt from the burst of light that filled her mind on swallowing the first morsel! Alas! the next moment she was enveloped by the furious waters, which, bursting forth, swept westwards, and carried the unfortunate lady with them, till they were lost in the great river which ever after bore her name.

Legends of foreign lakes afford an occasional parallel, not in detail, but in the idea of a supernatural origin, to these wild stories of our own. The following one, borrowed from Denmark, being curious, we give it welcome as a specimen :—

THE ORIGIN OF THE LAKE OF TIIS.

Soon after the preaching of Christianity in Zealand, a church was raised in Kund, and the cheerful clang of the bells was often heard, scattering their holy music abroad, and exciting devotion. But the chimes, as all other things connected with Christian ceremonial, were very distasteful to a troll who haunted the neighbourhood; and at last his annoyance became so intense, that he crossed over to Funen, and there abode.

Some time after he met a man from Kund, and made many inquiries about his old neighbours. At last, seeming to recollect something on a sudden, he changed the subject, and said to the man, "Will you oblige me by delivering this letter which I am dropping into your pocket, without showing you the address? There is a little secret about it, and you will oblige me by throwing it over the churchyard wall in Kund, where my friend is already expecting it." The man promised to do as desired, but on his return he forgot all about it. At last, being one day out in the low meadow, which now forms the basin of Lake Tiis, he suddenly recollected the letter, and, forgetting the injunction, he pulled it out of his pocket and looked at it. He observed with surprise that drops of water were trickling out of the corners. But terror soon succeeded to surprise when it flew open, and a mighty torrent began to rush from it. He had time, however, to escape before the hollow of the land in which he stood was filled with water. The revengeful troll had enclosed the whole lake in that pestilent letter; and if his evil design had succeeded, the church, and perhaps the whole town of Kund, would have been inundated.

The Celtic elves as well as the trolls have a great dislike to the intrusion of churches near their own residences, though they express it in a milder form. Sir Walter Scott has told how when they were going to erect a church at Deer, in the old ages, a chorus of the little people was heard to this effect :—

> "It is not here, it is not here,
> That ye shall build the Kirk o' Deer,
> But on Taptillerie,
> Where many a grave shall be."

THE BUILDING OF ARDFERT CATHEDRAL.

When St. Brendain, who went to search for the sunk isle of Hy-Breasil, was about to build his Cathedral of Ardfert in the kingdom of Kerry, he fixed on a spot where lay the remains of a deserted lios. This was a favourite resort of the red-capped gentry, a circumstance unknown to the saint. He cleared the foundation, and had made some progress in the building, when he was thus interrupted. The projected building would occupy a tolerably high rock, opposite to which stood another, and between them lay a wooded valley. One fine sunny morning as the trowel was making merry music on the stones, and the workmen were singing, a large crow came from the rookery in the valley, deliberately took up the measuring line in his bill, flew across the wood with it, and deposited it on the other eminence. The saint accepted the omen, and raised the sacred edifice on the spot pointed out by the fairy in disguise. We use the word fairy advisedly. If the messenger had been from another quarter, he would have made his appearance under snowy plumes.

The legend we are about to relate does not properly fall into the present category; but if we waited for a suitable niche, we should have probably to bring in St. Brendain again very unceremoniously, and here we have him without doing violence to good manners or classification. Our story-tellers sometimes represent the fairies,—either the original stock, or the human beings who have assumed their nature,—as showing good-will to mortals in distress. We would quote some instances of O'Donoghue's beneficence; but are they not sufficiently trumpeted in Killarney Guide-books? Such being the case, it would not be just or natural that our national saints should neglect their poor countrymen. But as our business in this section is not with legends of saints, but of fairies, we would not cite the following piece of supernatural interference were it not for its rather doubtful character:—

HOW DONAGHADEE GOT ITS NAME.

In the fine old kingdom of Kerry lived Donogha and Vauria, man and wife. Had they been a happy pair, their names and their little disagreements would not have reached our times. Donogha was lazy, Vauria was fiery in temper; and so food and fuel were frequently scarce, and words of anger and reproach frequent. On a fine summer day the master of the house was sitting by his hearth devoid of care, and doing no heavier work than smoking his pipe. Vauria coming in, rated him to such an extent for his idleness, neither sticks nor turf being under the roof to boil the supper, that he went forth into the wood to gather a *bresna*. Having taken twice the time it would have cost another to collect his bundle, he tied it up by a great effort, and then sat down upon it to lament at his ease his hard fate, cursed with poverty and a scolding wife. Our authority distinctly says that St. Brendain appeared to him then and there, and after speaking some words of kindness and encouragement, told him he would grant him two wishes, and advised him to think them over seriously before he would give them utterance. In our opinion the apparition was that of one of the fairy chiefs of the country. The lazy man returned thanks, and getting the fagot on his back trudged homewards. But the weight, multiplied by his native laziness, was nearly intolerable, and forgetting the late occurrence, he groaned out, "Oh, that this devil of a bresna was carrying me instead of *me* the bresna!" On the moment he found himself astride of the bundle, which was using the ends of its boughs as so many legs, and in a very short space of time he was thundering from the "bawn-gap," to the door. "Oh, Donogha, honey," says Vauria, "what's the meaning of this?" The fright inspired her with some politeness and good nature. He told her his good luck, and how they had still one wish left. "An', you anointed onshuch," said she, "is that the way you threw away your good fortune? I wish the bresna was in your stomach!" "It is well for me," said the easy man, "that it wasn't to you the saint appeared." Well, she went on *aggravating* him till he fairly lost patience; and cried out, "Oh, you serpent o' the world, I wish we were the length of Ireland separated from each other!" The next moment she and her cabin were at *Teagh na Vauria* (Mary's House), at the extreme end of Kerry, and he in the place called ever since Donaghadee (qu. *Teagh an Donogha*). They never saw one another more.

THE BORROWED LAKE.

A young chief once wooed the daughter of another chief, whose dun lay by the edge of Loch Ennel in Westmeath. The damsel was rather haughty and fastidious, and plainly told him that she would not require possession of his grianan as its mistress till she could see as beautiful a lake from its casement as that which lay before her father's house. This was annoying. The valley was suitable, but the hill sides were covered with cottages, and the rill which meandered in the bottom would, perhaps, take a score of years to fill it, after the dam, which it would require a dozen years to construct, should be finished. He would be an elderly man by that time. His foster-mother, an enchantress (this was during the times of the Danaans), seeing him take in his perplexity two or three vicious pulls at his long hair, induced him to unbosom himself, and ordered him to respect his flowing locks till to-morrow. She at once repaired through the air by the ordinary witch conveyance then in use, to the shealing of a Firbolg sister in the magic art, on the western bank of the Shannon. This hut was snugly seated on the brow of a hill above a pleasant lake, and the Danaan woman was hospitably entertained by her of the Firbolg race.

After their simple repast, the visitor unfolded the cause of her journey, and besought her sage friend for the loan of her lake till the next moon's day, deceitfully adding under her breath, "after the week of eternity." It was a difficult request to obtain, but at last obtain it she did, and triumphantly bore it in her cloak to the Leinster valley. The hill-side dwellers were awakened from their sleep that night by the noise, as it were, of ten thousand waterfalls. All made their escape to the upland, and were hospitably sheltered in the buildings of the dun; and at the dawn of morn, thousands of astonished eyes were gazing on the placid sheet of water that covered their dwellings of yesterday.

Thus the haughty bride was won. The misguided Conacht woman waited till the second moon's day, sorely annoyed by the muddy bed of her lake under the influence of a hot sun, and yet no appearance of the grateful waters returning. The patience even of a wise woman may be exhausted. She rode to the house of her deceitful fellow-witch in flying haste, and she was received with feigned welcome. "No time for compliments, gossip," said she; "the next moon's day and the moon's day after that have come, and, instead of my pleasant lake, I still see nothing but rocks, and mud, and decayed fish. Restore my lake, I say." "Alas, dear sister! your anger has driven away your memory. I promised you the return of your fine piece of water the moon's day after the week of eternity—not before; claim it when it becomes due."

The rage of the betrayed witch knew no bounds, but she was without remedy, owing to the treacherous self-reservation of the cunning Danaan. The result was tragic to most of the parties concerned, but the acquisition of Loch Owel to the pleasant plains of Meath is all that we are concerned with for the present.

KILSTOHEEN IN THE SHANNON.

The *Regia* of Ptolemy is supposed to be in existence, and inhabited by beings who once breathed the upper air. It lies in the bed of the Shannon towards its mouth, and is visible once in every seven years. Whoever is so unlucky as to get a sight of this buried city dies within a month. So late as 1823, fifteen men who had been down the river in a sail-boat, were seen by many people at mass in a neighbouring chapel, and even spoken to; but later in the day terror and grief prevailed in that neighbourhood, on finding that these poor fellows and their boat had been at the bottom of the river at the very time when they were supposed present in the chapel. A little vessel anchored one night near Beale, which is not far from the supposed site of Kilstoheen ; and next morning the crew on awaking found themselves by the quay of a magnificent city. A merchant coming on board engaged the vessel for a voyage to Bordeaux, for a cargo of wine. Thither captain and crew went in a few hours, laid in the commodity, and were back in Kilstoheen with very little delay. The freight being royally paid, the sailors went ashore, and enjoyed life in their peculiar way. One or two unfortunately approached some ladies who were taking the air, with coarse language and rough endearments, and at the same moment a storm began to blow, and the waters to rise. The crew made a hasty retreat to their vessel, and they had hardly gained it when they saw the beautiful city covered by the swelling waters, and their own bark dancing like a nutshell among the frothing waves. There was an unaccountable blank at this point in their after recollections; but next morning they awoke with their little vessel grounded on a sloping shallow portion of the bed of the river.

The people of Kilstoheen were reported to cultivate a fine breed of horses. A farmer in the neighbourhood found his hayricks invaded several nights in succession. So he set a watch, and found that the depredators, after making their meal, made their way into the Shannon,

THE ISLE OF THE LIVING.

Wonderful as were the stories concerning our lakes, islands, and sunk cities, related by native historians, they were excelled in some respects by the reports of foreign writers, who put down for subjects of general belief what were told to them by some individuals who were overcredulous, or wished to mystify the unfriendly visitor. Thus the choleric and disparaging Gerald Barry, after having told his Anglo-Norman admirers how the Shannon rises in a large lake, and after dividing Connaught from Ulster, flows into the Northern Ocean, gave them this notable piece of information :—

"In North Munster there is a lake with two islands

one large, the other small. In the former there is a church of ancient veneration; in the latter there is a chapel devoutly served by a few unmarried persons named Colidei (*Culdees*). If a woman or any animal of the female sex enters the larger church she dies instantly; but no person ever dies, or died, or can die a natural death in the smaller isle, and hence it is called the 'Isle of the Living.' Sometimes, however, they are grievously afflicted and brought to the last gasp by a mortal distemper; and when all hope is gone, and they feel that nothing of *living* life remains, . . . they get themselves carried in a boat to the larger island, where they yield up the ghost the moment they reach the shore."

This lake was known by the name of Lough Cre. The place once occupied by itself and its banks is now called Monincha (Bog of the Island). It lies near Roscrea. According to the same judicious writer, after the Isles of Arran had been blessed by St. Brendain, no corpse suffered decomposition there, nor rat could live. So the inhabitants had the privilege of pointing out their great-grandfathers, with their lineaments still recognisable —a questionable benefit; and if an ill-advised person brought over a rat from the neighbouring Galwegian continent, and gave him his liberty, he incontinently ran direct to the sea; if stopped and detained, he died on the instant. Irish writers, later in time than Giraldus, convicted him of error as to the antiseptic qualities of Arran of the Saints, but claimed them for Inis na Gloire, off the coast of Erris. However, the learned and credulous Roderic O'Flaherty, zealous as he was of the fame of that sacred island, pronounced the report altogether untrue.

With the following precious pieces of information, obtained from Giraldus, we close this section of our researches :—

"There is a well in Munster, and whoever is washed with its water becomes instantly gray. There is another well in Ulster, and whoever bathes in it never becomes gray. In Connaught there is a well salubrious for human uses, but whose very taste poisons flocks, and herds, and beasts of burden, and all sorts of animals. The pebbly sand of this well, if only applied to the mouth, at once assuages the cravings of thirst. There is a well in Munster which if touched or even looked at by a man, the whole province will be deluged with rain, which will not cease until a priest, selected for the purpose, and who has been a virgin in body and mind from his infancy, appease the fountain by the celebration of mass, and the sprinkling of holy water and of the milk of a cow of one colour (a custom barbarous enough, and destitute of reason)."

We shall not occupy our reader's time with such trifling legends of lake lore as that of Fion stamping on a mountain, and thus producing a cavity filled with excellent liquor, for the purpose of slaking the thirst of O'Sullivan Mhor, after a severe day's hunting.[1] Neither shall we relate all the particulars of Donal Gealach's dealings with his favourite shepherd, and how he enabled him to convert the waters of a certain mountain lough near Killarney into special strong beer, by merely dipping a bunch of heath into it. He and his family might have enjoyed their jug of beer for many a day, but the poor man's conscience troubled him from receiving any benefits at the hands of the "good people" He revealed his scruples the next time he went to confession, and was obliged to resign his privilege.

If our ancient chroniclers did not, in every instance, succeed in establishing the truth of their records, they certainly deserved more credit than some of them have received, so great was the interest they took in their favourite studies, and so firmly did they seek to establish the foundation of the literary structure they were em-

[1] This was the origin ef the "Devil's Punch-bowl," Killarney. The Donal Gealach mentioned above was the king of the Killarney fairies.

ployed in raising. One of them has even left on record, or invented, some particulars of the primal historian who witnessed some of the evil doings before the Flood.

FIONNTUIN MAC BOCHNA.[1]

In the days of Noah, and while the ark was being built, there dwelt in the forests by the banks of the Tigris, Bith, with his wife Birren, of the race of Cain. Near them lived their daughter, Kesára, whose husband, Finntan, was of the blood of Seth. Farther off was the wood-built habitation of their son Lara, and his wife, Blama. None of these paid adoration to the Creator but Finntan, and to him was revealed the approaching destruction of mankind by a universal deluge. He constructed a rudely-built vessel, and not until it was finished could he induce his relatives to escape with him from the impending danger. His unbelieving consort tenderly loved him, and though fearless of the coming danger, she determined to share his fate. The others joined them at the last hour; the bark went down the river, and in one year from that day they were entering a bay on the west coast of the then uninhabited woody island, afterwards called Erinn.

They lived by hunting and fishing, and moved inland till they reached that mountain in the centre of the island, which has since borne the name of Lara's wife, Blama. They were all in the prime of their age when they left the far-off eastern land, varying in age from four to five hundred years each. But now a couple of centuries seemed to have passed over their heads in one revolution of the year. Hardly had they reached the hill when Bith and Birren expired on the same day. Their sorrowing children had scarcely interred them, raised their pile, and sung their lamentation, when Lara and Blama followed them to the lone house. Now were Finntan and Kesára the only dwellers on the island; and as they sat in woe by the side of the neighbouring loch, and looked on the cromlechs laid over their relatives, Kesára burst into a wild passion of grief and reproaches

[1] Fair Wave, Son of Ocean.

against her gods and against the God worshipped by her husband. He spoke to her of a future state of rest and happiness for those who were submissive to the decree of the All-Wise and All-Good; but her fury only gathered strength. Just then a volume of white vapour arose from the dark loch. It went round and round, and at last wheeled out between the living pair; then in rapid whirls it sunk again on the lake, and Kesára was left desolate on the brink. She cried out wildly on her husband not to abandon her; but seeing nothing but the wild hill round her, the grey sky over her, and the dark water beneath, she flung herself wildly below its quiet surface to find her partner or perish with him. To the bright land of Tirna-n-oge was Finntan conveyed, and there was he conscious of the great flood that submerged the island, of its loneliness for three hundred years, of the landing of the parricide Partholan, and the speedy destruction of his colony by a plague at Ben Edair. Then in succession came the clans of Nemidh, the Fomorian pirates, the Firbolgs, the learned Danaans, the warlike Milesians; and after a thousand years of their sway, worshipping the Host of Heaven, and the spirits of the seas, the lakes, the forests, and the hills, it was told at the Court of Laeré that a strange Druid, in flowered garments, with a two-pointed ornamented birredh on his head, and bearing in one hand a book inscribed with characters different from the Oghuim, and in the other a double cross, was approaching from the country of Gallian (Wicklow, Wexford, &c.).

It was the Eve of the Sun's Fire (Beltiné), and the learned and the noble from every part of the island were assembled at Teamor, in the Midchuarta. In rows they took their seats, and five fileas in succession recited the deeds of dead heroes, the genealogies of the lines of Heber, Heremon, and Ith, and the different invasions of the island since the landing of Nemidh. The last orator had ceased, and a storm of applause burst over him from the assembled nobles. When silence fell on the benches, he again took up the theme. "More praise than we merit you have given to my brothers and myself. Alas! we have only preserved some of the inscribed staves on which the full chronicle of our country is engraved. There is only one to whom the whole story is known, Fionntuin, son of Bochna, son of Eathoir, son of Annadha, who, from the days of the great flood to this, has been preserved in life in the land of youth. Whenever a filea, endowed with untiring zeal and all the knowledge that can be obtained, appeared among now dead poets, he has at some period of his career been favoured with a visit from this being in the deep dark silence before the dawn, and missing staves of the past chronicles supplied.[1] From the revelations of some of these we learn that his life shall endure till a white Druid, whose writings are made on folded parchments, and not on the corners of staves, and who also bears a cross and wears a flowered garment, shall come to reveal to us a god whom we yet know not. This Druid of an unknown faith shall wash him from his earthly stains, and his freed spirit is then to depart [2] to some place, as much excelling the Land of Youth as that happy country surpasses this."

He was yet speaking, when every one in the vast hall was on a sudden seized with awe, united to a certain feeling of pleasure, as they observed a venerable figure in long robes, and with long white hair falling on each side of his agreeable and majestic countenance, gliding from the entrance to the centre where the fileas were seated. He needed not to announce his name. Every one felt that he was in the presence of Fionntuin, son of Bochna, son of Eathoir.

"Kings, chiefs, and men of learning," said the vision, "great is my joy to see this happy day, and behold so many of my kind on whose souls divine light will soon dawn, and not only on them, but on all who rule within our seas. This light will come from one who is at hand, and to whom I leave the glorious task of instructing you in the heavenly scheme, which I only know in part, and

---

[1] The Oghuim writing of the Pagan Celts was commonly cut on thin staves.
[2] *Soar* would be more poetical than *depart*; but the filea knew his audience. The cold upper air, with its fogs, snows, and harsh winds, was the Celtic Tartarus.

which I am unfit to reveal. What I am permitted, I shall speak."

Then he proceeded in flowing words, while his hearers with their hearts flooded with pleasure, sat entranced, to announce that, before man was sent on earth, spirits created for happiness rebelled against the Master of sea, land, sun, moon, and stars; and that they were since that moment suffering pains not to be conceived. He then went on to describe the creation of man and woman, their pristine happiness, their fall through the wiles of the chief of the evil spirits, the after-wickedness of mankind, and the destruction (one family excepted) of the human race. The remainder of the oration chiefly related to the fortunes of the ancestors of those before him. He told of the preservation of letters after Babel; of the wanderings of the early Scots, and of their relations with Moses, when he was conducting the people of God from their thraldom. From the remainder of the discourse the fileas afterwards completed the full tale of their inscribed staves, soon to be changed for the characters and the rolls of vellum introduced by Patrick, and hence the perfect state of the annals of the Scots of Ireland compared with those of all nations that see the sun rise and set.

That evening, no fire or lamp was found burning through the length and breadth of the land, and all were watching in silence from the summits of the hills, in the direction of Teamor for a tongue of flame from the next hill that lay between. Laeré, preparing to kindle the sacred fire in the great bawn of Teamor, whose flaming up was to set all the fires on all the hills in Erinn ablaze, was dismayed on beholding, a small distance to the east, a lamp suddenly enkindled, and a man of a most attractive and venerable countenance gazing by its light on the leaves of an open book.

This was the humble, the gentle, the fervent Apostle Patrick, who, being summoned to the royal presence, preached the Word of Life. Small was his difficulty to turn the hearts of his hearers (the king excepted) from the practice of idolatry. The ground had been prepared by Finntan, and the seed sown by Patrick at once struck root, and soon the land was white with the Christian harvest.

The practice of magic being resorted to for the acquisition of supernatural power, its form and nature must depend on the religion, true or false, which is supposed to influence the practitioner. And here we must take occasion to remark in what a satisfactory state our knowledge is with regard to the Teutonic, and how comparatively trifling and conjectural is our acquaintance with the Celtic, forms of belief before the light of Christianity dawned on the people. Soon after the Scandinavians became Christians, their Pantheon was epitomized in verse by Saemund, a priest; and about a hundred years later, the prose *Edda*, furnishing the adventures of the gods, the heroes, and the giants, was compiled by the turbulent and talented Snorro Sturlason.

Now, the great change among the Celtic peoples had taken place by the fifth century, and it happened that no Saemund or Sturlason was vouchsafed to them; or if vouchsafed, the writings left by him were early lost in the confusion attending the determined struggles between themselves and their dogged, troublesome neighbours of the Teuton stock.

Owing to this unfavourable state of things, our knowledge of the nature of religious usages among our ancestors is necessarily limited. It had been obtained from casual allusions in early Christian writers on serious subjects, and, to a greater extent, from ancient poems and romances, and the relics of their festivels—still celebrated, but changed in object, and devoted to honour events in the life of our Lord, or the memory of saints. We have already gone over this ground. The Sun and Moon; Mananan Lir, the sea deity, and peculiar patron of the Isle of Man; Dagdæ, the Danaan chief; Morrigu, his spouse, the Celtic Bellona; Crom; and the spirits of the hills, streams, and forests, received worship from the heathen Scots. Their Elysiums were delightful islands in the Atlantic—alas! no longer visible—meadows of asphodel, sun-enlightened, below its waves, and the placid lakes of Erinn; and grottoes under the sepulchral mounds of old Danaan kings and sages. When cruelty, inhospitality, and treachery developed themselves to a monstrous extent in any individual, his thin, shivering ghost[1] suffered in the winds, and rains, and cold rigours of upper air, after its separation from the body. Besides the worship given to the divinities mentioned, it is conjectured by some ardent Celtic scholars that a fetich reverence was paid to some traditional bulls, cows, bears, and cats; even Dallans were not without reverence of some kind.

Everything of a magical character connected with the history or social state of the early inhabitants of Ireland, is traceable to the people called the Danaans, of whom we subjoin a brief sketch, claiming the same belief for its certainty as we could for the exploits of Romulus or Theseus.

THE FIRBOLGS AND DANAANS.

Nemedius (a wanderer from the East) and his thousand men reached Erinn from Thule (Jutland, or the Belgian Peninsula), in thirty skin-covered corrachs. He employed four Phœnician or African architects to raise four palaces for him in different parts of the island; and to prevent their doing as much for any other chief or prince, and thus detracting from his own greatness, he

---

[1] James M'Pherson was only imperfectly acquainted with even the oral literature of the Highland Gael. The ghosts of his good characters look complacently from their bright clouds of rest on the actions of their former friends or their own brave descendants.

had each skilful artist pitched from the battlements as soon as his work was achieved. But there was such a principle as poetical justice extant in Erinn, even so early as the days of Abraham. The Fomorians from Africa—all cousins-german to Rog, Robog, Rodin, and Rooney, the murdered men—assailed Nemidh from the bleak northern Isle of Torry, deprived the four castles of their master, by sending him to Tir-na-n-oge, and scattered his people to east, south, and north. Some under the leader Jarvan sailed to the Danish Isles, and the south of Sweden; and their descendants established themselves in four cities—Falias, Gorias, Finias, and Murias—and taught the simple Scandinavians magic rites, and the other branches of the polite literature of the day. After a few hundred years, their descendants took the resolution of seeking out the pleasant isle of their forefathers, and set sail, bringing from city No. 1 a magic glaive, from No. 2 a magic spear, from No. 3 an enchanted caldron, and from No. 4 the *Lia Fail*, or "Stone of Destiny," at present resting in the lower part of St. Edward's Chair, in Westminster Abbey.[1]

At the time of their approach to the island, it was held by a kindred race, the Firbolgs lately returned from Greece, to which country they had fled when routed by the Fomorians. The new-comers, landing somewhere in the north-west, enwrapped themselves in a *druidical* (magical) fog, and were never seen by mortal till they had attained the plain of southern *Moy-tuir* (plain of the tower), near Cong. The Firbolg king, Achy (*Eochaidh*, Chevalier), sent a herald to demand their business. They said they merely wanted possession of the country, and would allow their cousins in the tenth degree—the Firbolgs—to retire to the islands of Arran, Inisbofine, &c.; moreover, that it was useless to brandish sword, or fling spear at them, as their Druids, on the morn after a battle, would pass through the slain, and by their

[1] Dr. Petrie insists that the Stone of Destiny is the Dallan still to be seen on Tara Hill. He may be right; but we are determined not to believe him while treating the present subject.

☞ This was written when we had the amiable archæologist still amongst us.

spells of power recall every dead warrior to his pristine life and strength. "We defy your Druids," said the Firbolg spokesman. "Every one of our *curai* (companions) shall be attended by a kern bearing twenty sharpened stakes of the rowan-tree; and as every Danaan warrior falls in fight his body shall be pinned to the sod by one of these charmed staves."

The threat had its effect; and the succeeding battles were fought without the aid of *draoideacht* on either side. The Firbolgs being defeated, were allowed to people the islands off the western coast; and it is supposed that Dun Ængus in Arran, and other stupendous *caisiols* (stone forts), are the architectural remains of this brave but unsuccessful people. The ancient martial games and marriage-fairs held at Tailtean, now Teltown, in Meath, were instituted in honour of Tailte, wife of the brave Firbolg king slain at Moy-tuir.

INIS NA MUIC.[1]

The fated children of Gael Glas sailed from Egypt into the Black Sea, and thence through the waters which filled the Riphean Valley,[2] and made a temporary lodgement in the southern part of Scandinavia. Their next voyage was to Spain; and at last, the great-grandchildren of those who had quitted Egypt (*temp.* Phar.) determined to make their permanent abode in the green island, which Breogan, their chief, had discovered from a watchtower on Cape Ortegal. The brave old historians occasionally omitted details: they have left no account of the construction of the telescope used in the operation.

The Danaan Princes, either through negligence or design, allowed the invaders to land without opposition, and then a parley ensued. They demanded of the newcomers their objects and conditions, and received an answer similar to that given by themselves to the poor

[1] Island of the Pig.
[2] The maps used by Homer, and the romantic annalists of Ireland, exhibited a sea (part of the great Ocean Stream) covering the sites now occupied by South Russia, Poland, and North Germany, thus connecting the Euxine with the Baltic.

Firbolgs some generations back. They rejoined that it was a most unhandsome thing to take people by surprise in that fashion; but if they only re-embarked, and withdrew nine waves from the land, they would then receive them in a manner meet for warlike visitors, and their own relations in the twentieth degree. The simple Milesians consented; and by the time that the nine waves were passed, a druidic fog had fallen between them and the shore. Occasionally a luminous rift was made in this dark curtain, and the island was seen in the guise of the back of a black swine, weltering on the waters, and shooting up huge spear-like bristles. A mighty storm next swept the vessels round the rocky shores. Some effected a landing in Kerry, others in Louth, and the rest on the bleak western coast. The wise and valiant Danaans at last found their spells and their arms too weak before the resistless might of the Milesians, and a new dynasty began.

Mrs. K——, of Cromogue, in the "Duffrey," is the only authority we have for the veracity of the following very ancient tradition. A version of it is to be found in Keating; but we have several reasons for believing that she and her authorities had got their legend through an oral channel. It is out of our power to settle the question of the navigability of the Slaney to Enniscorthy at the date of the story. The corrachs, as may be supposed, drew but few feet of water. Another admirer of past things, who only remembered a small portion of the story, placed this fortress some miles lower.

THE BATH OF THE WHITE COWS.

A great many years ago, when this county was so thick with woods that a very light person might walk on the tops of trees from Kilmeashal to the Lady's Island, a little king, or a great chief, had a fortification on the hill side, from the Duffrey gate in Enniscorthy, down to near the old abbey—but I don't know if there were any abbeys at the time.

This chief had three beautiful daughters, and all were

married, and themselves and their husbands lived inside of the fort; for the young families in old times were not fond of removing far away from the old stock. One fine morning in harvest, the watchman on the big ditch that ran round the fort struck his shield, for down below was the river covered with corrachs, all full of foreigners, and all with spears, swords, shields, and helmets, ready to spring out and attack the dun.

But my brave chief, and his son, and his *sons-in-law* had no notion of waiting an attack within their ditches and palisades. Out themselves and their kith, kin, and following, rushed, and attacked the Welshmen, or Woodmen, as they were called; and a bloody fight went on till the sun was near going behind the White Mountain. At last the captain of the strangers blew a great blast on his bugle-horn, and asked the Irish chief to lay aside the fight till next morning. He consented, and both sides separated, one party moving up to the great rath, and the other down to the boats that brought them up from the Bay of Wexford, that was called Loch Garman in old times. Well, just as they separated, a flight of arrows came from the hill on the far bank, and struck several of the Wexford men. No matter how small a scratch was made, the flesh around it began to itch, and smart, and turn purple, and burn, till the man dropped, crying out for water, and twisting himself in the greatest agony. Those that were untouched hung their shields behind their backs, and carried all that were not yet dead inside the gates.

The three sons-in-law were dead before they could cross the drawbridges, and in the chief's family there was nothing but lamentation. One of the married daughters fell on the dead body of her husband in a faint, after striving to pull out an arrow-head that had pierced into his side. But the beard of the arrow scratched her nice white wrist, and she was soon roused from her faint with the purple spreading round the mark, and the pain going to her very heart.

Well, they were bad enough before, but now they didn't know which way to turn; the poor father and the mother and brothers and sisters looking on, and no one able to do a single thing. While they were expecting every moment to be her last, three strangers walked in—an old and a young warrior, and a Druid. The young man came at once to the side of the dying princess, took hold of her arm, and fastened his lips to the wound. The Druid cried out to bring a large vessel, and fill it with the milk of a white cow and water from the Slaney; and to get all the milk from all the white cows they could lay hands on, fill vessels with it and Slaney water, and dip every wounded man that still had a breath of life in him. The young man sucked away until the bath was ready, and she was hardly lain in it till the pain left her, and in half an hour she was out of danger. All the still living men recovered just the same; and after a great deal of bustle and trouble, things got a little quieter, and it's a wonder if they weren't grateful to the strangers.

Just as the armies were parting in the evening, these men crossed the river about where the island is now. They left a hundred men at the other side; and when they all sat down in the rath to their supper, you may be sure there was *cead mile failthe* for these three.

The chief and his people were eager enough to know something about their welcome visitors, but were too well bred to ask any questions till supper was over. Then the old man began without asking, and told all that were within hearing that himself and his son, and all their people, were descendants of a tribe that was once driven out of Ireland by enchanters and pirates, and sailed away to Greece, where their own ancestors once ruled. They were badly treated by their relations, and made to carry clay in leather bags to the tops of hills. "And even my own daughter," said he, "was carried away from her home by the wicked young prince while I was away fighting for his father. My son, at the head of some of our people, overtook and killed him; and when word was brought to me I quitted the army at once. We seized some ships and sailed away, searching for the old island where our forefathers once dwelt. My daughter fell sick on the voyage; but our wise Druid foretold that a draught of water from the Slaney would bring her to health, and that on our reaching its banks we should save hundreds of lives."

Well, there was not much sleep in the rath that night. The friendly strangers on the other bank where the chief's sick daughter still stayed were provided with everything they wanted. Other things were looked to, and a little after sunrise the men of the rath were pouring out of their gates, and the men of the woods landing from their corrachs, and forming their battle ranks. Before they met, a shower of darts flew from the woody hill down on the Irish, but pits were ready, lined with yellow clay, and filled with milk and Slaney water, and the moment a man found himself struck he made to the bath. The ranks were on the point of engaging, when a great shout was heard from the hill, and the Woodmen were seen running down to the bank, pursued by the strange young chief and his men, that were slaughtering them like sheep. They were nearly all killed before they could get to the boats; and into these boats leaped the friendly strangers, and rowed across. So between themselves and the men of the fort rushing down hill, the Woodmen were killed to a man. No quarter was given to the people that were so wicked as to use poisoned arms, and no caoine was made, and no cairn piled over them, and no inscription cut on an upright stone to tell their names or how they perished. Their bodies were burned, and the ashes flung into the river; and the next night, though there was some lamentation in the fort, there was much rejoicing along with it.

The Druid did not allow his people to remain long there; he said that Scotland was to be their resting-place. Some of them stayed all this time in a little harbour near the place now called River Chapel, and there they set sail again. But the young chief and two friends would not leave without the three widowed princesses, and the only return he made was to leave his sick sister, that was now as well as ever she was, with the son of the chief of Enniscorthy. The lady whose life he saved was not hard to be persuaded to marry him after he risked his life for her, and her sisters did not like to let her go alone among strange people. Maybe that's the reason that the Irish and the Highlanders like one another still, and can understand one another when they meet and begin a conversation.

OSSIANIC AND OTHER EARLY LEGENDS

The party who brought such timely succour were descendants of the Nemedians, who had been driven out of Ireland by the Fomorian pirates after the defeat at Tory Island, and afterwards got the name of *Firbolgs* (Men of the Bags), from their forced employment in Greece. Keating says that King Heremon, jealous of this colony who succoured the Wexford men, obliged them, by a kind of moral pressure, to proceed to Scotland, where the children of the Irish ladies enjoyed ascendency over the rest. The Picts, according to the same authority, were the offspring of these people, and their country was called Caledonia, from Cathluan, the young chief of the tale. The western Highlands and Islands being colonized by other Irish tribes, got the name of Alba.

A high antiquity must be assigned to some of the Irish fictions, both in prose and poetry. We have mentioned some poems attributed to Oisin, preserved in the Book of Leinster, written in the early part of the twelfth century. The poems were copies in a dialect antiquated even then. The Tain-bo-Cuailgne [1] was copied into the *Book of the Dun Cow* by Maolmuire, a monk of Clonmacnois, whose death occurred in 1107; and the tale, in its construction and orthography, was less familiar to the scholars of the time than the first book printed by Caxton would be to a student of this day, whose favourite researches were bounded by the London journals. Moreover, there is a significant absence of religious rites, or reverence for beings higher than the hill folk—the men and women fairies residing in caverns, and favouring or persecuting the worthies of the epic according to circumstances.

THE QUEST FOR THE "TAIN-BO-CUAILGNE."

Among the Celtic fictional remains, the "Tain-bo-Cuailgne" is one of the most remarkable. It was in

[1] The Cattle Raid of Cuailgne.

such high consideration, that the author of the *Proceedings of the Bards* ascribed its production to the spirit of a dead hero. Seanchan, the chief bard of Erinn (contemporary with the magnanimous Guaire of Conacht), and his numerous suite, not only tried the patience of Guaire's people and Guaire himself, but even that of his sainted brother, Marvan, the swineherd (hence, probably, the saying, "You'd try the patience of a saint"). He bore all like a Christian, till they demanded that his favourite boar should be sacrificed for their entertainment. Under this last impertinence his patience broke down. For this valued pig used to search for, and drive home before him, all the vagrant silly swine that were attempting to get out at any of the nine passes of the valley on cold evenings. When the saint's feet were bleeding after the day's fatigue, as he lay resting himself in his hut before the fire, this boar would completely stop the blood, and heal the scratches, by licking them with his tongue. When the saint required a little relaxation from mental and bodily fatigue, he nudged his bristly servant with his foot, and he forthwith emitted *Cronan* (purring) music, such as could not be excelled by thrush or blackbird.

So in his resentment he laid *geasa* on the whole bardic body, that they should at once lose their powers of invention and composition, and that they should never sleep for two consecutive nights in the same place till they discovered and were able to repeat the tale of the Tain in perfection. They repaired to the palace of the King of Leinster at Naas, they crossed the sea to Mann, they explored the hills and lochs of Alba, and at last were obliged to return and implore St. Marvan to relieve them. Being satisfied with the amount of punishment already inflicted, he directed them to collect the Twelve Apostles (bishops or saints) of Erinn, including St. Colum Cille and St. Kiaran, to the grave of Fergus Mac Roigh, in Mayo, in order that they might induce the spirit of that defunct warrior (himself one of the personages in the great cattle spoil), to appear and reveal the story to them. The ecclesiastics assembled, and after three days' invocations, the shade of Fergus, "high, mighty as in life," issued from his mound, and told the weird, heroic legend. St. Kiaran, of Clonmacnois, produced the skin of his pet dun cow, on which he engrossed the narrative as it came from the mouth of the ghost, and when the task was achieved he re-entered his dark abode in the Tulach. This first draft has been lost, but we have the defective copy made (as already specified) some time prior to 1106; and the volume in which it is preserved derives its name from the skin on which the saint penned the original.[1]

Seanchan and his companions, having their proper faculties now restored, were ordered by the saint to disperse, and never again oppress or annoy king or chief by visitations in a large body, extravagant demands, or unlawful use of the terrible powers of satire. Evil usages and principles seem possessed of surprising vitality. Kings, and chiefs, and common men—even rats (if legends tell truth)—feared satire in the sixth century when St. Kiaran ruled Clonmacnois. So late as 1800, poetic satirists by profession had free bed and board in the provinces among the gentry and farmers, by whom a lampoon for stinginess or some domestic scandal was very much dreaded.

The subjoined historical tale is worth giving in outline, as illustrating the fear of satire which prevailed long ago among Irish kings, as well as other characteristic specialities of Irish life at the dawn of the Christian era:—

THE PROGRESS OF THE WICKED BARD.

There flourished in Ulster in the days of the Knights of the Red Branch and their Grand Master, Connor Mac Nessa, a poet named Aithirné the Importunate. He well deserved his *sobriquet*, for he seldom asked for anything easy or honourable to grant. At the time of our story the King of Ulster and his knights were in an uncomfortable state. They had subdued all the fighting forces in the island, were consequently at peace with everybody, and as uncomfortable as the great Neal Malone himself "for want of a batin'." Paddy Kelly

---

[1] This copy is reverently preserved in the Royal Irish Academy, Dawson-street.

trails his coat in the dust, and defies the world to tread on it;—King Connor sent the vicious master of satirical song through the kingdom to find out what prince would dare refuse his most insolent demand.

He first took his way to Cruachan in Conacht, and was disappointed by the ready assent given by the monarch to his unreasonable demands. He then sought the court of Achy, King of Mid-Erinn, at his fortress near the Shannon, on the borders of Clare and Galway, and after exhibiting his poetic powers, he demanded the king's eye for his guerdon. The poor monarch had only one, but rather than be considered ungenerous to a bard, or involve his people in a useless war, he tore it out at once and handed it to the wicked poet. Led by his servant to the nearest point in the Shannon to have his wound washed, "Alas! dear master," said the sorrowing follower, "the water is all red with your blood." "Let that circumstance give it a name for all future time," said the king. "Loch Derg Dheirc (Lake of the Red Eye) shall it be called while the Sionan runs to the sea." Let the tourist, as he approaches Killaloe through Lough Derg, remember this legend.

At the palace of Carn Tiernach, in South Munster, he met no refusal. At Fort-Brestiné, in the modern county of Carlow, he received from the King of South Leinster, Fergus Fairrge, a much valued brooch lost by his (the poet's) uncle in an unsuccessful fight near the same fort several years before.

At Naas, the seat of Mesgera, King of North and South Leinster, he abode a year, and at his departure insisted on getting seven hundred white cows with red ears,[1] sheep without limit, and a hundred and fifty of the most noble of the ladies of the province to be led into Ulster as slaves.

Even this detestable demand was not refused; but the Leinster nobles accompanied him and his convoy apparently through respect, till they came to the edge of the Avan Liffey (the then boundary of Leinster and Meath),

---

[1] If one of the most delightful of our bards, poor Oliver Goldsmith, had met with this tale in his youth, it surely supplied him with a hint for his " White Mouse with Green Eyes," in the charming story of Prince Bonbenin Bonbobbinet.

at a ford, near a deep pool, called Dubhlinn, from the circumstance of a lady named *Dubh* having been drowned there. It being found that the sheep could not be got across at this ford, a floating causeway was constructed with wattles and boughs, which being secured at each bank, they were conveyed safely over.[1] When all were fairly in the province of Meath, the Leinster men took their wives and daughters by the hand, and directed them to recross the stream. They would have also turned back the cattle, but a body of Ulster warriors, previously warned by the suspicious poet, and watching the proceedings from near the mouth of the Tolka, interposed. A terrible fight took place, in which the wrongdoers sustained defeat, though they managed to carry off the white cows with red ears and the sheep. They retreated with their spoil to a fort on the side of *Beann Edair* (Hill of Oaks—Howth), and held out against their foes till the siege was raised by new reinforcements from Ulster, under the command of the renowned Conall Cearnach.

Before this invincible champion the Lagenians were obliged to retire, and the furious Ulster chief, pursuing them through Dublin and Kildare in his war-chariot, at last came up with King Mesgera beyond Naas, and near to the Liffey. Neither warrior (an accident frequent in stories) had any of his men near him. So, with no fear of odds on either side, they fell to sword and shield play, and the beam of battle at last inclined to the champion of the evil cause. The savage Conall, taking the brains of the gallant king, mixed them with lime, and formed a ball, which having been dried in the sun, became a "*Lia Milidh*" (champion's stone), and in the end proved fatal to Conall's own master, King Connor.

Taking the chariot of the king for his prize, and carefully laying the head of its late master in one of its corners, he was proceeding northwards (the historian laying no stress on his having to pass through an enemy's country), when who should come that way but the widow

---

[1] This raft or bridge was thenceforward called "Ath cliath," the Pass of Boughs or Wattles, and the future city got the name of "Bailé Atha Cliath," the Town of the Pass of Wattles.

of the slain hero, the charitable Queen Buona, attended by fifty ladies. She was returning from a short sojourn in Meath. "Who art thou, O lady?" said Conall. "I am Buona, wife to Mesgera, King of Leinster." "Thy lord has sent me for thee : behold his horses and chariot." "My lord is generous ; he may have given them to thee as a present." "Well, you will at least credit this token," said the savage Curadh, worthy to be one of Homer's mailed butchers, and as he spoke he held up the bloody trophy. Wild shrieks rose from her attendants, but she neither uttered cry nor shed tear. "I am then free," said she, in a serene voice. "But give me my husband's head, that his spirit may not hereafter accuse me of neglecting his caoiné." She received it into her arms, kissed the pale bloody face, and then burst out into a wild lamentation. At its conclusion she fell lifeless on the turf, and her spirit rejoined that of her loved lord in the happy valleys of Tirna-n-oge. The rough warrior and his no less rough charioteer were affected. They interred the devoted wife, laying her husband's head by her side. The sepulchral mound lay a little to the north of the ford of Claen. In time a hazel sprung from the turf over her remains, and it was long known by the name of *Coll Buona* (Buan's Hazel).[1]

[1] The Irish *Ban* (white), *Bean* (woman), *Finn* (fair), and the Latin *Bonus*, are cognate words. Here follow some names of women in the Celtic :—Brighid, Fionula (fair shoulder), Grainné, Sorcha (bright), Dervorglan (true oath), Dunfla (lady of the fort), Eiver, Gormfla (blue *eyed* lady), Niamh (effulgence), Orfla (golden *haired* lady), Siobail (pr. *Shibail*, Elizabeth), Sioban (pr. *Shivaun*, Joanna). The six best women in Ireland and the world are mentioned in this quatrain :—

"The six best women that in the world were,
After Mary the Virgin-Mother,
Were Maev, Saav, and fair Sarai,
Faind, Eimer, and the sorrowing Acal."

Eimer was the hard-won bride of Cuchullain ; Acal, the wife of Erc, son of King Cairbré, before mentioned. Conall Cearnach slew him in revenge for the death of Cuchullain, and Acal, like Queen Buona, died of grief for his loss. All good women should be endowed with these gifts, viz. :—Beauty of person, a good voice, skill in music, in embroidery, and all needlework, the gift of wisdom, and the gift of virtuous chastity.

PART V

LEGENDS OF THE CELTIC SAINTS.

LEGENDS OF THE CELTIC SAINTS

BEFORE the name of a person, however ascetic may have been his or her life, can be formally enrolled in the list of those whom the Roman Catholic Church pronounces worthy to be invoked in her public prayers, she insists upon evidence of his or her having exercised devotion in a heroic degree, and of three miracles at least having been performed through his or her intercession. An advocate well trained in the canon law attends the examination of witnesses, and is supposed to exert all his ingenuity in finding out and exposing weak points in the testimony offered in support of the miracles. However excellent his intentions, he is styled the *Devil's Advocate* for his part in the procedure. If a strong case be made out for the eminent sanctity of the deceased, all the papers used in the process are sealed up, and not opened till after a lapse of years supposed sufficient for cooling the undue zeal of relatives, fellow-countrymen, or brotherhoods. Then a second hearing being appointed, the seal is removed from the collection, the documents and evidence *pro* and *con.* read, and the examination begun anew. With the various stages of the business we are not concerned, except the fact that in the brief of the canonization the miracles alleged to have occurred are set forth, as entitled to general credit.

With these miracles the present article has no concern, its object being simply to inform and amuse, not to awake controversy. The early martyrs under the Roman Emperors were judged to stand in no need of this tedious preliminary to inscription in the Hagiologies. Their public and heroic profession of faith in Christ, and their subsequent tortures and public martyrdom, sufficed.

Among the voluminous martyrologies are mentioned many saints whose "ACTS"[1] have been lost. This circumstance opened a field to the indiscreetly zealous, and to the successors of the bards and story-tellers of the heathen times. They had received, perhaps by tradition or hearsay, tales of miracles not mentioned in the ACTS. If they had not, it was easy to coin a few, or re-issue one of the old Pagan tales, with the stamp of the Christian mint, substituting this or that saint as the hero, instead of the original demigod or fairy king.

Our traditions, or legends, or whatever else they may be termed—many of them curious, others romantic or poetic in spirit—claim not of course the authority of the narratives inserted in the ACTS, and may be accepted or rejected by Roman Catholics without incurring spiritual censure. These are the legends which we here intend to discuss and quote.

ST. PATRICK.

Our subject requires that we should give the place of honour to St. Patrick, whose biography, divested of its legendary adjuncts, may be consulted in the great work of Rev. Alban Butler. Jocelyn, Monk of Furness, most credulous of hagiographers, is our darling authority. Scant would have been his patience in following day by

[1] Documents prepared at canonizations of saints, in which are mentioned the dates of their births and deaths, outlines of their lives, and three miracles proved at the examination.

day the footsteps of the great Apostle, preaching the word of life, and indefatigable in instructing his neophytes in the principles of the Christian faith, had not these unceasing works of mercy been enlivened by romantic and miraculous incidents. From the bushel of wheat and chaff we offer our readers a measure filled at good Father Jocelyn's granary; we give our readers the privilege of carrying away one or the other. The outlines of the saint's life may be given in a few words.

Patrick was born, according to the best authorities, in the Roman colony of Tabernia, afterwards named Bononia, now Boulogne-sur-Mer: his father, the Roman Calphurnus; his mother, first a beautiful Gaulish captive, then wife to the Roman officer. In a descent on the coast by Nial of the Nine Hostages he was captured, and the next seven years of his life were spent in herding swine in the North of Ireland. Making his escape, he regained France; and finding within himself a strong vocation for the preaching of Christ to the Pagan Irish, he entered on the course of theological studies, and being in time ordained and appointed to the mission, he returned to Ireland. After some conversions in the North, and using a barn as his first cathedral, he preached before King *Leoghairé* (*pr.* Laeré) and his court, and received the royal permission to teach the new faith through the island, provided he caused no social disturbance. From this period, A.D. 432, till his death, placed by some in 460, by others in 492, his missionary and episcopal labours never ceased, and before his departure the greater part of the island dwellers were Christian. Now, putting off the robe of the historian, we resume the easier garb of the legendary.

HOW ST. PATRICK RECEIVED THE STAFF OF JESUS.

When our saint was returning from Rome to France in his way to Ireland he stopped at a religious house in an isle in the Gulf of Genoa, and was entertained for a night by the inmates, whose self-imposed duty was the care of wrecked sailors. He revealed his name and mission, and observed that about half the community were young and

fresh-looking, and the rest very aged and infirm. One of
the younger brothers surprised him not a little by mentioning that the very old members were their children. "It
is," said he, " about a century since I and my companions
agreed to live here in community, labour with our hands,
and spend a certain time of the day in reciting holy
offices. We were all widowers, and children remained
to some of us. These are they (pointing to the aged
men). One night, it was our good fortune to entertain
a stranger pilgrim of a sweet and majestic countenance,
and when he was about to quit us in the morning he
spoke these words, handing to our superior the staff
which he had in his hands :—' In requital for your loving
hospitality, I leave you this staff. During its stay with
you years shall have no effect on your strength nor appearance. Retain it till my servant Patrick rests here
on his way to Erinn for the conversion of its people, and
give it into his hands when he quits you.' We all listened
with awe, and when the last word was spoken the
majestic form was no longer there. Our children entered
the community as they grew up, but, the blessing not
having been addressed to them, years have had their
natural effect. When you depart, bearing the sacred
staff with you, we expect our release from fleshly bonds."
This or some other staff attended the saint in his many
weary journeys through the length and breadth of Erinn ;
and when he died it was preserved in his cathedral at
Armagh. At a later date it was transferred to Christ-
church Cathedral in Dublin.[1]

THE FORTUNE OF DICHU.

On his first landing on the eastern coast a tall savage
man named Dichu, attended by a no less savage dog,
attacked him in presence of a large crowd, and both in
a moment became as stiff in joint and limb as if they

---

[1] These last two sentences have nothing of a legendary character about them. Our Dublin authorities of the sixteenth century having no opportunities of studying the works of Dr. Todd, Dr. Petrie, or either of our late lamented Irish professors, were little imbued with an archæological spirit. They broke and burned the *Bacal Iosa* on the High Street, to testify their zeal against image worship.

were made of stone. At the saint's intercession they were restored to power and flexibility, but their savage nature had quitted them, and Dichu becoming a convert, granted his large barn to the Apostle for the purpose of worship. The tradition of the incident was transmitted in the name of the better-built church which succeeded it, and was called *Sabal Phadruig* (Patrick's Barn).

Patrick approached the royal fortress at the end of Holy Week, and on Easter Saturday evening was reading the offices suitable to the occasion in his temporary lodging, some distance eastward from Tara. It happened to be the eve of the *Bealteiné*,[1] when no fire was to be seen through the length and breadth of the land. As darkness fell, the king, and his nobles, and his Druids, all assembled on the hill and the neighbouring plain, were awaiting the propitious moment for lighting the Sun's Fire. Watchers were stationed on every high hill through the whole island at the moment, their eyes turned in the direction of Tara; and as each caught sight of the blaze on a height in that direction, he lighted his own heap of dry brush with sparks struck from flint stones. A portion of the rest of the night's occurrences is legendary.

ST. PATRICK'S CONTEST WITH THE DRUIDS.

At the moment when the high pile of brushwood, crowned with flowers, was about to be lighted up by the hands of the Chief Druid, the King's eyes sparkled with rage, for eastward a weak but steady light was beheld glimmering. "Who," said he, "has dared to commit this sacrilege?" "We know not," was the answer from many voices in the assembly. "O King," said the Chief Druid, "if this fire be not extinguished at once, it will

[1] The latest day on which Easter Sunday falls is the 26th of April. *Bealteiné* was held on May 1st; no authority hitherto consulted by us has alluded to this discrepancy.

never be quenched. It will put out our sacred fires, and the man who has enkindled it will overcome thee, and he and his successors rule Erinn to the end of time." "Go, then," said Leoghairé, "quench his light, and bring him hither." "We go," was the answer; "but let all in the assembly turn their backs toward the magic blaze. Meanwhile let our own sacred fires be kindled, and all the dwellers in Erinn rejoice in its light. When we have brought this stranger into the presence, let no one rise to do him homage."

So saying, the Chief Druid set fire to the pile, and, accompanied by two other Druids and some guards, proceeded till he came to where the saint and his assistants, in their white robes, were chanting their psalms. "What mean these incantations?" cried the Druid, curiously glancing at the books so unlike their own wooden staves and tablets; "or why this flame on the eve of Bealteiné, contrary to the orders of the Ard Righ and the Ard Druid? Accompany us to the assembly at Tara, and account for your disobedience; but first extinguish that ill-boding light."

Of all that sat or stood in the presence of the King, no one arose to show respect to the newly-arrived but Dubhthach, an aged Druid, and the young poet, Fiech, who thus braved the King's displeasure. He, fixing his eyes sternly on the saint and his followers, sharply addressed them. "Know ye not the law of this land, that whoever on the eve of Bealteiné kindles a fire before the blaze is seen from Tara, is devoted to death?"

Patrick then commenced, by declaring the Unity of the Godhead in a Trinity of Persons, the creation and fall of man, the necessity of a Mediator, the Incarnation of the Son of God, and our redemption thereby; the necessity of true Christian belief, and the rejection of all creature worship, not excepting that of the genial life-cherishing Beal. He then alluded to his former captivity and the object of his present mission, and besought king and people not to resist the good impulses which would be vouchsafed by God's goodness to every one who did not wilfully offer opposition to them.

The hearts of the King and the greater part of the

Druids remained obdurate; but such persuasive strength was vouchsafed to the words of the saint, that very many hung on his lips with veneration and enthusiasm. The Ard Righ observed this with regret; but his power was much restricted, and he did not venture to express open dissatisfaction. He ordered apartments to be assigned to Patrick and his companions, and appointed him to argue with his Druids on the morrow.

Thousands were assembled next day on the wide plain, and the stern-looking Druids filled the greater part of the space enclosed for the disputants. After some explanations and arguments were adduced by the missionary which told heavily on the priests, the Chief cried out in an arrogant tone, "If the Son of God has redeemed the human race, and if you were sent by Him, work a miracle to prove your mission." "I will not seek to disturb the order of Providence to gratify mere curiosity," modestly answered the saint. "Then will I approve the truth of druidic worship by effecting what you fear to attempt," cried the infuriated pagan; and beginning to describe lines in the air with his wand, and to chant spells, a thick veil of snow shut out the light and heat of the sun, and covering the ground several feet, an intense cold was felt, and the teeth of every one in the assembly chattered. Cries of discontent arose, and the saint addressed the Druid: "You see how the assembly suffer; banish this snow and cold, and admit the warm sunshine." "I cannot do so till this hour on to-morrow." "Ah! you are powerful for evil, not for good. Very different is the gift bestowed on the messenger of the Giver of all good." He made the sign of the cross, invoked the aid of the Holy Trinity, and the snow sunk in the soil, the grass again emerged green and dry, and the blue air again appeared, warmed by the bright and comforting sunbeams. All the people invoked blessings on the head of the beneficent Apostle.

"To convince you all," cried the Druid, "of our power and that of our gods, behold what I am empowered to do!" In a few seconds darkness such as seldom shrouds the earth fell on the assembly, and they groped about and murmured. Again was the thick black cloud dispersed at the prayer of the Apostle, and thousands of tongues blessed him.

The King, wishing other proofs, cried, "Each throw his book into the water, and let him in whose book the letters remain uninjured be declared the minister of truth!" "I will not consent," said the Druid; "he has a magic power over water of which I know not the extent." "Well, then," said the King, "let the ordeal be by fire." "Nay, his magic also embraces the fire." "Well," cried the King, "we are tired; let this last trial be made. Each priest enter a tent filled with dry boughs; which shall then be set on fire." "Nay," said the Saint, "let one be filled with the branches still green, and this I resign to the opponent of my sacred mission."

Young Saint Benin, who attended night and day on St. Patrick, besought his leave to enter the hut of dry boughs, and his request was granted, he bearing the Druid's mantle, and the Druid bearing his. Both huts were fired at the same moment, and in the twinkling of an eye the Druid and the green twigs full of sap were reduced to ashes by the devouring flames, nothing being spared but the cloak of the young saint, in whose hut nought was consumed but the Druid's garment. This was the last trial which the assembly would suffer, thousands, including the queen and her daughters, openly professing their belief in the God of Patrick.

THE BAPTISM OF AONGUS.

The Apostle passing into Munster was kindly received by Aongus, King of Cashel, who on being duly instructed presented himself for baptism. St. Patrick, as already mentioned, bore with him in all his journeys the *Bacal Iosa*, which he had received from the monks in the Tuscan Sea. As he was administering the Sacrament, filled with holy ardour, he raised in his left hand the staff, whose lower extremity was pointed with bronze, and, seeing in spirit the arch enemy of mankind prostrate at his feet, he forcibly struck it into the ground. He did not stir that arm until the ceremony was over, but then, on lifting the staff, he found the spike driven into the floor, through the instep of the king. "My son," said he, sorrowfully, "why did you give no notice when you found your foot pierced through?" "Father," said the king, "though the torture was great, I strove to endure it. I looked on what you did as a necessary part of the rite." Patrick, stooping, and making the sign of the cross on the wound, the blood ceased to flow, and the sufferer was relieved of pain. He was then gladdened by these words addressed to him by the saint:—"For your piety and faith it shall be allowed to ten monarchs of your line to wear your crown in succession; and, one excepted, all shall be blessed with prosperous reigns."

THE DECISION OF THE CHARIOT.

St. Fiech, when a Druid at the court of the Ard Righ, was one of the two who stood up to receive the saint. He assisted him afterwards in his apostolic labours, and, becoming infirm, was indulged with a chariot. St. Sechnal, or St. Secundus, from whom the old town of Dunshaughlin received its name, and who was another of the saint's coadjutors, considered himself as well entitled to the privilege as his brother Fiech. "We shall," said St. Patrick, "leave the decision to the beasts themselves, or rather to Providence, whose favours are shown even to the dumb animals." Next morning the two beasts were yoked and put on the highway, and on they went at their ease till evening. Being then near St. Sechnal's home, they turned into his bawn, ate the provender offered them, but would suffer no one to unyoke them. When daylight came, they resumed their journey, entered another bishop's bawn in the evening, took supper, and again objected to being unharnessed. The third evening found them in St. Fiech's bawn, and most eager to be rid of their trappings. St. Sechnal humbled himself, and no one afterwards grudged St. Fiech his hard-seated, block-wheeled car, unprovided with springs, for such was the vehicle to which the lofty name of chariot was given.[1]

[1] Both saints left behind them hymns in honour of their great patron. St. Sechnal composed his during St. Patrick's life, and rather against the inclination of the humble servant of Christ.

CONVERSION OF THE ROBBER CHIEF, MACALDUS.

A district adjoining the Boyne was infested by a band of robbers, under the command of a chief named Macaldus. Some of these had been converted from their evil ways by the missionaries, and their chief was very wroth in consequence against St. Patrick. Hearing that he was to pass along a road in their neighbourhood on a certain day, he and some of his band took up a position by its side, intending to murder him; but as they caught sight of him slowly approaching, and apparently sunk in profound contemplation, they found themselves deprived of all desire to injure him. Still they would not let the opportunity pass without endeavouring to bring ridicule on him by some stratagem. So one of them lay down by the side of the woodland path as if dead, and Macaldus, as the saint passed by, besought him to restore his dead comrade to life. "I dare not intercede for him," said the saint, and passed on. Though very well inclined to offer him some insult, they could not muster resolution for the purpose, and, when he had gone on a little way, Macaldus ordered the man to rise. But while the poor wretch had been feigning death, life had really deserted his body, and consternation and remorse now seized on his comrades. Macaldus, foremost in wickedness, was first to feel repentance. Following St. Patrick, and throwing himself on his knees before him, he besought him to return and intercede for his comrade's restoration, acknowledging the deception they had attempted, and his own readiness to undergo the severest penance the saint might impose.

The Apostle, retracing his steps, knelt by the dead body, and did not cease to pray till the breath of life entered it again. All the band present vowed on the spot to embrace the faith preached by Patrick, and Macaldus besought the imposition of some most rigorous penance upon himself. Patrick conducted him to the Boyne, and taking a chain from a boat lying by the bank, he flung it round him, secured the ends by a padlock, and threw the key into the river. He then made him get into the boat, and trust his course to Providence. "Loose not your chain," said he, "till the key which now lies at the bottom of this river is found and delivered to you. Strive to maintain (with God's help) a spirit of true sorrow; pray without ceasing." He then unmoored the hide-covered canoe; it drifted down the river, out by the old seaport of Colpa, and so into the open sea.

In twenty hours it was lying by a little harbour in Man, and those who assembled wondered much at the robust form of the navigator, his dejected appearance, and the chain that bound his body. On making inquiry for the abode of a Christian priest, he found that the bishop of the island lived near. He went to his house, told him his former life and present condition, and besought instruction. This was freely given, and the man's conversion found to be sincere. Feeling a strong vocation for the clerical office, he studied unremittingly, and at last came the eve of the day on which he was to receive holy orders. On that evening the cook, suddenly entering the room in which the bishop and postulant were conferring, cried out, "Behold, O my master, what I have taken from the belly of a fish just brought in." Macaldus catching sight of the key in the cook's hand, at once recognised it as the one with which St. Patrick had secured his chain. It was at once applied to its proper use, and he had the happiness of being ordained next day, unencumbered by spiritual or material bonds. At the death of his kind patron and instructor, he was raised to the dignity of Bishop of Man.

BAPTISM AFTER DEATH.

The saint was not insensible to the charms of poetry, nor to the merits of the pieces in which the heathen bards of Ireland celebrated the fame of their dead heroes. He lamented the fate of so many noble-minded and heroic men, who had gone from the earth before the light of Christianity was vouchsafed. Passing one day by the tomb of one of these heroes lately deceased, he stopped, seemingly disturbed and grieved, and entered into prayer. Tears fell fast from him as he was on his knees, and when he rose he ordered the tombstone to be removed. Looking on the serene noble features, he prayed earnestly that life might return for a short time to its former tenement. The supplication was heard; the now living man half raised himself in his tomb, was instructed by the great-hearted saint, and baptized. Then laying himself down with heavenly joy stamped on his features, he again surrendered his soul to its Maker.

THE VISION OF ST. BRIGID.

Brigid, daughter of the converted Druid, Dubhthach, was distinguished from her girlhood by an intense spirit of piety. Once while listening to one of St. Patrick's discourses she was observed to fall asleep, and those who observed it made signs to the preacher to arouse her. He did not take the hint, but when the sermon was at an end and Brigid wide awake but sorrowful, he begged her to reveal the vision which he knew must have been vouchsafed her. "Alas, Father!" said she, "my soul is sad from the sights that succeeded one another while I slumbered. I seemed standing on a high eminence with all Erinn in my sight, and from every part of it were issuing bright flames that joined above and filled the atmosphere. I looked again, and behold, fires were still burning on mountains and hills, but the sight was poor compared to the former general blaze. The third time I cast my eyes abroad, nothing brighter than the puny flames of torches and candles met my gaze. This was sad enough, but when I looked again, the land was covered with ashes, except where a few solitary torches burned in caverns and in the shadows of rocks. I shut my eyes and wept, but was comforted on again opening them to see a steady bright flame blazing in the north, and which spread, scattering itself from its focus till the whole island was once more cheerfully lighted up."[1]

DEATH AND BURIAL OF ST. PATRICK.

As St. Patrick was approaching his hundredth year, he received assurance of his labours being near their end,

[1] This vision is explained by the great sanctity of the people at and after the death of St. Patrick, the gradual decay and almost extinction of piety during the Danish irruptions, and its revival under St. Malachy, Archbishop of Armagh.

and his reward at hand. He accordingly turned the heads of his oxen towards his cathedral seat at Armagh. St. Brigid and her nuns being warned in a vision, repaired to Down with his grave-clothes, which they had already prepared, and there they found Patrick, who had been able to proceed no further, stretched on his last earthly bed. Heavenly were the words spoken on either side, and when the pure and beneficent spirit left its earthly companion, they prepared to spend the night in singing hymns and psalms of mingled joy and sorrow. Notwithstanding their resistance, they were overcome by deep slumber, and through the long night they enjoyed the presence of choirs of angels singing and playing on their golden harps. This continued for twelve nights, and during these twelve nights and days men and women in countless numbers entered the room where the body was laid, gazed on the fresh and heavenly features, kissed the hands, and gave place to others.

At the end of this time the good people of Dunum were much troubled, for the people of Armagh were there in force, and insisted on their right to bear the holy remains to his own cathedral. The prize was too precious to be given up, and each party determinedly confronted the other. Arms of iron or bronze they would not use, but neither party would resign the custody of the saint's body.

At last when anger was waxing hot on either side, the men of Down were surprised and rejoiced to see the men of Armagh filing away orderly and peaceably to the west, till not a man was left behind. They lost no time, but conveyed the saint's remains to their church, and there deposited them in a richly-ornamented tomb.[1]

A vision had appeared to the Ardmachians of the coffin of the saint laid on his own chariot, and his milk-white oxen conveying it in the direction of Armagh.

[1] The Anti-Archæologists of the sixteenth century, holding an annual meeting in Down, converted the rich shrines of the three saints into ordinary coin of the realm, for their own special convenience. The silver case in which the right hand of St. Patrick was kept, somehow escaped their sharp eyes. It is known to be in very safe keeping at this moment, but we are not at liberty to publish all we know on the subject.

They followed the phantasm, but as it appeared entering a ford near the city of Armagh, oxen, chariot, and coffin vanished, and the saddened multitude sought their respective homes. The body of St. Brigid was laid near that of St. Patrick after her decease, and the church was afterwards further enriched by the remains of St. Colum Cillé, concerning the translation of whose body the following legend is told :—

THE CORPSE-FREIGHTED BARQUE.

Colum Cillé, who had preached the Gospel to the heathen Picts, and built the monastery of Iona in the Hebrides, the chief seat of religion in the Highlands and isles for centuries, died there after a most active life, telling his monks in his last hours that he wished his remains to be laid by those of the blessed Patrick and Brigid. *Festina lente* was the order of the day. Most leisurely was their haste in the execution of his wishes. In fact, they could not bring themselves to expedite the removal of the holy relics from the scene of his past and their own present labours. Perhaps they might find courage to commence the voyage to-morrow, next week, next year. No one could tell what might occur if sufficient time were given. However, they were rather dismayed one fine morning on finding the coffin absent from its accustomed place. Dire was the alarm, earnest the search ; but instead of recovering coffin or body, a little barque, which yesterday floated at its mooring beside the quay, was also missing. The pious but procrastinating community did the wisest thing under the circumstances. They sent three of the brethren, men skilled in the simple navigation of the time, with directions to explore all the waters that lay been Iona and Down, and, if unsuccessful so far, to make inquiries of the ecclesiastical authorities of the latter place concerning the missing body of St. Columba.

The legend says nothing of the voyage till the questing barque was made fast to a post within the loch of Down. As the three monks disembarked they discovered an old brother of theirs, from whom they had been separated for years. Salutations, questions, and answers crossed one another rather confusedly on both sides at first, each party being full of the one absorbing subject. The following is the account given by their recovered friend, divested of the ejaculations and interruptions which accompanied it :—

"A week since, just as the sun was directly in the south, the loiterers and labourers on the shore observed a small object far at sea making for the harbour, but their wonder was great when, as it approached, they found it to be a decked boat with sails closely furled, yet proceeding at a rapid speed through the water. No oars were visible, but still it came swiftly onward, leaving a long, straight line of foam behind. The crowd that thronged the shore as it came in, were on their knees, as much from fear as piety, and praying earnestly, but no one dared to enter the enchanted boat till the bishop and three of his clergy, who had learned the news, came from the cathedral, in their robes, and went on deck, scattering incense and singing hymns. They went below, and after what seemed a long hour to the crowd, they came up again bearing a coffin, which they laid upon the deck. The bishop then addressed the assembly, informing them that within the coffin lay the still undecayed body of St. Colum Cillé, evidently sent by Heaven to repose beside those of St. Patrick and St. Brigid. The whole multitude broke out at once with the hymn, 'Laudate Dominum,' and when it ended, with the 'Gloria Patri, Filio, et Spiritui Sancto : sicut erat,' &c. The precious burden was removed on the shoulders of the clergy to the cathedral, and at this moment our most skilful artificers are preparing a fitting monument to be placed beside those of our other patron saints."

Our three voyagers shared but moderately in the general joy that prevailed among all classes. They visited the cathedral along with hundreds of the curious and devout, and were hospitably entertained by the bishop and chapter. The people of Down would have gladly retained the miraculous boat, but in a council held by the clergy and Brehons it was resolved that it should be sent back to its owners in I. Colmkil. It was not fitting that the loss sustained by the islanders should be aggravated. These last, on the return of the exploratory expedition, resigned themselves as well as they could to their loss, and went on their noiseless and useful course. Concerning the abode of the saints in Down, we quote the distich :—

> " Hi tres in uno tumulo tumulantur in Duno—
> Brigida, Patricius, atque Columba pius."

> "These three rest in one tomb in Down—
> Brigid, Patrick, and pious Columba."

ST. BRIGID'S CLOAK.

The King of Leinster at that time was not particularly generous, and St. Brigid found it not easy to make him contribute in a respectable fashion to her many charities. One day when he proved more than usually niggardly, she at last said, as it were in jest : " Well, at least grant me as much land as I can cover with my cloak ; " and to get rid of her importunity he consented.

They were at the time standing on the highest point of ground of the Curragh, and she directed four of her sisters to spread out the cloak preparatory to her taking possession. They accordingly took up the garment, but instead of laying it flat on the turf, each virgin, with face turned to a different point of the compass, began to run swiftly, the cloth expanding at their wish in all directions. Other pious ladies, as the border enlarged, seized portions of it to preserve something of a circular shape, and the elastic extension continued till the breadth was a mile at least. "Oh, St. Brigid ! " said the frighted king, "what are you about ? " " I am, or rather my cloak is about covering your whole province to punish you for your stinginess to the poor." "Oh, come, come, this won't do. Call your maidens back. I will give you a decent plot of ground, and be more liberal for the future." The saint was easily persuaded. She obtained some acres, and if the king held his purse-strings tight on any future occasion she had only to allude to her cloak's India-rubber qualities to bring him to reason.

ST. BRIGID AND THE HARPS.

It was not in the nature of things that a Celtic saint should despise music or poetry. St. Brigid being once on a journey, sought hospitality for herself and her sisters in the *lios* of a petty king. This king and his chief officers, including his harpers, were absent, but some of his sons did all that religious reverence and a hospitable spirit could for the suitable reception of their honoured guests. After a frugal meal the hosts and guests continued an interesting conversation, during which Brigid, observing the harps suspended on the wall, requested the princes to favour her with some of the ancient melodies of the country. "Alas, honoured lady!" said the eldest, "our father and the bard are absent, as we have mentioned, and neither my brothers nor myself have practised the art. However, bless our fingers, and we will do all in our power to gratify you." She touched their fingers with the tips of her own, saying some prayers in a low voice; and when the young men sat down to the instruments, they drew from them such sweet and powerful melody as never before was heard in that hall. So enthralling was the music that it seemed as if they never could tire of playing, nor their audience of listening. While the performance was still proceeding the king and his suite entered the large hall, and were amazed at hearing sweet and skilful strains from the untaught fingers of the princes. Recognizing the saint and her daughters, their wonder ceased. The gift was not conferred for the occasion, for the princely performers retained their power over the harp-strings while they lived.

At one time the three isles in the Bay of Galway were ruled by Corbanus, who acknowledged Aongus King of Munster for his liege lord. St. Enda, brother to Aongus, considered the wild lonely condition of Arranmore the best possibly suited to the needs and spiritual discipline of one or more religious houses. So the king purchased the largest isle from Corbanus, and bestowed it on his pious brother: thus far we are within the historic limits.

"ARRAN OF THE SAINTS"[1] AND ITS PATRONS.

Corbanus, who was still a heathen, and a churl to boot, vacated the isle, and conveyed his people and their property to the opposite coast. There he met with St. Enda and his monks preparing to cross in their slender corrachs, and seemingly ill provided with food and furniture. There were several sacks and casks of corn and meal on the shore belonging to Corbanus, and as the frail boats were putting off he said in a jesting fashion to the saint, "Here are some barrels and sacks of good corn which I would gladly give to save you and these poor men with the shorn heads, from starvation, but your wretched boats could not bear their weight across." "Do not mind that," said the saint; "let the gift be from your heart—that is the main thing." "Surely!" said the other, "I make a free offer!" At the word, sacks and barrels, with much bustle, shot forward in an upward sloping direction over the boats and over the men in them, and in a direct line to the eastern landing-place of Arranmore, while the chief looked on with confusion and chagrin, and his people with anger in their hearts for the vain-glorious offer which was so unexpectedly taken. He and they would have made a voyage to Arran for the recovery of the goods, but they were shrewd enough to feel that they would have to do with beings of unknown and terrible power.

ST. FANCHEA'S VISIT TO ARRAN.

St. Enda's sister, Fanchea, accompanied by three of her nuns, once paid a visit to Arran to see how the good work was proceeding. She and they were much edified by the praying, and fasting, and labouring, and building, and the copying of Latin gospels and missals, all in busy progress. When she was departing, she would not allow her brother to withdraw a couple of his monks from their labours to row them across to the mainland. "We will," said she, "trust to God for a passage." Coming to the

[1] So called from the number of monastic institutions that once distinguished it, and the many canonized saints that it produced.

shore, she made the sign of the cross on the water, and spread her cloak on it.

The garment at once assumed the qualities of a stout board, and the sisters, each taking her position at a corner, went tranquilly over the rough waters of the bay. Fanchea observing one corner of the raft rather shaky, and inclined to let the salt water invade the feet of the sister placed there, exhorted her to acknowledge the fault which occasioned this partial failure. "Dear mother," said the repentant lady, "while on the island I coveted a nice pipkin for which we have much need at home, and so I secretly brought it away with me." "Ah, dear daughter, you have done wrong. One venial sin deliberately committed may lead easily to a mortal sin. Throw the cause of your fault into the sea." It was done, and the remainder of the voyage was pleasantly effected.

ST. BRENDAIN'S VOYAGE.

The story-tellers of kings and chiefs among the Gael had their repertory very exactly arranged, the chief sub jects, as before mentioned, being huntings, adventures in caverns, stormings of forts, pitched battles, enchantments, love stories, voyages, &c. A modification of the principal will be discovered in the saintly legends that were invented or tampered with by the successors of the pagan and the early Christian bards. Of the voyage division we have a good specimen in the celebrated course undertaken by St. Brendain for the discovery of the Blessed Isle of Breasil. This legend appears to have been translated from a Celtic original for the entertainment of Adelais, wife of Henry I. of England. It was admitted into the *Legenda Aurea* of John Capgrave, and copied over and over. In the *University Magazine* for May, 1852, may be read an English translation by our national bard, Denis Florence M'Carthy, and in his collected poems a charming metrical version.

We need not quote at any length from the incidents of the voyage, which, though exhibiting fancy and invention, are generally vague and purposeless. One of the most poetic of the passages is that respecting

THE ISLAND OF THE BIRDS.

St. Brendain's barque having sailed long in a south-westerly direction in beautiful weather, came to anchor by a delightful island in which the fragrant turf came down to the very water. There were hills in the centre of the isle, where some grey rocks appeared among strips of green turf and red flowered heath; the rest of the island was occupied by delightful woods and sloping meadows, the trees furnished with the finest fruit, and shrubs everywhere presenting the loveliest flowers. No cloud obscured the sunshine, and the trees and shrubs were filled with birds of varied and beautiful plumage, whose voices united in forming music that entranced the souls of the listeners. St. Brendain felt that there was something supernatural about the little creatures; so he adjured them to explain the mystery. "Welcome, sainted man!" cried out one of them, who at that moment perched on his arm. "It is delightful to us to hear the voice of one of God's creatures who loves and fears Him as we do ourselves. When the rebel angels were plotting their evil designs in heaven, we were tempted by the arch-fiend to join his party; and, though we yielded not, we dallied with the temptation. So when the unfortunte and wicked legions were flung headlong into the lower sea of fire, this island mercifully received us; and since then we have never ceased night and day to sing hymns of joy and gratitude for being spared. We can still see the glorious companions of our former happiness gliding fleetly through space on their heavenly errands, and we wait with patience for our own release." The saint and his eleven companions sometimes sitting down to listen to the choristers, at an early hour in the morning, would find the sun about to set when no more than half an hour seemed to have gone by.

All the incidents of the voyage were not of this agreeable character. Once landing on a sort of purplish-grey slippery island, with a kind of tough hard reeds springing up here and there, they lighted a fire; but as it blazed up they were amazed to find the isle shaking itself uncomfortably, and moving away. It was a very large fish, which, finding itself incommoded by the fire, thus showed its discontent. The reader will remember the same incident in the voyages of Sinbad, in the *Arabian Nights*.

THE SINNER SAVED.

On a Christmas-eve the barque reached an island, and brought comfort and joy to the heart of its only inhabitant; for he had seen seven Christmas-days in this solitude without having been present at a mass or heard the human voice. He feasted his guests on roots and dried fish, in a comfortable cavern. The devotions of the festival were duly performed, and the solitary then gave an outline of his history. He had been one of the monks of Inis-na-Gloire, on the coast of Erris, and, like their lost comrade, had been guilty of hidden sins of gluttony and incontinence. Stung at last with remorse, and urged on by despair, he flung himself into the sea; but touched by a feeling of true penitence, he exerted himself, and gained a boat moored near the spot. Fearing to return, he loosed the chain and let himself drift out to sea. The boat was driven west, and for some days he endured hunger and loss of sleep. A violent gale of wind upset the boat at last, and he hoped his last hour had come. He fell into a sweet sleep, and found himself, when he awoke, lying on the strand of an unknown island, being unable to tell whether his lethargy had lasted for hours or days. He returned heartfelt thanks, and then explored his new territory. It appeared to him that death by hunger and cold awaited him; but while he was humbly resigning himself to God's will, an otter appeared before him with a fish in its mouth, and laid it at his feet. By means of flints and dry leaves, seaweed and sticks, he soon kindled a fire and broiled the fish. So soon as he was enabled by natural means to procure necessaries, he was deserted by his dumb servant.

This penitent was carried away by the monks, and filled a vacancy that had occurred in a terrible fashion.

In Keightley's *Fairy Mythology of Scandinavia*, saints are frequently assisted by the trolls in the erection of their churches, subject to be dealt with severely by the said trolls, unless they can discover their names before the keystone is inserted. The Patron of Ferns, St. Aidan (or Mogue), knew better than to employ such dangerous assistants. He raised the walls of the cathedral to the wall-plate in one night, without any unholy aid. The peasantry of Wexford delight to boast how a late Protestant Bishop paid a hundred pounds to an Italian sculptor for repairing the nose of his statue.

The dwellers under Mount Leinster, who have had no personal experience of the matter, are, or were some time ago, firmly persuaded that the bells in Ferns Cathedral could not be heard across the neighbouring stream. We ourselves have seen the statue of St. Mogue lying as described, and believe that the care of the Bishop in having it restored has been in the main correctly reported. There is a strong desire through the neighbouring country for interment in the cemetery of Ferns, owing to a supposed promise of the saint, on his death-bed, that he would take five hundred times the full of the churchyard to Paradise along with himself.

A LEGEND OF ST. MOGUE[1] OF FERNS.

When St. Mogue was Bishop of Ferns, he had a wild brother that gave him a great deal of trouble, and at last ran away from him altogether. Well, the saint wasn't to be daunted. After waiting for a long time to see if he

[1] *Mogue*, erroneously supposed an equivalent to Moses, is an abridgment of *Mo-Aodh-Oge*, "My Lord, young Hugh." St. Mogue, otherwise Aidan, spent some time with St. David of Wales. He died A.D. 632.

would come back, he took a short stick in his fist, and searched the European world all over for him, and at last found him playing ball again' the walls o' Jerusalem. So he over-persuaded him to return, and help him to build his cathedral; but a figary took the young fellow again, and, instead of assisting the saint, he took it into hishead to make a church for himself the other side of the river Bann. St. Mogue was mighty incensed at this, and says he to his brother, "The bells I'll put up in my steeple," says he, " will be heard seven miles on every side ; but for all that, not a jangle of them will ever reach across the stream to your parish." And sure enough, the finest day that ever came down in Ferns, not a sound of them is ever heard in the next parish, where the brother's church was built.[1]

So after all the bother the saint got with his brother and that, he thought he might as well set about the work at last. So they began to clear out the foundation at sunset one harvest evening, and the cars to bring down the stones from Slieve Bui, and the stonecutters to square them, and the masons to fit them in the wall, and others to pitch in the pebbles between the inner and outer layer, and spill in the hot lime mortar. Up went the walls like anything, and they were very near the eaves, and a grey horse was bringing down the last load along the side of the hill. The sun was within a foot of rising, when the devil bewitched a red-haired woman that was sleeping in the upper room of a house not far from the churchyard to put her head out of the window to see what was going on. "Oh, musha, St. Mogue, asthore!" says she, " is that all you done the whole night ? " The saint was so moidhered with the assurance of the bosthoon that he couldn't say a word. He let his two arms fall by his side, and every workman stopped his work, as if he was shot. The grey horse stood fast on the hill-side ; up went the car, and down tumbled the load. If any one doesn't believe me, let him go up Slieve Bui any day he has time, and he will see it lying among the heath, the size of three houses. And that's the reason the cathedral

[1] This legend prevails in the Duffrey, few of whose inhabitants ever resort to Ferns on Sundays, to verify or disprove the assertion.

of Ferns was never finished. All that's left of the old building is the statue of the saint, and the nose of it was broke about fifty years ago. The Bishop, although he was a Protestant, got an Italian man that used to make images, and paid him a hundred pounds to come over and repair it. The next time that there's a funeral, any of you will be welcome to go inside and look at it.

Somewhat more hasty was the proceeding of another saintly architect.

St. Declan, when he was building the great round tower at Ardmore in Waterford, was much annoyed by the chatter and questions of an inquisitive woman (the colour of her hair is not recorded). So just as the cap was being placed on the lofty building, he took a shovel that happened to be at hand, and putting it under her feet, skilfully pitched her to the summit, where her skeleton was afterwards discovered *in situ!*

In the monastery of Innisfallen there flourished, in the days of Brian Boroimhe, a remarkable scholar, by name Maelsuthain O'Carroll, who enjoyed the honour of being confessor and private secretary to the Irish Alfred. There is a specimen of his handwriting extant in old Latin (Irish letters), made in the year 1002, in the Book of Armagh, in the presence of King Brian himself, on occasion of one of his visits. The object of the entry was to confirm the supremacy of the Archbishop of Armagh over him of Cashel, and the other Irish dignitaries. The translation is subjoined. The curious may see the original in the College Library, at folio 16 of the book:—

"St. Patrick, going up to heaven, commanded that all the fruit of his labour, as well of baptisms as of causes and of alms, should be carried to the Apostolic City, which is called *Scotice* (in Gaelic) ARDD MACHA. So I have found it in the book-collections of the Scots (the Gael). I, Calvus Perennis (*Mael-Suthain*, bald for ever), have written this in the sight of Brian, Emperor of the Scots; and what I have written, he has determined for all the kings of Maceriæ (Stone Fort, Cashel)."

This same churchman and scholar is supposed to have commenced the annals of the monastery in which he dwelt. Here is the legend attached to his memory:

O'CARROLL'S WARNING.

Three Ulster students spent some time under him, and at last they formed a design of performing a pilgrimage to Jerusalem. They asked his permission, which he granted on one condition. "You will die," said he, "before you return. And now give me your solemn promise that, when your spirits are freed from their mortal bonds, you will not ascend to heaven till you come and announce to me the time of my own death, and whether I shall obtain eternal happiness or not."

"We make that promise," said the three together.

They died at Jerusalem: and when St. Michael was about to conduct their spirits to heaven, they mentioned the necessity they were under of returning to their preceptor, and making the revelation demanded. "Go," said he. They appeared before the great scholar, and thus revealed his destiny:—"You have made changes in the canon—you have been incontinent—you have neglected to sing the *Altus*[1] for seven years. In three years you shall die, and hell is your destination."

"Not so," said the frightened man. "I will never more make a letter of alteration in the canon; I will lead a pure life; I will sing the *Altus* seven times every night; I will turn with true contrition to my Maker. Is it not written, 'the impiety of the impious, in whatever hour he shall turn from it, shall not injure him'?"

So he changed his practices; he lived a mortified and

[1] The *Altus* is a hymn in praise of the Holy Trinity (still extant) composed by St. Colum Cille in his monastery at Iona. O'Carroll had a beloved and pious son, for whose recovery from illness he had got the *Altus* seven times solemnly chanted. The youth, however, died the death of the just, and the father never sang the hymn again till after the warning.

pious life; and at the end of the three years, on the day of his decease, he was again visited by the three spirits who, in the appearance of doves, came to give him an assurance of salvation, and bring comfort to the assistants at his death-bed.

A smith, whose forge was on the Kerry side of the Shannon, was disturbed one night by an impatient traveller, whom he afterwards discovered to be one of the provincial fairy kings proceeding to make war on the fairy tribes of Cork, and anxious to have his horse shod. The steed was so fiery and impatient of restraint that the smith dreaded to touch his hoof, whereupon *Fear Dhoirche* at once plucked the leg off and handed it to the artist, who was thus enabled to do his office without risk of being pranced on or kicked. The inventor of the following legend had some such fiction as the above in his mind, when he told the world—

HOW ST. ELOI WAS CURED OF PRIDE.

Before St. Eloi[1] became religious, and while he was still but a working goldsmith, he sometimes amused himself with shoeing horses. He was very proud of his skill, and often boasted that he never saw that thing done by a man that he couldn't match. One day a mounted traveller stopped at his forge, and asked leave to fasten a loosened shoe on his horse. Eloi gave permission, and was very much surprised to see him twist a fore leg of the beast out of the shoulder joint, bring it into the forge,

[1] Eligius, called Eloi by the French, was born near Limoges, A.D. 588. Having acquired the knowledge of working in metals, he was distinguished by the patronage of Clothaire II. and his successor Dagobert. His life at court was distinguished by works of charity; and so great was his reputation for sanctity, that on the decease of the Bishop of Noyon and Tournay he was elected his successor, and could hardly obtain time for receiving the successive grades of holy orders. It was the era of transition from Paganism to Christianity, and our saint's efforts were attended by miracles of conversion and reformation of morals. He died, universally regretted, A.D. 659.

and fasten on the shoe. This being done, he rejointed the leg, patted the beast on the shoulder, and asked the smith if he knew any one who could do such a neat piece of work as that. "Yes, I do," said the conceited man; "I will do it myself." So he ordered one of his horses to be brought, and the fore-leg twisted out. He was not able to get this done so satisfactorily as was desirable. There was some blood-shedding, and tearing of muscle, and skin. He made as nice a shoe as could be seen however, and fastened it on in such style as elicited even the applause of his rival; and here his triumph came to a close. When he brought the leg into the yard, the poor animal to whom it belonged was lying on his side expiring, and his tender-hearted though conceited master burst into a passion of grief for what he had done. "Oh, what a proud, worthless creature I am!" cried he, "My poor beast tortured and killed by my heartless presumption!" "Are you sure you are cured of pride and vanity by this mischance?" said the stranger. "Oh, I am, I am! at least I hope so. I will never again, with God's help, indulge a proud thought. But why did you induce me to do this wicked thing by setting me the example?" "My object was to root a strong vice out of your heart. Give me the leg." So saying, he applied the broad end of the limb to its place, tapped the animal on the shoulder, and the next moment he was standing up strong and uninjured; but there was no appearance of the stranger or his steed. While Eloi stood wrapped in joy and surprise, he was sensible of these words distinctly uttered, but he could not tell whether they were heard in his heart or his brain :—"Eligius, remember the promise made to your Guardian Angel."

Some collectors or inventors of saintly legends could not divest themselves of a taste for the grotesque in their misdirected zeal. We quote a narrative of this class—that of

ST. LATEERIN OF CULLIN.

St. Lateerin lived at Cullin, near Millstreet, and her sisters lived in her neighbourhood. They visited one another once a week, and because they had to pass through bogs and brakes, the angels made a fine road for them connecting Kilmeen, Drumtariff, and Cullin, where they respectively lived. St. Lateerin took only one meal in the day, and when it was dressed she let her fire go out. Every evening she went to the smith's forge for the "seed of the fire," and carried it home miraculously in the skirt of her long gown. One unfortunate evening, the smith, who had been "looking at some one drinking," that day, said, as she was walking away with the bright coal in the fold of her robe, "Ah, Saint Lateerin, what a darlin', purty, white foot you have!" Vanity took possession of her pure mind for a moment, and she looked down, but what did she see and feel? The red hot coal burn through her gown, and scorch her ankles. She was naturally vexed with the smith, as well as with herself, and exclaimed, "May there never more be a smith or his forge in Cullin!" Curious readers will do well during the excursion season to call at Cullin, and ascertain whether the wish has been fulfilled.

If any fair or gentle reader, touched by the poetic or romantic spirit of some of these saintly legends, desires to make acquaintance with more of the same stamp, he or she will save time, trouble, and expense by *not* buying or borrowing the authorized Roman Catholic work on the subject—*Lives of the Saints*, by the Rev. Alban Butler. They will meet with much biographical, historical, and archæological information, and the principal events in the lives of his subjects, but a total absence of romantic and a sparing use of supernatural events.

We are not to suppose that such legends as we have given were deliberately fabricated by the early biographers of the different holy personages and committed to writing. They were the result of oral tradition, altered and enlarged by many transmissions, till some scribe or other secured the eightieth or hundredth version of some simple narrative. A saint's memory falling into the hands of a professional story-teller fared still worse. His imagination went to work. He cared to a certain extent for the reputation of his subject; but he cared, to an extent unlimited, for the impression to be made by his narrative upon his audience. He consequently borrowed passages from the pagan poems and stories, Christianized them slightly, and connected them without scruple with the memory of the humble-minded and earnest worker in God's vineyard.

If any of our readers feel disposed to apply the test, *Cui Bono?* to our light labour, we beg to say, that it can scarce ever be uninteresting to learn something of the circumstances, the habits, or the language of those who, in succession, held our native soil before us for thousands of years. Well, we are often in doubt as to their implements of labour, their dress, their merry-makings, their funerals, or the terms on which they held their lands. But here in these wild, purposeless, and artlessly-constructed tales, we have the very words, and assemblages of words, that have, for two or three thousand years, filled their ears at their comfortable fireside gatherings, or travelled with them in their tedious and difficult progresses from the far East. We certainly did nothing for the Greeks and Romans, but our gratitude would be not small to those writers who might have left us, but unfortunately did not, a correct report of their fireside stories, if they were accustomed to the indulgence of such. So rapid have been the changes in our social customs, and so altered our tastes in many things; so powerful is becoming the influence of the mighty dollar and splendid shilling; and so terrible the battle of life, that if such task as we have undertaken be not now achieved, it would become impracticable, even within a score of years from this our present epoch. The *Gentleman's Magazine* has existed a hundred and thirty odd years, and will, as we hope and wish, be still young a hundred years hence. Its chief object is to preserve in memory former modes of existence, and everything connected with them. We readily grant that many of the treasures of its museum are of far more importance than such relics as we are striving to save from the remorseless teeth of time, but certainly others there preserved are much inferior. But the world of literature is wide enough for us all : we only scramble each to get his own collection in a place of honour. We are hopeless of literary fame for ourselves in this struggle; but we are truly in earnest that the memory of those things which were of interest to our forbears should be recorded and preserved for the knowledge of those who succeed us to the fiftieth generation. We are doing for them what we should be very glad that the Greeks and Romans had done for us.

What is here presented is a mere fraction of the wealth of Gaelic fiction.